Crossing Memories

The Harriet Tubman Series on the African Diaspora

Paul E. Lovejoy and Toyin Falola, eds., *Pawnship, Slavery and Colonialism in Africa*, 2003.

Donald G. Simpson, *Under the North Star: Black Communities in Upper Canada before Confederation (1867)*, 2005.

Paul E. Lovejoy, *Slavery, Commerce and Production in West Africa: Slave Society in the Sokoto Caliphate*, 2005.

José C. Curto and Renée Soulodre-La France, eds., *Africa and the Americas: Interconnections during the Slave Trade*, 2005.

Paul E. Lovejoy, *Ecology and Ethnography of Muslim Trade in West Africa*, 2005.

Naana Opoku-Agyemang, Paul E. Lovejoy and David Trotman, eds., *Africa and Trans-Atlantic Memories: Literary and Aesthetic Manifestations of Diaspora and History*, 2008.

Boubacar Barry, Livio Sansone, and Elisée Soumonni, eds., *Africa, Brazil, and the Construction of Trans-Atlantic Black Identities*, 2008.

Behnaz Asl Mirzai, Ismael Musah Montana, and Paul E. Lovejoy, eds., *Slavery, Islam and Diaspora*, 2009.

Carolyn Brown and Paul E. Lovejoy, eds., *Repercussions of the Atlantic Slave Trade: The Interior of the Bight of Biafra and the African Diaspora*, 2010.

Ute Röschenthaler, *Purchasing Culture in the Cross River Region of Cameroon and Nigeria*, 2011.

Ana Lucia Araujo, Mariana P. Candido and Paul E. Lovejoy, eds., *Crossing Memories: Slavery and African Diaspora*, 2011.

Edmund Abaka, *House of Slaves and "Door of No Return": Gold Coast Castles and Forts of the Atlantic Slave Trade*, forthcoming

The Harriet Tubman Institute for Research on the Global Migrations of African Peoples

CROSSING
MEMORIES
Slavery and African Diaspora

Edited by

Ana Lucia Araujo

Mariana P. Candido

Paul E. Lovejoy

AFRICA WORLD PRESS

TRENTON | LONDON | CAPE TOWN | NAIROBI | ADDIS ABABA | ASMARA | IBADAN

AFRICA WORLD PRESS
541 West Ingham Avenue | Suite B
Trenton, New Jersey 08638

Copyright © 2011 Ana Lucia Araujo, Mariana P. Candido,
and Paul E. Lovejoy
First Printing 2011

Book and cover design: Saverance Publishing Services

Library of Congress Cataloging-in-Publication Data

Crossing memories : slavery and African diaspora / edited by Ana Lucia
Araujo, Mariana P. Candido, Paul E. Lovejoy.
    p. cm.
Papers presented at a conference held in Quebec City in 2005.
Includes bibliographical references and index.
ISBN-10: 1-59221-819-9 (hardcover : alk. paper)
ISBN-10: 1-59221-820-2 (pbk. : alk. paper)
ISBN-13: 978-1-59221-819-6 (hardcover : alk. paper)
ISBN-13: 978-1-59221-820-2 (pbk. : alk. paper) 1.
Slavery--History--Congresses. 2. Slave trade--Africa--History--Con-
gresses. 3. Memory--Social aspects--Congresses. 4. African diaspora-
-Congresses. I. Araujo, Ana Lucia. II. Candido, Mariana P. (Mariana
Pinho), 1975- III. Lovejoy, Paul E.
HT855.C76 2011
306.3'6209--dc22
                        2010054213

The Harriet Tubman Institute for Research
on the Global Migrations of African Peoples

Dedicated to
Bogumil Jewsiewicki

Table of Contents

Tables

• • • • • • • • • • • •

Maps

Illustrations

Acknowledgements

This book arises from an international conference, *Crossing Memories: Slavery and African Diaspora/Mémoires Croisées: Esclavage et Diaspora Africaine*, which was held at the Université Laval (Quebec, Canada) from May 3 to May 5, 2005. Ana Lucia Araujo organized the conference, which was sponsored by the Canada Research Chair in Comparative History of Memory (Université Laval), under the direction of Bogumil Jewsiewicki; the Centre interuniversitaire d'études sur les lettres, les arts et les traditions (Université Laval); the Canada Research Chair in the African Diaspora History (York University), under the direction of Paul E. Lovejoy, and at the time, the Harriet Tubman Resource Center (subsequently, The Harriet Tubman Institute for Research on the Global Migrations of African Peoples, www.yorku.ca/tubman). This volume includes papers from the conference, as well as the contribution of Mariza de Carvalho Soares, which was added.

The aim of the conference was to encourage exchange between different generations of scholars whose work, mainly in English and French, deals with the history and memory of slavery. The international context in which the conference was planned was important. The year 2004 was the bi-centenary of the independence of Haiti and was declared the International Year for the Commemoration of the Struggle Against Slavery and its Abolition. In focusing on how slavery has been remembered or forgotten and how the slave past has been reconstructed and manipulated, the conference participants focused attention on the study of memory from a transnational perspective. The chapters in this volume deal with the history and the memory of slavery in multiple geographical areas and time periods. Using diverse approaches, the contributors examine archival documents, life-stories, autobiographies, interviews, commemorative monuments, engravings, watercolors, music and dance in examining how memories have been shaped.

The editors wish to thank Université Laval for hosting the conference, the Department of History, Princeton University, for financial assistance in editing the volume, and to Henry Lovejoy for translating several of the chapters into English. The cover is based on a photograph of the sculpture at the Gate of No Return in Ouidah, Republique du Benin, by Gnonnou Dominique Kouass (Photographed by Ana Lucia Araujo, 2005). Finally, the editors wish to thank the contributors for extreme patience in the editing and translation process, which delayed publication.

The book is dedicated to Professor Bogumil Jewsiewicki, without whose inspiration and scholarship the conference and this volume would not have come into being. The editors present this volume to him in tribute.

Ana Lucia Araujo
Mariana P. Candido
Paul E. Lovejoy

Chapter 1

In the Empire of Forgetting: Collective Memory of the Slave Trade and Slavery

Bogumil Jewsiewicki

Collective memory lives and breathes inside of memory.[1] We are presently living from the past of the slave trade and slavery. That horrific past must be analyzed in relation to a plurality of times[2] wherever, whenever and however it is recorded or remembered. I will avoid writing about time because it is not necessarily the continuity between certain moments of time that present themselves to us in instantaneous photographs or snapshots of memory. These collective representations of the past give absent memories a full sense of meaning to present ones, whereby the past is felt as if it were being remembered or relived in the present.[3] Such *véritables représentations* articulate moments or images of the past, conveyed in the present, often through narration and/or performance. At the same time, the memories of slavery depend on the existence of collective representations in order to convene the collective memory (*cadres sociaux de mémoire*) within the limits of social frameworks, including religious organizations.

Breaking the Chains of Slavery

"Being chained up" and "breaking free" are two images, neither of which has a beginning nor an end (much like the chicken and the egg debate), but which extend the experiences of slavery from the past into the present. The collective memory associated with such images also brings the experiences of slavery closer to the present; it exhibits a potential for narration and/or performance, it represents collective representations of absent moments and lost memories, it reveals how memory is culturally inherited (i.e., *patrimonialisé*),[4] and how historical artifacts are indeed fact.

The framework of the Christian Bible, whose relevance is confirmed by historical artifacts, replicate three processes related to the production of meaning (*mise-en-sens*): First, there is the process arising from a pact between a chosen people and God, based on the biblical account of slavery in Egypt and deliverance to the promised land; second, there is symbolism that arises from the use of devices of restraint, such as chains, to restrict the mobility of slaves; and, third, there is the equally symbolic rupture of chains, as portrayed by abolitionists to represent the transition of the slave from being an object to being a subject, especially as a means of affirming that the human is an alternative to servility.

Collective memory can emerge from any of these three processes. The collective memory can engage or otherwise determine the meaning of an image, so that a single *patrimonialized* memory can close or validate a memorialized development. For historical reasons that are impossible to describe or analyze here, Christianity and Islam, each one in its own way, have offered to enslaved people ideological and social means, sometimes even political, to dispute the dehumanization of slavery, to claim emancipation, and sometimes even to achieve freedom in an individual capacity. Those individuals scattered by the slave trade and put into circulation like commodities were "legally" dehumanized by institutions, but the two monotheisms provided a framework for a return to humanity and for a reconstruction of identities, and even communities. I emphasize the framework since the corpus came from elsewhere, and those who transmitted memories relied on sounds, images, gesture and shared sensibilities that held their own memories.[5] People turned to monotheistic religions – above all Christianity – as a grammar to reconstruct the world in its diversity and time depth.[6]

While scholarship recognizes the syncretism involved in the interaction between "African" religions and Christianity, today we realize that the interaction was more complex because there were a variety of Christian denominations.[7] The Atlantic "world" comprised the North Atlantic, sometimes referred to as the "Black Atlantic,"[8] but also the South Atlantic,[9] where the diversity of the Christian impact can be seen. In the North Atlantic, the image of chains and their rupture has structured the memory of slavery and the memory of the individual self as a descendant of the slave, while in the South Atlantic this association is less evident.[10] Collective memory has revealed how conceptions of the imaginary in Christianity have sifted through the history of anti-slavery campaigns, the fight for African independence, and the civil rights movement in the United States. The explicit influence of Christian imagery seems to be weaker in the South Atlantic where "Africanized" religions occupy a much greater space. Moreover, the vision of chains seems to be absent from the imagery of slavery structured within Muslim frameworks of memory.

The colonization of Congo and its subsequent independence draw attention to differences in how representations of "the enchained slave" have been adapted. Breaking the chains can involve a "symbolic rupture," as revealed through the concept of imagination. The local memory of colonization was built around the centrality of the enchained slave, but who was transformed into an enchained worker. Through an inversion of the usual meaning for the imagery of chains, the Congolese chains symbolized liberation, whose rupture represented the end of colonialism, not the end of the slave trade.[11] During the early years of the twentieth century, resistance to colonialism was primarily directed against the Leopoldian system of labor exploitation in the rubber industry. In effect, the imagery mobilized the same framework used earlier by abolitionists. While there is certainly no local memory of the campaign against the transatlantic slave trade in Congo, slavery is remembered through the transference of local memories and also missionary propaganda. The colonial and Christian justification of conquest had been a campaign against slavery, and the association of colonialism with liberty was perceived as a "civilizing" mission for the Congolese population.[12] The imagery of broken chains became part of the collective memory, as revealed in

Patrice Lumumba's inaugural speech on June 30, 1960. The image of breaking free from the chains of the colonial past provided a vivid representation of this past for the popular mind. The image of chains haunted and shaped the collective memory. Despite its paradoxical appearance, to enchain and to break the chains pervades the political memory of the former Belgian Congo.

The social framework of memory leaves a strong impression, despite variable directions, on the expression of collective representations and the memory of experiences, whether or not culturally inherited or a quasi-remembrance appropriated as historical. The impressions of memory can also be a flash of recognition (a déjà-vu of what one had never been able to see) and the narration or the performance attached to the memory, the collective identity or a path towards the representations of the political. Living and dead representatives have their places, such as their deputies "elected" by the abolitionists of the past. Collective memory, which also includes a collective forgetting of time and history, makes certain remembrances more audible, more visible and more public while facilitating their transmission.

Under the Empire of Forgetting

Besides the concepts of memory and remembrance, the concept of forgetting is also an essential point of consideration when thinking about the history of slavery and the slave trade. First of all, there is the voluntary sense of forgetting, whether the failure to transmit is with the individual or through cultural disinheritance. Forgetting having been slaves sometimes has marked social, cultural and political identities asserted by individuals and the group. Acting like a black hole in outer space, forgotten memories collect, absorb and swallow all other memories. The forgotten voids remembered experiences of their substance, leaving nothing more than a gaping hole. As a result, memories of slavery either become "nothing" or become "too full" of violence. In the (re)-construction of identities, (re)-founding a community must then be claimed from remembrances that are very often virtual, such as, those selected by God, who has tested those who He cherishes, and from those identified as the founders of a civilization, or religion, who were once persecuted by impostors. The attraction of the black hole of forgotten memories and the force of equating racial prejudice with the slave, or black skin with servitude, prevented the descendants from capitalizing on their achievements in establishing identity. In areas outside of the direct control of slave masters, such as music, dance and religion, individual creativity and its social circulation were amplified through a non-Darwinian mode of division, that is to say, horizontal rather than vertical.[13]

The American phenomenon of "passing,"[14] whereby a person can assume an identity as "white" and thereby deny and even forget African ancestry, is in fact a "product" of a social and political framework which normally qualifies as "black" any person having at least one ancestor, even remote, of African origin. Hence, "passing" serves as an example of how memory is constructed under the empire of forgetting. In this framework, it is necessary to forget and make others forget the existence of an African ancestor, once a slave. By erasing specific cultural markers, the patrimony of the descendants of slaves was tied to the color of the skin (although this was not necessarily so elsewhere in the world).[15] By denying the two faces of the patrimony of slavery (personal property and natural color of skin through racialization), "passing" indeed transformed forgetting into invisible legacy, an inheritance onerous to carry. One sought, indeed, to make invisible two heritages – the memory of the forgotten legacy of slave ancestry and the reality of exclusion from general society, inherited on racialized grounds. Fatally, the double denial has commemorated what it has denied.

The phenomenon of "passing" is not unique to the descendants of enslaved Africans. To lesser degrees, the social ascension of the descendants of the serfs, the children of Eastern European peasants, could follow a similar path of social ascension, just as the descendants of Jewish parents, such as the Marranos, also could achieve integration. These specific historical cases reveal attitudes that were similar to the idea of "passing."[16] Forgetting history and refusing to reinforce memory has led to the memorialization of a double-faced stigmatization, one that was the result of contempt, combined with exclusion, while the other was based on forgetting.

Such forgetting generates its own work and contains its own interconnected elements of memory. The remembrance, sometimes disseminated in secrecy, is shared and carried on, despite itself. Remembrance constitutes a true act of identity representation: the absent is essential in the present, it produces a *déjà-vu* effect inscribing itself in the presence of the past, as if they were Russian nesting dolls. The forgetting contains a materiality and historicity that reveals a double heritage of having been slave and having been forgotten and obliterated. By attempting to raise the lid to find out what is underneath, one finds another lid and so on. As time passes, this forgetting "implodes" causing other forgetting and thereby imposing multiple layers of lost heritage.

Slavery and the slave trade introduce a specific feature into the generation of memory and the identification of places of memory. This work of memory connects in a loop with remembrance and forgetting and, especially, the painful and accusing remembrance of forgetting. The specific feature of slavery is the duration of its effects which condition the work of forgetting as memory. The generation of memory for Holocaust victims is comparable, although the Holocaust is a paradoxical model, since it was based on a singular event,[17] but nonetheless, like all contemporary initiatives at memorialization, the process includes forgetting. The remembrance of the survivors, their descendants and the state of Israel memorialize it as heritage as a means of survival. In the case of slavery, the length of time that is suppressed and forgotten and the force of the denial and obliteration have extended over generations, thus crystallizing forgetting as heritage that reinforces external exclusion and internal withdrawal. Over time, "popular" culture, including the religious field, offered a place of refuge where the dialectic of memory and forgetting was associated with the work of identity. More than in any other collective formation of memory, the work of forgetting (moved by the subdued memory of the forgetting, memorialized) is central to the genesis of memories of slavery and the slave trade. The racial stigmatization, imposed by this heritage, resulted in the naturalization of a heritage that became "invisible"[18] since it was "biological" and "natural." Thus, racialization of the slavery heritage led to forgetting and even denial of the role of historical slavery and to forgiveness for the actors of enslavement. In the place of an action arising from voluntary human actions, and by forgetting history, the slave trade becomes an expression of biological inequality and the inequality in destiny (the curse of Ham). This "naturalization" of the slavery heritage is conditioned by forgetting history. This is why the memory of slavery and the slave trade is based on forgetting; like a black hole, this forgetting swallows the past.

Plurality of Memories and Forgetting

The central role of the work of forgetting enables a periodization and spatial distribution of the work of memory spread out under the empire of the forgetting. We must distinguish some spaces, which overlap, that highlight the role of the social framework (especially the religious framework). The best known of these spaces is the Black Atlantic, that is, the North Atlantic, then there are the South Atlantic, the Caribbean, and the islands of the Indian Ocean (Mauritius, Réunion, Madagascar) – in which the memory of slavery is [re]constructed vis-à-vis the memory of indentured labor – and finally the Muslim space. In the Muslim context having been a slave means having been a non-believer rather than being black, and a black could claim being the descendant of one of the Prophet's companions. For the African continent, these different spaces overlapped with an internal diversity of situations in which the work of memory and forgetting was carried out. In Africa, stigmatization associated with slavery was not inherent. The continent has a social and political character in which the memory of slavery works as a collective and an individual heritage. Because of overlapping and telescoping memories, the memory of having been colonized (*indigenism* in the French system and the statute of *indigènes* during Belgian colonization) is more pervasive than the slave trade.[19] This later interference in the public space overshadowed the memories of slavery (or slaveries) and the social inequalities that had resulted in the internal context from warlike aristocracies and the taking of captives. The recent wave memorializing the memory of the slave trade, especially along the Atlantic coast, diversifies this landscape by connecting the continent again to the Atlantic.

The historical periodization allows us to highlight the transformations of the social framework and their impact on the work of memory and forgetting. The celebration of the independence of Haiti, long neglected by historians, marks the emergence of new forms of representation of what was the past. For at least a half-century before the independence of most African countries, the work of memory was forgetting.[20] Since then, the transnational process of recognition, the demand for reparations and the quest for full access to the rights of citizenship indicate the emergence of a framework for a revamped memory. This slow process started with the fight for civil rights in the United States, and the elimination of the infamy of the memory of having been enslaved, as represented in "black is beautiful," and the corresponding stigmatization of the former masters and slave traders. The memory of the Holocaust is then convened as a model for comparative recognition.[21] The comparison gives a new importance to counteracting the racialized identity of the victims of slavery and their descendants, who now claim moral and material reparations.

While historical reconstruction can help us to understand the periodization of memory, it is important to identify specific periods in the work of memory. The most contemporary element (and also the most relevant to analyze the work of memory, since memory always operates in the present) is related to the revalorization of work, from forced labor to wage labor paid by another individual. The experience of enslavement had transformed men into commodities and units of work. In the industrial era, men became a work force in circulation in the market. This new situation could be perceived as a transformation of slavery; was it relevant to the individual if the master was a man or capital? Abolition of slavery did not leave possibilities of survival, other than to become part of the workforce. This experience was perceived and remembered as slavery. Thus, the memory of colonization is linked directly with the slave past.

Recently, the representation of work has changed. The redress results from the claims for citizen rights, including equal access to working opportunities as well as to the job market. To get a job that corresponds to one's skills is a test of full citizenship. At the same time, the memory of having been enslaved ceases being infamous. Instead, the past becomes a source of authorized social and cultural capital and even political recognition. It is difficult to separate the [re]valorization of the memory of slavery from the claims for economic, moral and political reparations. Perhaps, in consumer societies, getting respect is less a question of honor and more the effect of having access to the market for goods and services. Labor rhymes with respect as long as it makes possible for individuals to occupy public space, where respect is negotiated on the basis of consumption. In Brazil, for example, taking a seat on a symbolic slave ship during a performance with religious overtones promotes a new black identity released of the ideology of racialized democracy. The place of memory represented in the slave ship drawn on the ground constitutes a "distinctive" feature of the strategies claiming full citizenship.[22] Being a citizen means to recognize that the forced labor performed in the past contributes to the present collective wealth and is the basis for a claim for equality in the labor market. In Central Africa, the post-independence generation reproaches the previous generation for having appropriated work as personal property, to the point not to leave any work for their children. The deep rupture between the generations, particularly in urban settings, is related not only to the memory of colonization but also to the memory of past labor.[23]

In facing a history that assigned slaves and their descendants the status of property owned by others, it is necessary to break the sequence "memories-forgetting-denial" and demand a recombination of the past, based on experience. Under slavery, the best relationship that could be achieved with masters was that of a stranger. In the reconstruction of memory, it is essential to "recognize a past and a heritage as belonging to the people who were enslaved," so they can never be owned by others again and will never live "without memory and faith, the world of the men of [their] time."[24] The points raised in this introduction are developed in the chapters edited by Ana Lucia Araujo, Mariana P. Candido and Paul Lovejoy. This general framework is meant to inform the specific historical situations examined in this volume and enable a comparative reading of the chapters that follow.

Notes

1. I use the term *temps* as defined in Pierre Nora, ed. *Les Lieux de mémoire* (Paris: Gallimard, 1984, 1987 and 1992) instead of the common meaning in current French. A translation of a selection of Nora can be found in Lawrence D. Kritzman, ed. *Realms of Memory: Rethinking the French Past*, trans. Arthur Goldhammer (New York: Columbia University Press, 1998).

2. Here the term *temps* extends the meaning of *régime d'historicité* (regime of historicity), as discussed in François Hartog, *Régimes d'historicité: présentisme et expériences du temps* (Paris: Seuil, 2003).

3. See Paul Ricoeur's extensive discussion of the occurrence of time, specifically the meaning of its presence or its absence in *La mémoire, l'histoire, l'oubli* (Paris: Seuil, 2000). For a discussion of political representations in the sense of delegation, see the work of Pierre Rosanvalon. For the notion of *représentation* and its applications, see Maurice Halbwachs, *Les cadres sociaux de la mémoire* (Paris: Presses Universitaires de France, 1952), originally published in 1925. Unfortunately, the analysis of collective memory has not advanced beyond this examination of social frameworks. My seminar, "*Mémoires historiques d'ici et d'ailleurs: regards croisés*," involved an exchange among Mirel Banica, Christian Décobert, Danièle Hervieu-Léger, Philippe Joutard, and myself on the collective memory of religion; see www.anamnesis.tv.

4. Here, *patrimoine* or *patrimonialiser* (patrimony or patrimonialize) means the transmission, actualization and collective representation of the past, whether material or immaterial. As displayed in public spaces, such markers represent a selective presence of the past that directs the shaping of memory and prompts strong ideas of identity. To maintain flow in the translation the verb "to patrimonialize" will be used accordingly.

5. Regarding the impact of memory in which ideas are carried by "messengers," see Ian Hacking, *Historical Ontology* (Cambridge, MA: Harvard University Press, 2004).

6. Very little attention has been paid to the epistemology of non-universal knowledge, although some Indian historians have compared differences in Christian monotheism and decentralized religious thought.

7. Roger Bastide, "Mémoire collective et sociologie du bricolage," *L'Année sociologique* (1970), 65-108, and Marie-Claire Lavabre, "Roger Bastide, lecteur de Maurice Halbwachs," in *Maurice*

Halbwachs: espace, mémoires et psychologie collective, ed. Yves Deloye et Claudine Haroche (Paris: Publications de la Sorbonne, 2004), 161-171.

8. The most influential is Paul Gilroy, *The Black Atlantic: Modernity and Double Consciousness* (Cambridge, MA: Harvard University Press, 1993).

9. Today, the "South Atlantic" is more cultural in conception than academic. Historically, the South Atlantic involved interaction between Brazil and west-central and southern Africa. See Ana Lucia Araujo, "Mémoires de l'esclavage et de la traite des esclaves dans l'Atlantique Sud: enjeux de la patrimonialisation au Brésil et au Bénin" (PhD diss., Université Laval, 2007), and Luiz Felipe de Alencastro, "Le versant brésilien de l'Atlantique-Sud : 1550-1850," *Annales: Histoire, Sciences Sociales* 61, no. 2 (2006), 339-382.

10. The "imaginary" is now a legitimate concept in the social sciences; see Charles Taylor, *Modern Social Imaginaries* (Durham, NC: Duke University Press, 2004). For the connection between memory and cultural history, see Alon Confino, "Collective Memory and Cultural History: Problems of Method," *American Historical Review* 105 (1997), 1386-1403. For concepts related to cultural memory, see Jan Assmann, *Religion and Cultural Memory* (Stanford: Stanford University Press, 2006). See also Karel van der Toorn, *Scribal Culture and the Making of the Hebrew Bible* (Cambridge, MA: Harvard University Press, 2007). He suggests that the texts produced in the workshops at the time of the Second Temple were products of an intellectual culture of the scribes' universe who were working there. These scholars have pioneered the comparison and differentiation of individual and collective memories within the intellectual framework in which the exceptionality of the author emerges as creator.

11. Bogumil Jewsiewicki, *Mami wata. La peinture urbaine au Congo* (Paris: Gallimard, 2003).

12. Martin Kalulambi Pongo, *Être Luba au XXᵉ siècle* (Paris: Karthala, 1997).

13. While it is dangerous to develop biological comparisons when referring to slavery, I would nonetheless suggest that the great cultural creativity (including in the religious sphere) has arisen because of the large number of individuals (in particular in the United States and Brazil) who were able to communicate horizontally, with the transfer of information from one individual to another. Social and political

structures that could transmit transfers within communities, through a vertical transfer, did not exist. Despite the challenge of dehumanization, the slaves produced a rich and dense cultural universe. Today, as reflected in theories of globalization, horizontal transfers are seen as even more important. The societies formed by immigrants benefit from horizontal transfers of information and creativity. As Freeman Dyson has written, "Cultures spread by horizontal transfer of ideas more than by genetic inheritance. Cultural evolution is running a thousand times faster than Darwinian evolution, taking us into a new area of cultural interdependence which we call globalization." See Freeman Dyson, "Our biotech Future," *New York Review of Books* (July 17, 2007), 6; see also Carl Woese and Nigel Goldenfeld, "Biology's Next Revolution," *Nature* 445 (Feb. 8, 2007), 1-3.

14. The notion of *passing* arises from the literary genre autobiography, as examined by James Weldon Johnson, or the history of the family (the work of James M. O'Toole). For analysis of "passing" in the literature, see the work of Nella Larsen, Gayle Wald, Elaine K. Ginsberg, and Katleen Pfeiffer. For "passing" as the expression of individualism, the work of memory and forgetting developed just accidentally; see James W. Johnson, *The Autobiography of an Ex-Coloured Man* (New York: Dover, 1995); James M. O'Toole, *Passing for White: Race, Religion, and the Healy Family, 1820-1920* (Boston: University of Massachusetts Press, 2003); Nella Larsen, *Passing* (New York: Penguin Classics, 1999); Gayle Wald, *Crossing the Line: Racial Passing in Twentieth Century U.S. Literature and Culture* (Durham, NC: Duke University Press, 2000); Elaine K. Ginsberg and Donald E. Pease, ed. *Passing and the Fictions of Identity* (Durham, NC: Duke University Press, 1996); Kathleen Pfeiffer, *Race Passing and American Individualism* (Boston: University of Massachusetts Press, 2003).

15. The American specificity is institutionalized, due to the telescoping of the political condition that arose from the denial of citizenship, initially because of the status of slave and later as a result of being colonized, and also as a result of physical appearance, in particular and more generally, at least in the Occident, the color of skin; see Myriam Cottias, *La question noire. Histoire d'une construction coloniale* (Paris: Bayard, 2007). I refer to the "Occident" because, as Duvalier has observed, the same drop of blood that makes one individual a Black in the United States makes a person a White in Haiti, according to how one attributes the marker.

16. For the United States, see Gwendolyn Audrey Foster, *Class Passing. Social Mobility in Film and Popular Culture* (Chicago: Southern Illinois Press, 2005).

17. See Nicole Lapierre, "Le cadre référentiel de la Shoah" in *Mémoires plurielles, mémoires en conflit*, special issue edited by Michèle Baussant, *Ethnologie française* 37, no. 3 (2007), 475-482.

18. This specificity is relative, imposed mainly through the institutionalization of racial segregation. In Central and Eastern Europe, by comparison, the marginalization of the peasants, as descendants of the serfs, Jews or Roma, was accompanied by racialization based on alleged physical characteristics that passed to their descendants. Obviously, a stigmatizing historical heritage can be naturalized in other ways, including speech, manners of the body, etc.

19. The articulation and the interferences between the memory of having been slaves and that of being colonized operate differently in the Caribbean and the Indian Ocean, among other things owing to the fact that the masters of yesterday became later the colonists. In Africa, the masters were part of the same societies as the slaves, and the slave traders recast themselves as colonists.

20. In the United States, there is extensive documentation on the memory of slavery, including oral data of the accounts of the descendants of slaves, and visual images (pictures, paintings, etc) collected during the Great Depression. This material became public only in the 1960s and 1970s. In Brazil, the key period corresponds to that of the Utopia or "racial democracy" smoke screen.

21. See Daniel Levy and Nathan Sznaider, "Memory Unbound: the Holocaust and the Formation of Cosmopolitan Memory," *European Journal of Social Theory* 5, no. 1 (2002), 87-106.

22. I take this notion from Michel de Certeau, who designates it as a place which the control constitutes the condition of passing from the tactic to the strategy.

23. Donatien Dibwe dia Mwembu and Bogumil Jewsiewicki, ed. *Le travail hier et aujourd'hui. Mémoires de Lubumbashi* (Paris: L'Harmattan, 2004).

24. Baussant, "Penser les mémoires," 394. This quotation is from Albert Camus, *Le premier homme* (Paris: Gallimard, 1994). See the proceedings of a conference organized by the Canada Research Chair of Comparative History of Memory, *Du vrai au juste*, ed. Michèle Baussant (Québec: Presses de l'Université Laval, 2005).

Chapter 2

Personal Memory and the Collective Experience of the Slave Trade in the Autobiography of Gustavus Vassa, Alias Olaudah Equiano

Paul E. Lovejoy

The poignant account of Gustavus Vassa, whose description of the slave trade and the notorious "Middle Passage" influenced the course of British abolition, confronts the issue of authenticity.[1] Vassa presents his experiences as an Igbo boy, as an autobiography, his traumatic separation from family and home and corresponding quest for survival during transport to the Americas. There is no question that Vassa's account, and the many public lectures he gave where he reiterated his story, was a powerful influence in swaying public opinion in Britain against the slave trade, a fact that was acknowledged in his day and has been attested by scholarly analysis. The corner stone of his story was his claim to having been kidnapped as a boy of about eleven, which underlay his sale to the coast and subsequent captivity on a British slaver bound for Barbados.[2] Vassa's description helped to convince an increasingly sympathetic public that the slave trade was evil and had to be abolished. Public awareness of his story had a common theme of slavery, revealed most forcefully in the images of the horrible

"Middle Passage." In articulating a collective experience, as well as his personal odyssey, Vassa's account was intended to highlight the importance of investigative reporting. As an astute observer, he invariably had to confront the tension between autobiography and the tradition of a shared history. The problems in the accuracy of memory that is inherent when individuals recount events from their childhood, and attempts to understand trauma, are well known. As he observed in the opening sentence of *The Interesting Narrative*:

> I believe it is difficult for those who publish their own memoirs to escape the imputation of vanity; it is also their misfortune, that whatever is uncommon is rarely, if ever, believed; and what is obvious we are apt to turn from with disgust, and to charge the writer with impertinence.[3]

Vassa was able to weave together fragments from his memory, what he was able to learn from others about his homeland and the "Middle Passage," and the reflections of a mature man grappling with his life experiences. Confusion over chronology and inaccuracy of details are understandable, however rationalized. In Vassa's case, he was able to correct some details about his early life in subsequent editions of his autobiography, which provide some insight into how he conceptualized his fusion of a text for political action with a personal account of his experiences and observations.

The authenticity of *The Interesting Narrative* was a subject of concern in Vassa's time. In a letter to William Hughes, Bath, October 10, 1793, William Langworthy, recommending Vassa and his book, noted that "the simplicity that runs through his Narrative is singularly beautiful, and that beauty is heightened by the idea that it is *true*; this is all that I shall say about this book."[4] The emphasis on truth was in the original. Langworthy noted "the active part he [Vassa] took in bringing about the motion for a repeal of the Slave Act, [which] has given him much celebrity as a public man; and, in all the varied scenes of chequered life, through which he has passed, his private character and conduct have been irreproachable."[5] Vassa was "engaged in so noble a cause as the freedom and salvation of his enslaved and unenlightened country-men."[6] If he was not born in Africa, then he lied, perhaps with noble political motives, but nonetheless propagating a falsehood, since kidnapping and sale into slavery were the central features of his autobiography, intended for political reasons to advance the cause of abolition. His book sold well because he was an "authen-tic" African.

But what is to be believed in *The Interesting Narrative*? Where he was born is perhaps the most crucial element in the narrative because his account was particularly useful in the aboli-tion movement because of his kidnapping and his experience of the "Middle Passage." The reliance on memory as portrayed in his autobiography is the issue being addressed here. What did he remember? What did he forget? What is not clear? What did he hide? According to his own assessment of his autobiography,

> My life and fortune have been extremely chequered, and my adventures various. Even those I have related are considerably abridged. If any incident in this little work should appear uninteresting and trifling to most readers, I can only say, as my excuse for mentioning it, that almost every event of my life made an impres-sion on my mind, and influenced my conduct. I early accustomed myself to look at the hand of God in the minutest occurrence, and to learn from it a lesson of morality and religion; and in this light every circum-stance I have related was to me of importance.[7]

His observation certainly extended to the name that he was given, probably with some degree of humility because of its significance, but which he adopted and exploited for political ends.

Vassa appears to have attached significance to his assigned name because it drew on public knowledge of the history of his Swedish namesake. He seems to have interpreted his experiences in the context of his perception of destiny, which derived from a religious conceptualization based on his childhood acculturation as Igbo. As Paul Edwards and Rosalind Shaw have demonstrated, the concept of "*chi*" pervaded Igbo cosmology and was a factor in the psychology of Vassa.[8] As a child, he would have learned that the relationship of an individual with the supernatural was special, depending upon a personal *chi*. As he stated in *The Interesting Narrative*, "I regard myself as a *particular favourite of Heaven*, and acknowledge the mercies of Providence in every occurrence of my life."[9] His apparent reluctance when named Vassa appears to have been related to the necessity of accepting his fate. Indeed his comments on his personal destiny are consistent with this interpretation. On board ship to England with his new master, Pascal, he noted that he was "still at a loss to conjecture my destiny." He wanted to return to Africa, but he came to accept the fact that he "was reserved for another fate."[10] His recognition of this Igbo philosophical construct must have become more coherent to Vassa as he grew older and reflected on his life. He was, after all, the acknowledged leader of the black poor of London and he was determined to lead his people out of bondage.

Vassa claimed that when he sailed with Pascal for England in late 1754 "I could smatter a little imperfect English," and he claimed that

> Some of the people of the ship used to tell me they were going to carry me back to my own country, and this made me very happy. I was quite rejoiced at the idea of going back; and thought if I should get home what wonders I should have to tell.[11]

His friends and colleagues later testified to the veracity of Vassa's assertion that he did not speak English, but they could not know if he was telling the truth about where he was born. However, they could confirm his claims that he had stated publicly that he had been born in Africa. Indeed in 1759, the same year he was baptized, according to *The Interesting Narrative*, he had "frequently told several people...the story of my being kidnapped with my sister, and of our being separated." As improbable as it may seem, he briefly thought she had been found while he was at Gibraltar later in 1759, but the young woman in question turned out not to be his sister.[12] In 1779 in a letter to the bishop of London, he described himself as "a native of Africa," while he said he was "from Guinea" in the *Morning Herald* of London on 29 December 1786.[13] When Vassa subscribed to Carl Bernhard Wadstrom's, *An*

Essay on Colonization, in 1794, he listed himself as "Gustavus Vassa, a native of Africa," and when his wife died in February 1796, the *Cambridge Chronicle and Journal* reported on "On Tuesday died at Soham, after a long illness, which she supported with Christian fortitude, Mrs. Susannah Vassa, the wife of Gustavus Vassa the African."[14]

The critiques of *The Interesting Narrative* highlight a recurrent problem of verification and perspective in using autobiography for scholarly purposes. It is fortunate for this discussion that Vassa had to confront skeptics in his own day, and those who wished to discredit him focused specifically on the issue of where he was born. As the London newspaper, *Oracle*, clearly stated in 1792, "*Ex hoc uno disce omens* – this one fact tells all."[15] That he was a great writer is not in question, since his text has survived and is widely praised. Where he was born is nonetheless relevant. Since Vassa has been widely recognized as an African, and his political clout was based on this very detail, it is worth reconsidering the available evidence. Moreover, the contradictions among the various sources are worthy of reflection because of the methodological issues of how conflicting evidence is assessed.

In his own day, Vassa had to face charges that he fabricated his childhood experiences. His answers to these charges at the time to some extent anticipated the questions that Vincent Carretta has asked about the veracity of Vassa's account of his birth. In 1792, it was claimed that he had been born in the West Indies, not in the British colony of South Carolina but on the Danish island of St. Croix. Stories were published in two London newspapers, the *Oracle* and the *Star*, that challenged him to substantiate his African birth, not on the basis of any documentation, only rumor. Specifically, the editor of the *Oracle* (25 April 1792) charged him with deceiving the public.

> It is a fact that the Public may depend on, that *Gustavus Vasa*, who has publicly asserted that he was kidnapped in Africa, never was upon that Continent, but was born and bred up in the Danish Island of Santa Cruz, in the West Indies…. What, we will ask any man of plain understanding, must that cause be, which can lean for

support on falsehoods as audaciously propagated as
they are easily detected?[16]

These charges were spurious, with malicious intent, no doubt to
undermine the abolitionist movement. By contrast, Carretta is
cautious about actually claiming Vassa to have been born in South
Carolina, but the thrust of his scholarship points him in that direction. Still, it is still worth considering how Vassa responded to his
contemporary critics because there may be clues that help to place
the baptismal entry at St. Margaret's Church and his enlistment
records on the Arctic expedition of 1773 in perspective. Hence the
question: Was Vassa telling the truth about being born in Africa
when there is documentary evidence that suggests otherwise?

The response of his friends and professional associates to
accusations that he was born in the Danish West Indies is instructive, providing some verification of Vassa's account of his Igbo
origins. In a letter to Thomas Hardy, the founder of the London
Corresponding Society, with whom Vassa and his wife lived in
1792, Vassa wrote, "Sir, I am sorry to tell you that some Rascal or
Rascals have asserted in the news papers viz. Oracle of the 25th.
of april, & the Star. 27th. – that I am a native of a Danish Island,
Santa Cruz, in the Wt. Indias." The tone of the correspondence
suggests that Hardy certainly believed Vassa was born in Africa,
and hence the reason Vassa wanted Hardy to get a copy of the *Star*
"& take care of it till you see or hear from me" – Vassa signed
the letter "Gustavus Vassa The African."[17] Vassa was clearly concerned that gossip would adversely affect the sale of his book and
thereby prove a discredit to the abolition movement. Indeed if his
kidnapping, sale to the coast, and his rendition of the "Middle
Passage" were fictitious, then Vassa's credibility would have been
compromised, which it seems that his critics in the *Oracle* and the
Star consciously tried to do. Vassa responded to these charges on
the first page of the 9th edition in 1794:

> An invidious falsehood having appeared in the Oracle
> of the 25th, and the Star of the 27th of April 1792, with a
> view to hurt my character, and to discredit and prevent
> the sale of my Narrative, asserting, that I was born in
> the Danish island of Santa Cruz, in the West Indies, it

is necessary that, in this edition, I should take notice thereof, and it is only needful of me to appeal to those numerous and respectable persons of character who knew me when I first arrived in England, and could speak no language but that of Africa.[18]

This was a worthy response and should be remembered in considering more recent suspicions of his birth in South Carolina. Vassa never claimed that the details of the interior of the Bight of Biafra were entirely based on his own experiences. He specifically noted that his account was an "imperfect sketch my memory has furnished me with the manners and customs of a people among whom I first drew my breath," and he acknowledged that he had gained information from some of the "numbers of the natives of Eboe" he encountered in London.[19] His discussions in London influenced what he wrote, just as his quotations from Benezet and other sources did, but the weight of evidence still indicates that Vassa had firsthand knowledge of Africa.[20]

Vincent Carretta claims that documents on the birth of Gustavus Vassa and his subsequent employment in the British navy "cast doubt" on the early life of the person usually recognized as Olaudah Equiano, author of *The Interesting Narrative of the Life of Olaudah Equiano, or Gustavus Vassa, the African. Written by Himself.*[21] The two documents in question are his baptismal record at St. Margaret's Church in London from 1759 and the muster records from the Arctic expedition of Sir John Phipps (later Lord Mulgrave) in 1773, both of which attest to his birth in South Carolina. Carretta casts his web of doubt even broader, suggesting that Vassa/Equiano was born in 1747, not 1745 as claimed in *The Interesting Narrative*, and certainly not in 1742, as I have argued elsewhere.[22] For Carretta, the author of *The Interesting Narrative* was a "self-made" man, adopting a public image as Olaudah Equiano, who had been born in Africa, when in fact he was known as Gustavus Vassa, and had been born in South Carolina. For Carretta, "self-made" has a double meaning, including both his success in achieving his emancipation and becoming famous through the fictionalization of his childhood to achieve this end.

According to Carretta, the evidence suggests that "the author of *The Interesting Narrative* may have invented rather than reclaimed an African identity," and if this is the case, then it follows that "he invented his African childhood and his much-quoted account of the Middle Passage on a slave ship." In short, a documented birthplace in South Carolina and problems in Vassa's memory of his youth are sufficient grounds to express "reasonable doubt" about Vassa's claim to an African birth. Indeed, Carretta considers that "the burden of proof . . . is now on those who believe that *The Interesting Narrative* is a historically accurate piece of non-fiction" and that "anyone who still contends that Equiano's account of the early years of his life is authentic is obligated to account for the powerful conflicting evidence."[23]

The methodological issues here relate to how historians engage oral tradition, memory, and other non-written sources with the written record. If Equiano was an eyewitness to events and practices in Africa, that's one thing. If his account is a composite of stories and information gathered from others, it's another matter. Despite some qualifications, Carretta essentially claims that the first part of *The Interesting Narrative* is a fictionalized account of life in Africa and the horrors of the Middle Passage, whereas I think that there is sufficient internal evidence to conclude that the account is essentially authentic, although certainly informed by later reflection, Vassa's acquired knowledge of Africa, and memories of others whom he knew to have come from the Bight of Biafra. The reflections and memories used in autobiography are always filtered, but despite this caveat, I would conclude that Vassa was born in Africa and not in South Carolina.

The controversy arises from the interpretation of Vassa's life before the summer of 1754, and here my reconstruction varies considerably from Carretta's. Perhaps we are pursuing historical understanding in different ways. Carretta pushes the evidence that casts doubts on what Vassa says. While Carretta appears to have uncovered evidence that Vassa was a fraud and that he knowingly lied, I ask: What if he was telling the truth? Then how do we account for evidence that conflicts with what he said? Moreover, when would he have invented his narrative, what evidence is there that helps to explain the construction of the narrative, and why would he deliberately have altered his natal home? How did he sustain the deception, if he constructed an African birth but in fact was born in South Carolina? As Carretta notes, "Vassa himself of course may not have been responsible for the information or misinformation regarding the place and date of his birth recorded at his baptism, but the correct information was presumably available to the future Mrs. Baynes, who Vassa later said first knew him as African."[24] This contradiction alone raises questions about the baptismal record. Similarly, the fact that he worked for Dr. Charles Irving on the Arctic expedition in 1773, and later was involved with Irving in the abortive plantation scheme on the Mosquito Shore in 1776, has not been examined carefully. On the Arctic expedition, Vassa registered his birthplace as South Carolina, while Irving hired him for the Mosquito Shore venture because he could speak the language of his "countrymen," i.e. Igbo.[25]

The biggest lacuna in Carretta's scholarship is the answer to the question: Where did Vassa acquire his understanding of Igbo cosmology and society, and indeed his knowledge of the Igbo language, as revealed in the vocabulary that he mentions in *The Interesting Narrative*? Did he learn it in the Carolinas before he was sold to Pascal? This is unlikely, since there were few Igbo in South Carolina, and he was not in Virginia long enough to meet any one with whom he could speak, according to his own testimony, even though there were relatively many Igbo speakers in the tidewater region. He clearly did not speak English, although by this time if he had come from Africa he would probably have begun to learn some words. If he had been born in South Carolina, he would have known English in the form spoken on plantations, a pidgin but nonetheless English. If he did understand Igbo, then, where and when did he learn it?

According to Carretta, Vassa's account of Africa is a combination of printed sources, memory, and imagination.[26] But is it really safe to conclude that because Vassa had great literary skills he made it all up? I think not. Anthony Benezet has been cited as a source, and it is clear that Benezet was an influence on Vassa's political development, which he duly acknowledges in *The Interesting Narrative*. But what could Vassa have learned from him? A close reading of Benezet's books and pamphlets reveals that he had absolutely nothing to say about Igboland or Igbo culture and society.[27] His work, with its noble antislavery polemics, is nothing more than long quotes from different sources to prove his point that slavery is evil and that everything possible should be done to stamp it out. Benezet's ideological and moral position was an important influence in Vassa's comprehension of the political and religious aspects of abolition, but he was not a source of information on Igboland.

According to Carretta, "Despite claiming to describe distinctively Igbo manners, he [Vassa] conflates accounts of various African ethnic groups to construct a kind of pan-African identity, a sort of essential African."[28] Carretta does not make it clear which ethnic groups are conflated, and I would argue, to the contrary, that Vassa provides the earliest information on several important Igbo institutions, including some insight into how these institutions operated before the middle of the eighteenth century. Most important, in my opinion, is Vassa's description of the *ichi* facial markings and their significance. Indeed, I would assert that Vassa's description of his country and his people are sufficient confirmation that he was born where he said he was, and based on when boys received the *ichi* scarification, that he was about 11 when he was kidnapped, as he claims, which suggests a birth date of ca. 1742, not 1745 or 1747. This shift in the chronology is warranted on the basis of internal evidence in *The Interesting Narrative* and the fact that Pascal arrived in England in December 1754 with the slave boy he had named Gustavus Vassa.

If Carretta is correct about Vassa's age at the time of baptism, accepting the documentary evidence, then he was too young to have created a complex fraud about origins. The fraud must have been perpetrated later, but when? Certainly the baptismal record cannot be used as proof that he committed fraud, only that his godparents might have. But why would they have done so is the question, not what a slave might have said in St. Margaret's Church, where the Members of Parliament met for morning prayers before opening session. Vassa was in the sanctuary of power, one of the few slaves ever baptized in St. Margaret's, and he was given a birthplace of Carolina. Was this a social event, a fraud of another kind, a joke? He was, after all, none other than Gustavus Vassa, the savior of his people, named after the liberator of Sweden, and seems to have believed that he had been promised manumission on baptism. The text itself points to authenticity, not fraud. It is the detail in the baptismal registry that requires explanation. As Carretta observes, Vassa provides details during and after the Seven Years' War, which, when possible to verify, are remarkably accurate.

Vassa's descriptions of Igbo cultural features are not generic African practices or some garbled merging of accounts, as Carretta claims. Moreover, Carretta is not accurate in stating that "modern scholars rightly point out that of the surviving brief eighteenth-century descriptions of the kingdom of Benin, Equiano's account of Igboland is the most fully developed."[29] In my opinion, this is inaccurate because Vassa's account has nothing to do with the kingdom of Benin, which Vassa added to his narrative on the basis of reading Benezet, who specifically did not discuss Igboland. Vassa was attempting to situate what he knew within the framework of what was known about Africa, and similarly he used such terms as "Libyan" and "Ethiopian" to try to achieve the same results. He also contrasted his people with Jews and Muslims, once again to establish similarities and differences with his own memories of his homeland. The relationship with the kingdom of Benin is in fact plausible, but only parts of Igboland west of the Niger River were tributary to Benin in the eighteenth century, and the area that Vassa was from almost certainly was not that part of Igboland, but rather central Igboland, to the east of the Niger River. While Vassa drew on published sources for what he knew about other parts of Africa, there is nothing in any of the known sources that he used that actually has anything to say about Igboland. His information had to have been derived from his own experience and whatever he learned in London from some of his "countrymen."

Vassa also engaged in comparing the customs of his own people with others, and these comparisons further attest to his Africanity. He observed that Europeans did not sell each other,

> as we did...and in this I thought they were much happier than we Africans. I was astonished at the wisdom of the white people in all things I saw; but was amazed at their not sacrificing, or making any offerings, and eating with unwashed hands, and touching the dead. I likewise could not help remarking the

particular slenderness of the women, which I did not
at first like, and I thought they were not so modest and
shamefaced as the African women.[30]

When Vassa was on board the *Aetna*, he became friends with
Daniel Queen, who taught him to read the Bible, with which Vassa
was fascinated for reasons that again highlighted his interest in
understanding his recollections of his country:

> I was wonderfully surprised to see the laws and
> rules of my country written almost exactly here [in
> the Bible]; a circumstance which I believe tended to
> impress our manners and customs more deeply on my
> memory. I used to tell him of this resemblance; and
> many a time we have sat up the whole night together
> at this employment.[31]

Carretta concludes that these accounts demonstrate that Vassa
was beginning to invent his past, but I would suggest that he was
making the comparisons that were necessary for him to comprehend his childhood in Africa and that would ultimately help
him to convey its meaning to his readers.[32] Vassa compared the
customs of his people with Jewish traditions, which is the first and
independent tradition of Hebrew origins in southeastern Nigeria,
now a wide spread tradition that is seemingly unconnected with
Vassa's examination of common myths. Similarly, he observed
practices in his brief visit to Symrna (Izna) in Ottoman Turkey
that also brought forth comparisons. These reflections, in my
opinion, reflect an astute mind.

Why his birth was recorded as South Carolina when he was
telling people otherwise is a puzzle, but the consistency in his
testimony, in my mind, cannot simply be dismissed and certainly
reduces the likelihood of fraud; indeed a close reading of the
available texts makes it most likely that he was born where he said
he was.Vassa visited South Carolina several times in the 1760s
but gives no hint that he had previously been there as a child,
had family there, or that he knew anyone or anything about the
area, which seems an odd omission (and only could have been
consciously introduced in a manner constituting fraud). Admittedly he may well have been the "self-made man" that Carretta

conjures up in his thoughtful biography, but if he falsified his place of birth and the story of the "Middle Passage" for purposes of political and indeed literary purposes, in which he advanced the cause of abolition, and ultimately emancipation, he intriguingly mixed fiction and autobiography in a successful experiment in English literature. Nonetheless, it seems to this historian, that the difficulty in establishing the literary license taken by authors has to be recognized.

Generally, historical methodology is a process of assessing the evidence in the context of known documentation and other source materials, never trusting any document or other piece of evidence more than it can be verified. The degree of speculation and interpretation are matters of reflection. If Vassa invented his origins, as Carretta suggests, then he had to find a means of establishing his African birth without undermining what would be the basis of his credibility in his adult life, when his political image was significant. If he falsified his place of birth later in life, after confessing to a South Carolina birth when he was a teenager and when he was on the exciting and well publicized Arctic expedition of Constantine Phipps, seven years after he had purchased his own emancipation, but then subsequently suppressed the fact of a South Carolina origin that he commanded a degree of foresight that would honor of the memory of the original Gustavus Vassa, who mythically liberated his people. The suppression of the "creole" birth suggests a degree of consciousness that makes Vassa too clever.

Vassa is one of first to say he was an African, and in accordance with contemporary usages in Europe, to be equated with Ethiopians and Libyans. As Alexander Byrd has demonstrated, Vassa's use of these concepts reflects evolving meanings of nation and citizenship as discussed in the late eighteenth century.[33] The term "Eboe" as used by Vassa had various meanings. In the eighteenth century, apparently, it was not a term that described a common ethnic identity because its implication was pejorative; it meant "other" people. It meant both neighbors and foreigners, who presumably spoke a dialect of Igbo, and who in fact would now be recognized as Igbo. Vassa's use of these various terms, and others such as "countrymen" and "nation" are important examples of how Vassa, and by extension, others from Africa and of African descent were grappling with issues of identity and community. He also used the term "African" to designate his place of birth in Africa, which occasionally he also refers to as Lybia.

Hence, it may appear that Carretta has a good case, much better than that of Vassa's critics who first challenged his claim of an African birth in 1792. The baptism record states age and place of birth, as does the Arctic muster book (despite differences in the derived date of birth, the baptism record suggesting a date of birth in 1747, and the Arctic list indicating 1745). The weakness in Carretta's argument arises from his understanding of the ethnography and history of the interior of the Bight of Biafra. Moreover, Carretta's chronology for Vassa's life is not supported by the available evidence, and it is more likely that Vassa was born before he says he was, rather than later. This reconstruction suggests that he was about 12 when he first arrived in England, as he states in *The Interesting Narrative*, which we know to have been in December 1754. If he had been born in 1747, as Carretta has concluded, it is unlikely that he could have earned his freedom between 1763 and 1766, in fact earning much more than the cost of his ransom because he suffered from theft and non-payment. It would have meant that he earned his freedom by the time he was 19. If this were the case, he would have been a most unusual young man indeed. If however, he were born in 1742, he would have been baptized when he was 17, earning his freedom by the time he was 24, which seems more plausible.

The baptismal and naval documents raise important issues, especially since "Equiano" has been claimed as "American" and *The Interesting Narrative* the archetypal "slave narrative."[34] In fact, Vassa spent only a few months in Virginia in 1754, and later visited for brief periods on ships trading to South Carolina, Georgia and Philadelphia as a slave, and then as a freeman trading to Georgia and South Carolina. As a free sailor, he also visited Philadelphia and New York in 1785 and 1786.[35] As a Briton, he displayed a keen interest in science through his friendship with Dr. Irving, expressed himself musically through his mastery of the French horn, participated in debating societies (most notably the London Corresponding Society, as one of its first members), and demonstrated his commitment to interracial marriage through his liaison with Susannah Cullen. Hence the issue is not the validity of autobiography, whether something is being remembered accurately or being distorted for some purpose of obfuscation or political intent, but whether or not subsequent generations and scholarship choose to interpret ambiguities in a particular fashion. Vassa was a prominent, historical figure, and it matters whether or not he was telling the truth about his birth.

Autobiography does not necessarily reflect memory accurately, since what is written is selective, embellished or simplified depending upon the conscious or unconscious will of the author. Moreover, memory is not a replica of what actually happened but an interpretation of context and circumstances, which often were incompletely understood and require interpolation. Autobiography can be used in the reconstruction of events that are clouded in memory, but to use autobiography as a means of understanding what people remember, and why, requires examining the details being presented in the narrative in context and checked against all available evidence, not just written documentation. The methodological issues surrounding where Vassa was born confront memories of slavery and abolition and their meanings. The fact that Vassa may *not* have been born in Africa is a significant detail that casts a shadow on the veracity of the eyewitness accounts recorded in his life story. The challenge of *The Oracle* that "*Ex hoc uno disce omens* – this one fact tells all" foreshadowed recent accusations that he falsified his place of birth, even if for noble political motives. Sometimes documents may suggest that an individual lied, when in fact that may not have been the case at all.

Methodologically, the early life history of Gustavus Vassa, when he had the name Olaudah Equiano, raises interesting questions of verification and context. Independent written documents claiming a Carolina birth conflict with personal testimony and ultimately the oral account of the person whose place of birth is in question. While the baptismal record at St. Margaret's Church is difficult to explain, the record of Vassa's name on the Arctic expedition of 1773 is more understandable. It is unlikely that Vassa would have contradicted the information on his baptismal record at the time of the Arctic expedition. As a former slave, he undoubtedly relied on his document of manumission, which he published in his *Interesting Narrative*, and most likely his baptismal record, too. The existence of separate documents that claim a Carolina birth may seem difficult to reconcile with Vassa's own account of his birth in Africa, but perhaps less so than some have thought. The veracity of documents that seem irrefutable is called into question when placed in context. The contradictory testimony of the sister of Vassa's god-mother, who attended his baptism in 1759, and then in 1792 verified that he only knew an "African" tongue when she first met him, raises questions about baptism and whether or not Vassa provided the information for the record. This is not known, but according to a number of sources, it is clear that he was not familiar with the English language until after he became Pascal's slave. Only in 1759, at the time of his baptism was he able to "speak English tolerably well, and I perfectly understood every thing that was said."[36] Hence he may have known what was being entered on his baptismal record, but whether he conspired in the inaccuracy contained therein is impossible to know.

Vassa clearly told the man he worked for, Dr. Charles Irving, that he was an African and spoke Igbo, and on that basis, the Mosquito Shore expedition was planned. It is unlikely that Dr. Irving would have otherwise later employed him in a plantation scheme unless he had knowledge of Igbo. Hence it is a question of when he told the truth, whether in his autobiography or at the time of his baptism and the voyage to the Arctic. It is likely that as a former slave that he kept with him key documents that could be used to verify his status as a freeman, including the letter of emancipation from King, which is reproduced in *The Interesting Narrative*. It would have been unwise to contradict his baptismal record but rather inevitable that he would use it, in which case he would not have said that he was born anywhere other than South Carolina.

Because there is conflicting evidence, the documentary information in itself is not sufficient to prove that he was born in South Carolina. Wherever he was born, he embraced an African birth, which affected his conscious development of an Igbo identity and his association with an African community, but ultimately he was committed to a multi-racial society, as evidenced in his marriage. In my opinion, the preponderant evidence derived from culture and context confirms his African birth and the documents that claim otherwise have to be interpreted accordingly. What appears to establish his place of birth as South Carolina disappears when the chronology of his *Narrative* is more carefully reconstructed. Vassa was likely two or three years older than he thought, not younger as Carretta has concluded.

When all factors are considered, especially in consequence of what he reveals about eighteenth-century culture and society in Igboland, the most reasonable conclusion in assessing whether or not Vassa was born in Africa or in America is to believe what Vassa claimed, that he was born in a place called "Essaka." Hence his account of his homeland and the terror of the "Middle Passage" should be considered as being derived from his memory, which he attempted to place in the context of what was known in Britain about Africa. As Vassa's account demonstrates, the collective experience is reconstructed through the medium of memory, political and social motives, and efforts to interpret fill partially understood experiences.

As Vassa's account demonstrates, autobiography is based on selective memory, which is interpreted in the context of later knowledge, the efforts of the individual to provide analysis and explanation, and the attempts to disguise or underplay information deemed inappropriate for the exposition. As Carretta has argued, in one sense it matters not whether or not Vassa personally experienced a kidnapping or the traumatic "Middle Passage" because his account reflects a collective memory that has been verified in its descriptive power through contemporary evidence. As in other autobiographical accounts, his description of his childhood was flavored with additional information learned later in life, which he admitted informed his reflections on what he remembered and how he attempted to understand his early experiences. A variance in detail between what he stated and what probably happened exposes a methodological problem that faces anyone working with autobiography.

Notes

1. Funding for this research has been provided by the Social Sciences and Humanities Research Council of Canada. Mark Duffill has assisted in researching Dr. Charles Irving and related subjects and has provided commentary on aspects of Vassa's life that are incorporated here as appropriate. Ana Lucia Araujo and Henry Lovejoy made useful suggestions for improving the paper, which I acknowledge with thanks.

2. See Vassa's account in *The Interesting Narrative of the Life of Olaudah Equiano, or Gustavus Vassa, the African. Written by Himself* (London, 1789), which has been republished many times. The version used here is edited by Vincent Carretta, *The Interesting Narrative and Other Writings* (New York: Penguin, 2003). When Vassa's text itself is cited, reference is to Vassa, *Interesting Narrative*; when other materials from this edition are cited, the reference is to Carretta, *Interesting Narrative and Other Writings*.

3. Vassa, *Interesting Narrative*, 31.

4. William Langworthy to William Hughes, Bath, October 10, 1793, originally published in the 1794 edition, and reproduced in Carretta, *Interesting Narrative and Other Writings*, 11-12.

5. Langworthy to Hughes, October 10, 1793.

6. Langworthy to Hughes, October 10, 1793.

7. Vassa, *Interesting Narrative*, 236.

8. Paul Edwards and Rosalind Shaw, "The Invisible *Chi* in Equiano's *Interesting Narrative*," *Journal of Religion in Africa* 19 (1989), 146-56.

9. Vassa, *Interesting Narrative*, 31. Emphasis in the original.

10. Vassa, *Interesting Narrative*, 64.

11. Vassa, *Interesting Narrative*, 64.

12. Carretta, *Interesting Narrative and Other Writings*, 79-80. As James H. Sweet has noted, Vassa's anxiety about his sister is a "powerful clue" that has to be recognized; see "Mistaken Identities? Olaudah Equiano, Domingo Álvares, and the Methodological Challenges of Studying the African Diaspora," *American Historical Review* 114, no. 2 (2009), 302-303.

13. Cited in Vincent Carretta, *Equiano the African: Biography of a Self Made Man* (Athens, GA: 2005), 3.

14. *Cambridge Chronicle and Journal*, 20 February 1796, cited in Carretta, *Equiano, the African*, 363.

15. *The Oracle*, 25 April, 1792.

16. The article also charged that Wilberforce and the Thorntons were "concerned in settling the island of Bulam in Sugar Plantations; of course their interests clash with those of the present Planters and hence their clamour against the Slave Trade." *The Oracle*, 25 April, 1792; in Carretta, *Interesting Narrative and Other Writings*, 237. For the attack in the *Star*, see ibid., 238.

17. Vassa to Thomas Hardy, Edinburgh, May 28, 1792, TS 24/12/2 (National Archives), and reprinted in Carretta, *Interesting Narrative and Other Writings*, 361-362.

18. The passage was addressed "To the Reader;" see Carretta, *Interesting Narrative and Other Writings*, 5.

19. Vassa, *Interesting Narrative*, 38.

20. For a discussion of Benezet's likely influence on Vassa, see Maurice Jackson, *Let This Voice Be Heard: Anthony Benezet, Father of Atlantic Abolitionism* (Philadelphia: University of Pennsylvania Presss, 2009), 155, 194-199.

21. Vincent Carretta, "Olaudah Equiano or Gustavus Vassa? New Light on an Eighteenth-Century Question of Identity," *Slavery and Abolition* 20, 3 (1999), 96-105.

22. Paul E. Lovejoy, "Autobiography and Memory: Gustavus Vassa, alias Olaudah Equiano, the African," *Slavery and Abolition* 27, no. 3 (2006), 317-347.

23. Carretta, *Equiano the African*, xiv-xv.

24. Carretta, "Olaudah Equiano or Gustavus Vassa?" 101.

25. It is clear to me that Irving understood that Vassa would recruit his own "countrymen," meaning those who spoke the African language that he knew. He later added the epithet "Lybian," which Alexander X. Byrd and James Sweet exaggerate, in my opinion; see Alexander X. Byrd, "Eboe, Country, Nation and Gustavus Vassa's *Interesting Narrative*," *William and Mary Quarterly* 63, no. 1 (2006), 123-148; and Sweet, "Mistaken Identities," 303. Vassa used the terms "African" and "Lybian" at different times and in ways that suggest that the terms were synonymous, meaning that they came from Africa.

26. Carretta, *Equiano the African*, 7.

27. Anthony Benezet, *Some Historical Account of Guinea, Its Situation, Produce and the General Disposition of its Inhabitants with an Inquiry into the Rise and Progress of the Slave Trade, its nature and lamentable effects* (London: Frank Cass, [1771] 1968). Benezet quoted at length various European observations of western Africa, but nothing on the interior of the Bight of Biafra, skipping from the kingdom of Benin to Kongo and Angola in his descriptions and reports. He quotes some information on Barbados that presumably Vassa could have used, but not on his homeland. However, as Jackson has noted, Vassa probably transferred descriptions from elsewhere in Africa to his homeland; see Jackson, *Let This Voice Be Heard*, 194-199.

28. Carretta, *Equiano the African*, 312.

29. Carretta, *Equiano the African*, 319.

30. Vassa, *Interesting Narrative*, 68.

31. Vassa, *Interesting Narrative*, 82.

32. According to Carretta, "Queen played a crucial role in Equiano's later reconstruction of an African past," although how this was so is not explained. Queen did help Vassa with his education, however. See Carretta, *Equiano, the African*, 82.

33. Byrd, "Eboe, Country, Nation," 123-148.

34. But contrast the approach of Gates and others with that of Paul Edwards and James Walvin, *Black Personalities in the Era of the Slave Trade* (London: Macmillan, 1983), 16-34; and Folarin Shyllon, *Black People in Britain 1555-1833* (London: Oxford University Press, 1977).

35. Carretta, *Equiano the African*, 201.

36. Vassa, *Interesting Narrative*, 77.

Chapter 3

"The 'Brazilians' Are Us:" Identity and Gender in the Memory of the Atlantic Slave Trade in Ketu

Lorelle D. Semley

Residents of the Yoruba town of Ketu in southeastern Republic of Benin talk about Brazilians living in their midst. These Brazilians reputedly live a few miles away in the small village of Ofia, which used to be part of the Ketu kingdom. When I arrived in Ofia curious about Brazilians living there, the king of Ofia responded matter-of-factly that, "The 'Brazilians' are us." Ketu residents began calling Ofia villagers "Brazilians" after the king developed a smaller version of a slave route site similar to the one established in Ouidah, Benin in 1993.[1] While Ketu residents misunderstood and perhaps derided Ofia's slave route project, in the end, the site has very little to do with Brazil or the Atlantic slave trade. Instead, it displays local history and gender relationships through art, history, and myth. Why create sculptures of a mermaid, a hunter, or a masquerade festival as part of a slave trade exhibit? This chapter argues that the history of West Africa and the Atlantic slave trade displayed in the Ofia exhibit poses important intellectual and methodological challenges that force scholars to rethink African diaspora history.[2]

The history of Ketu and Ofia engages West African and African diaspora history through two broad themes: identity and gender. First, Ketu defies our sense of African identities based on discrete cultural groups and political states. Ketu was a Yoruba kingdom composed of numerous dependent villages including Ofia. Ketu also sat at the nexus of multiple, diverse towns and states and was itself heterogeneous. For its part, Ofia claims an alternate history that challenges social and political power of Ketu during the era of the Atlantic slave trade. Ketu and Ofia are not the sites of actual returned Brazilian ("Aguda") communities found on the West African coast, so the exhibit in Ofia raises questions about how West Africans remember and represent their connections to the African diaspora. Second, scholars often overlook how Africans and their descendants in the Americas evoke gender in their history and memory of the Atlantic slave trade. Some Afro-Brazilians claim that enslaved women from Ketu founded Candomblé, an African-derived religion, in Bahia, in northeastern Brazil. While the Ofia exhibit does not tap into that history, references to gender in the history, myth, and religion throughout the site recast local African and African diaspora histories.

Recent African diaspora scholarship by Africanists and Americanists highlight a "return" to Africa. The Nigerian Hinterland Project based at York University tackles the historical effects of the Atlantic slave trade in the African diaspora *and* Africa.[3] Such studies recognize specific groups of enslaved Africans not as "unitary" or "static" but as "varied, complex, and fluid."[4] But African diaspora scholarship from this "new" perspective often speaks less to the complexity of African society itself than to the diverse influences of returned slaves and their descendants on Africa.[5] Much of this newer scholarship which embraces Africa as part of an Atlantic world focuses on people whom Ira Berlin names the "Atlantic creoles" of the West and West Central African coast.[6] Sitting almost sixty miles inland, beyond a stretch of thick marsh, Ketu provides a different context for the examination of West Africa's role in an Atlantic world.

Ketu also raises important questions about the role of gender in the history of the Atlantic slave trade. How did women move along the networks that linked Ketu, other parts of West Africa, and the Americas? How have people on both sides of the Atlantic remembered and portrayed gender and the Atlantic slave trade? While African diaspora studies are paying more attention to women and are exploring the rich discourse of black masculinity in the Americas, more work remains to be done on gender relationships and the construction of femininity.[7] Joseph Miller challenges scholars to shed modernist assumptions about identities and understand how Africans sought to "restore" an idea of the self and community. Any discussion of the African diaspora must grapple with issues of identity, gender, and power on the African side of what J. Lorand Matory aptly calls a "Afro-Atlantic dialogue."[8]

Defining The "Children of Ketu"

Scholars continue to debate if the people who physically bridged West Africa and the Americas traveled in specific "groups" or in more amorphous "crowds."[9] Still, most studies focus on how oppressive conditions and intense cultural interaction in the Americas forged new ideas about African ethnicity and race. But, by the eighteenth and nineteenth century, West Africa, particularly in the Bight of Benin region, already exhibited the cultural contact and innovation occurring in slave societies in the Americas during the same era. The Ketu kingdom, in particular, sat at a cultural crossroads between fellow Yoruba-speaking towns and Gbe-speakers, particularly the Dahomey kingdom. Looking broadly at the links between Ketu, Yoruba, Gbe, and other communities, I will show how Ketu was part of the flow of people, goods, and ideas that define the Atlantic world in the modern era. In many ways, Ofia claims many of the same political and cultural Atlantic world connections for itself in its slave route exhibit.

The Ketu kingdom was one of the diverse subgroups and towns that comprise the Yoruba-speaking community of Nigeria, Benin Republic and Togo.[10] By the seventeenth century, the Oyo subgroup founded an empire at Oyo-Ile to the northeast of Ketu. Other major Yoruba subgroups in Nigeria include the Egba, Yewa (Egbado), Ijesha, Ife, and Ijebu. Yoruba-speaking groups in Benin Republic include Shabe to the north of Ketu, Anago to the south, and Dassa to the west. The presence of numerous distinct towns, dialects, and kings did not mean that Yoruba communities did not recognize shared histories and cultural practices between them. In 1853, Alaketu[11] Adebia claimed to be the elder of three brothers who founded the Yoruba towns of Ketu, Oyo, and Abeokuta. The

Alaketu's declaration appeared boastful and exaggerated but not entirely: Ketu did predate the newer Abeokuta state formed in the 1820s and New Oyo was founded after the desertion of Oyo-Ile in 1836. Alaketu Adebia also ostensibly linked the cultural practices of Ketu, Oyo, and Abeokuta because in the same breath, he described the king of Gbe-speaking Dahomey (perhaps with some irony) as a "true friend and neighbor."[12] Indeed, Yoruba groups lived in isolation neither from one another nor other ethnic groups.

Gbe-speaking villages composed one part of the Ketu kingdom. The large Gbe-speaking state of Dahomey lay only two days away to the west of Ketu. While Dahomey paid tribute to Oyo-Ile during the eighteenth century, eighteenth century visitors to Dahomey claimed that Ketu fought wars with Dahomey.[13] When Oyo-Ile began to decline in the late eighteenth and early nineteenth century, Dahomey raided many Yoruba-speaking towns, destroying Ketu in 1886.

But the relationship between Ketu, its Yoruba neighbors, and Dahomey was not only about war. For example, Dahomey borrowed a range of religious and cultural practices from Yoruba to the east, the Mahi to the North, and as far as the Akan to the west.[14] John Peel argues that Yoruba towns, especially those to the north and west implicitly and explicitly incorporated Muslim influences in terms of dress, Ifa divination, and perhaps even the recognition of a Creator God.[15] Matory describes a "transatlantic Djedji/ Jeje" (Gbe) identity that migrated back and forth between the Bight of Benin and Bahia between the mid-nineteenth century and the 1930s.[16] War and various forms of exchange brought diverse African neighbors into contact but social boundaries allowed people to move between status as insiders, outsiders, and those in-between.

By the nineteenth century, Ketu, like many West African towns, consisted of a walled center and a series of dependent villages and farming hamlets. Residents of the central town and the outlying villages identified as "omo Ketu" meaning "children of Ketu." But villages also sought new protectors/allies or claimed outright autonomy as the situation changed.[17] Likewise, the connection between village and town (capital) changed over time and space. For example, in 1825, when Hugh Clapperton traveled through the towns of the Yewa (Egbado) region, his Muslim guides from Oyo-Ile told him it was a "department of Oyo" and the people were all "servants of the King" (of Oyo-Ile) some thirty days journey away. An era of Oyo expansion into the region beginning in the eighteenth century turned the corridor from Oyo to the coast into a province of the Oyo empire.[18] But some of these major Yewa (Egbado) towns may have had an earlier link to Ketu. Then, in the 1830s, with Oyo-Ile's light fading, the Yewa (Egbado) region faced a second devastating change. In retaliation for the region's support of Ibadan, Abeokuta decimated the Yewa (Egbado) region.[19] By the 1850s, the most western edge of the Yewa (Egbado) region claimed allegiance to Ketu. Though, today, the border with Nigeria marks the end of Ketu territory toward the east, in the first half of the nineteenth century, Ketu's influence reached just beyond the Yewa River in Nigeria to a village called Ijale about twenty-five miles away. War and displacement that erupted across Yorubaland in the nineteenth century contributed to shifts in borders and influence. John Peel astutely refers to the nineteenth century as an "age of confusion."[20] But the nineteenth century also was an age of cultural diffusion, albeit under violent circumstances.

In 1851, when American Baptist missionary Thomas Bowen approached Ketu's walled town, an African man greeted him in Portuguese. Bowen believed the man to be a returned slave from Brazil but the man retreated when he realized that Bowen did not speak Portuguese. Most studies of returned Brazilian populations argue that Brazilians had to stay on the coast for fear of enslavement in the interior.[21] With little information on this particular individual, his presence says little about a specific Brazilian presence in Ketu. Instead, the brief appearance of this man illustrated the range of identities in a place like Ketu in the nineteenth century. Although Ketu did not have an open slave market, a number of war captives and other slaves passed through the town during Bowen's visit because Abeokuta had defeated Dahomey in the weeks before. Abeokuta traders brought Dahomey captives to Ketu in order to ransom them to Dahomey traders. One captured Dahomey soldier was a Ketu woman. Rather than allow her anxious relatives to purchase her freedom, she decided to "go back to her master." The woman represented an untold number of Ketu women and men living in neighboring communities as wives, slaves, traders or soldiers.[22] Enslaved outsiders also could become part of Ketu's population. Bowen met a female trader who had been kidnapped from a market to the east the Oyo-Yoruba region. The woman had passed through several slave markets before arriving in Ketu. She asked her owner to let her speak to Bowen whom she implored to purchase her. This woman had heard stories about the slave trade and desperately fought to avoid the ships on the coast.[23] But slaves were not the only outsiders visiting and living in Ketu. Muslims resided in the town and Bowen assumed that they formed part of the hostile coalition that cheered his departure after his one month stay.[24]

As the first eyewitness account of Ketu, Bowen's account opened a series of questions about Ketu identity and the impact of the slave trade. Did people retain a Ketu identity if they found themselves living as a stranger or slave in a different land, such as Dahomey? Did strangers, including Muslims and slaves, living in Ketu view themselves as "children of Ketu" or citizens)? Did gender affect the nature of one's movement through the region in specific ways? Subsequent descriptions of Ketu illustrated that mobility, danger, and multifaceted identities remained part of nineteenth century Ketu realities.

When famed Yoruba missionary Samuel Crowther of the Church Missionary Society (CMS) visited Ketu in January 1853, he observed the vitality of the economic and social exchange between Ketu and its neighbors. The vibrant market every four days featured traders from up to two weeks travel away, as well as traders from neighboring Dahomey and the coastal town of Porto-Novo. Ketu served as a meeting point of trans-Saharan and Atlantic trade routes as cloth from the interior was traded for the rum and tobacco of the Atlantic trade.[25] Ketu's apparent openness brought temporary residents and migrants who became part of the fabric of the town. The head of the Baatonu (Bariba) caravan of traders had a home in the walled center.[26] Crowther expressed suspicion toward the Muslims who resided in the town, though Alaketu Adebia never singled out Muslims, in particular, as troublemakers. Female traders also frequented Ketu and along with ordinary female residents they "walk[ed] freely at night."[27]

The mobile female traders served as an important point of contrast for Crowther who expressed pity for the "wretched" wives of the Alaketu whose shaven heads and simple clothing indicated their special status in the community. With a large number of "aya oba" or royal wives, Ketu king shared in regional practices of displaying wives and dependants as symbols of wealth and prestige. However, royal wives embodied contradictory forms of freedom and power, whether as messengers in the former Oyo-Ile empire or as ministers and soldiers in Dahomey.[28] Even in Ketu, royal wives reflected conflicting images about the power and subordination of women. The wives of the Alaketu served as frequent emissaries to visiting nineteenth-century missionaries. Ketu residents I interviewed expressed a slight disdain for the confined women with shaved heads, on the one hand. But they also explained how the royal wives carried calabashes in public to serve as seats because no one could reuse a chair once a royal wife sat there. The royal wives in Ketu provided one glimpse into important West African ideas about gender and power that circulated in the Atlantic world in the modern era.

Ketu residents also experienced the fragility of political power. A few months after Crowther's visit, West African CMS catechist James Barber visited Ketu upon the death of the powerful Alaketu Adebia and found deep political fissures in the community.[29] Divisions and alliances erupted between the ministers, town residents, villagers, and the newly intended Alaketu. A faction of the town proclaimed that several of the Alaketu's messengers should perish along with the Alaketu. A coalition from Meko (an outlying village now located in Nigeria) apparently arrived at the request of those agitating for the ritual death. According to Barber, the group of men from Meko pillaged farms and held the town hostage.[30] Local oral histories also claim that between 1853 and 1858, a civil war and a treacherous plot led to the successor Alaketu's suicide.[31]

CMS missionary Charles Gollmer visited in 1859, when the tumultuous events of the 1850s reached a brief resolution. Gollmer's valuable account highlighted an important, different aspect of Ketu's engagement with an Atlantic world: the presence of Islam. A man described as the Muslim chief and "a wealthy and influential man" offered a gift of sheep and cowries and visited Gollmer several times while another Muslim resident provided drinking water for Gollmer and his entourage.[32] In Meko – the village so implicated in political intrigue and dissension – Gollmer received a visit from "twenty young Mahomedan men" inspired by the scripture readers' preaching in town.[33] Historian Biodun Adediran argues that this shift indicated a "truce" between Muslims and local chiefs when feared attacked from Dahomey and sought protection from Christian missionaries.[34] On another level, Muslims acted as members of a large, heterogeneous society who advocated their interests, greeted visitors, worked, and lived as members of the community, thereby expanding the nature and meaning of Ketu identity.

Gollmer also provided different insight into gender relationships in Ketu and the larger West African region. Some local notables introduced Gollmer to three elderly women whom they referred to as "the mothers of all Ketu." Rather than inquire about their significance or duties, Gollmer brushed them off as "heads of large families."[35] But the term "iya"or "mother" often marked political titles in Ketu and neighboring states. It is impossible to know what, if any, official position these women held in Ketu but in Oyo-Ile and Dahomey, elderly women held specific government offices. But these mysterious women who Gollmer briefly met represented neither the status nor the opinion of all women in Ketu. In Ketu, a small group of women attended one of Gollmer's sessions and according to him, they were prepared to forsake their orisha (deity, god) worship.[36] Yet, a female initiate of Shango in a village on the road between Ketu and Abeokuta countered the preaching and singing by Gollmer's entourage with an intense dance.[37] Women expressed a range of reactions to Christianity that indicated their mobility and level of influence in the local community. Gollmer did not distinguish greatly between the women he met, but titled "mothers," ordinary wives, and orisha devotees also reflected the range of power and gender relationships in Ketu.

By the final decades of the nineteenth century, insecurity engulfed the Ketu region. The Alaketu who met Gollmer fled to Meko as controversy and dissension between that village and the central town continued to fester. In 1875, CMS missionary Valentine Faulkner found decimated communities as he traveled along

Gollmer's 1859 route to Ketu. In Ijale, he met a small group of defiant men who declared their allegiance to Ketu but the men also had sequestered the town's remaining women, indicating a severe and dire situation indeed.[38] A man claiming to be from Ketu joined Faulkner briefly before fleeing during a raid by Abeokuta soldiers. The man actually had been from Meko and the distinction between Ketu and Meko had become significant after Meko offered refuge to the Alaketu in 1867. Then Abeokuta accused Meko of treachery and threatened to destroy it. As the man who traveled some distance with Faulkner and shifted his identity from Ketu to Meko, these markers proved malleable but not meaningless. Shifting political alliances did not preclude meaningful ties to town and community.[39] Ultimately, Dahomey destroyed Meko in 1882 and razed Ketu in 1886. Five years later a French Catholic priest named Pied traveled to the region south of Ketu, he found a camp of refugees claiming their Ketu identity and recognizing their own Alaketu.[40] Fehetona, the locally proclaimed Alaketu, complained that raiders from Abeokuta had kidnapped several Ketu men. He asked Father Pied to forward his message to French administrators stationed in Porto-Novo. Unlike the sequestered women in Ijale, Pied encountered women and men moving about the abundant cultivation and indigo dyeing that supplied clothing. But these Ketu refugees were not isolated from the larger region. As Pied continued north to New Oyo, more men joined him and his Ketu guide in order to visit relatives sheltered there. En route, Pied's non-Muslim guide did not miss the opportunity to stop in Isheyin in order to greet heartily a Muslim friend.[41] Ketu residents remained mobile and continued to interact with diverse African communities and an expanding European presence, even during the nadir of the kingdom's history.

Engendering History and Identity

The slave route exhibit in Ofia engages debates over identity, conflict, and political autonomy which continued through the colonial period into the present.[42] Since multiparty elections began in 1991, Benin's government recognizes a Council of Benin kings and certain official holidays for Vodun ceremonies. While the nine tourist sites in Ofia are clustered around the center of the village only cover a fraction of the territory covered by the slave route in Ouidah, the king of Ofia admitted that he hoped to attract tourism and revenue to the village. A "self-proclaimed" king, he had been a friend with the late king of Ketu, Alaketu Adetutu and traveled to Brazil with the king of Ketu in 1990. Following a dispute with the king of Ketu, he convinced the village of Ofia to recognize him as king; he has since been quietly deposed. Still, the exhibit is not simply a power play. The potent historical, political, and cultural images about identity and gender also make claims to kingship. By making local history part of the slave trade, the exhibit provides an example of West African understandings of the slave trade and African diaspora.

In many ways, the history and art displayed at Ofia revisit many of the themes that prevailed in the nineteenth century context in Ketu. Ofia claims a diverse history punctuated by intrigue and war. An undated manuscript entitled "The Story and the Biography of Abiodun Adebi Osungade Adedeji Family" gives a brief version of the history that serves as a background for the slave route exhibit. The short document explains that the original leaders of Ofia came from Oyo-Ile and descended from Alaafin Abiodun. One of the sons, a hunter named Abidogun Adebi, founded Ofia. Once established, the inhabitants of Ofia were a diverse lot from Oyo-Ile, other Yoruba-speaking towns, and Gbe-speaking groups. The town then faced several challenges in the form of disease and fire and eventually succumbed to an attack by King Agaja of Dahomey in 1727. The fateful war with Dahomey killed the last historical king of Ofia. His top two ministers committed suicide but the third minister, with the title "Essiki," was caught, chained, and ostensibly consumed by the Atlantic slave trade along with six other ministers.[43] The anachronistic references to the reigns of Abiodun of Oyo-Ile (1774-1789) and Agaja of Dahomey (c. 1716-1740) are less important than the political implications of an historical association with Oyo-Ile and Dahomey. Other than the statue of the Essiki minister chained and kneeling, eight sites (discussed below) highlight history, religion, and gender and attempt to erase Ketu literally from the town's history.[44] Gender runs through Ofia's presentation of its history and culture even if the ties to the Atlantic slave trade remain remarkably tenuous throughout the slave route exhibit. Other than the figure of the kneeling and chained Essiki minister, the other sites depict gender, religion, masculinity, and femininity.

Indeed, the first tourist site is not the masculine hunter-who-would-be-king, Abidogun Adebi. Instead, the tour begins with another key figure in Ofia's history, a "foreign" woman known as Iya Abiya. Iya Abiya, who lived in water beneath a tree, was a mermaid who performed miracles and cured illnesses. Iya Abiya also was a prophecy; the founder of Ofia was told to search for "a woman under a tree" to determine where to build Ofia. But Iya Abiya not only allowed Ofia to be born, but also gave her life for Ofia's survival. After enduring an attack orchestrated by the king of Ketu, she blessed and vowed to protect Ofia before disappearing.[45] In these ways, Iya Abiya represents the quintessential "female" power to give birth, nurture, and protect – but she also embodied the trope of female self-sacrifice. In her name "Iya" also operates like a given title as a "mother." But any power or respect as a "mother" explicitly was undercut by her position as a wife. Indeed, Abidogun Adebi depended on Iya Abiya to found Ofia but his figurative role as her "husband" makes him her superior.[46]

Other religious sites in the exhibit serve as potent cultural markers and also make claims about gender. First and foremost, the site dedicated to the Gelede masquerade evokes fertility, "female" power, and social harmony. Known as the dance "to honor our mothers," Gelede has been said to denounce witches.[47] Many Gelede scholars deem the festival a celebration of motherhood and female power – a profound power which cannot be expressed openly in a patrilineal society.[48] But Gelede songs also discuss history and politics critically.[49] Accordingly, Gelede in the Ofia exhibit addresses gender and history. The founder of Ofia used the Gelede masquerade to protect his infants from death by tapping into the spiritual power in his hometown located in modern-day Nigeria.[50] On a popular level in Ofia, Gelede claims to aid infertile women or mothers plagued with infant deaths. But, here, the political implications are also important. Through the power of the Gelede dance, the past Ofia kings claimed ties to Nigeria and other Yoruba towns peopled with their descendants.

The remaining religious elements in the Ofia exhibit focus more explicitly on the role of masculinity in religion and society through

Ifa divination, worship of the Orisha Ogun, and the practice of Oro. The relationship between women, religion, and "traditional" culture is both implicit and often assumed in numerous examples from African and Western history. Scholars often contrast "feminine," indigenous practices with patriarchy of Abrahamic religion and Western and Muslim society. Similarly, in Yoruba culture, Ifa divination differed significantly from other Orisha worship as a primarily masculine domain controlled by *babalawo* or diviners (literally, "father-of-secrets").[51] In the specific case of the Ofia exhibit, the homage paid to a diviner named Fadairo has a distinct political message like the Gelede display. Fadairo tried to warn the king of Ofia of the false intentions of the kings of Ketu and Dahomey, who requested reconciliation with Ofia. When the Ofia king ignored the "clairvoyance, lucidity, and loyalty" of the diviner, it spelled the beginning of ofia's decline. The other sites that evoke masculinity, religion, and politics include a display honoring hunters and their primary *orisha,* Ogun, and a portion of "sacred forest" dedicated to the cult of Oro. Ogun as the deity of iron is associated with hunters, warfare, mobility, and empire-building.[52] Oro is a male society that punishes criminals and restores order. The celebration of Oro also is gendered as it excludes and limits the movement of women so explicitly; women are forbidden to appear in public when the "bull-roarer" sounds.[53] Both Ogun and Oro are deeply political in their association with the enforcement of social order. Oro more notably opposes the other images of women and femininity in both Africa and the African diaspora – namely, the mobility and autonomy often associated with market trade, marriage, motherhood, and elder status.

These ongoing debates over identity in the Ketu region have profound implications for the study of African identities in the Americas. Individuals potentially carried a range of identities with them from Africa to the Americas. How should we interpret the formation of identities in the Americas – as memory or creation? Ketu poses particular problems for the study of the Atlantic slave trade and African diaspora because it has a specific place in Afro-Brazilian culture that does not mesh with the historical record in West Africa. Because gender flows through narratives about Ketu on both sides of the Atlantic, gender may provide a useful framework to examine how African identities traveled in an Atlantic world.

Mothers of an Atlantic World
●●●

In Bahia, Brazil, the term "Ketu" is used to describe the type of religious practices among the most studied and renowned groups within the Afro-Brazilian Candomblé. Candomblé generally combines divination, spirit possession, and dance in religious ceremonies. Though scholarship associates Candomblé closely with Yoruba practices, elements and terms from West Central Africa, the West African Gbe cluster, Islam, and Native American cultures are crucial.[54] Moreover, a specific connection between Ketu in modern-day Benin and Bahia, Brazil actually is hard to prove using slave ship records and military history from West Africa. Ketu was a small kingdom wedged between much more powerful neighbors by the nineteenth century. Though individuals may have been kidnapped from Ketu and enslaved in Brazil, the ascendance of Ketu as a major cultural marker in the Americas still is hard to explain. Specifically, oral histories recorded about the origins of Ketu Candomblé claim that three freed female slaves named Iya Adeta, Iya Kala, and Iya Nasso (or combination thereof) established Candomblé in Bahia by the first half of the nineteenth century. One of the three women, Iya Nasso, headed the first Candomblé house, Engenho Velho (Old Sugar Mill), also known as Ile Iya Nasso (House of Iya Nasso).[55] It is difficult to trace this story to a specific person, though specific ties to an individual Ketu girl have been claimed in another Candomblé house known as Ilê Maroiálaji or Alaketo.[56] Although historical evidence challenges these links to Ketu, I argue that the intellectual, political, and symbolic work behind this popular history still provides a new, fruitful perspective on African and African diaspora identities.

Scholars, mainly anthropologists, have used two major approaches to view the prominence of Ketu in Brazil: retentions or creolization. Both models undercut the founding stories of Ketu Candomblé in Brazil without giving us the tools to analyze the meaning or significance of the oral histories. "Retentions" models, first made famous by Melville Herskovits, require specific links between Bahia and Ketu. The "retentions" argument does not work well for Ketu and Bahia for a couple of reasons. A massive deportation of Ketu war captives could be used to explain the prevalence of the term and identity marker in Brazil but Ketu

47

did not suffer its devastating military defeat until 1886, well after the end of the Atlantic slave trade and the beginnings of Candomblé. By the end of the eighteenth century more Yoruba-speakers began to turn up in the slave ships departing the Bight of Benin. Even the term, Nago, used to describe Yoruba-speakers in Brazil probably is derived from a Yoruba subgroup to the south of Ketu – the Anago – who were particularly vulnerable to slave raids by the late eighteenth century.[57] But even if one believes in explicit connections between Ketu and Bahia, some of the Yoruba terms in Ketu Candomblé actually evoke the Oyo-Ile region to the far northwest of Ketu. For example, the term "Iya Nasso" was a title in Oyo-Ile that was awarded to female leader of the followers of Shango – a mythologized king of Oyo and the deity who becomes manifest in the form of lightning.[58] One of the splinter houses that formed after the death of Iya Nasso took the name Ile Axe Opo Afonja. Afonja was an infamous provincial chief who led a Muslim uprising that contributed to the fall of Oyo-Ile in 1817. The actual practices in Ketu Candomblé ultimately support a creolization argument. Some scholars now emphasize the "eclectic" nature of Ketu Candomblé rather than its self-proclaimed "purity." Rachel Harding argues that the Ketu marks a "liturgical" difference rather than an ethnic marker.[59]

However, the underlying assumption of creolization defined by Sidney Mintz and Richard Price is that innovation can only occur in the American context. One assumes that whole and specific identities necessarily were fragmented, melded, and "creolized" because Africans were socially and culturally marginalized and could not replicate their societies in the Americas. Without denying that subjugation in American slave-holding society forced innovation in the Americas, the Bight of Benin during the eighteenth and nineteenth century already exhibited cultural exchange through trade, migration, marriage, and enslavement. Indeed, Andrew Apter has argued for attention to an original "syncretism" in West Africa itself. He argues that understanding West African practices as a critical discourse avoids the notion of discrete African ethnicities frozen in the form of disembodied "Africanisms."[60] As Bowen's conversations in Ketu in 1851 indicated, people knew the dangers of "the coast" because they had heard stories or experienced it firsthand. Movement and the sharing of knowledge began on the African side of the Atlantic before people found themselves enslaved in the Americas.

Women were particularly mobile and vulnerable to enslavement and cross-cultural marriage patterns in different ways from men.[61] The importance of marriage across town and ethnic boundaries is difficult to trace and quantify during this period but limited slave narratives offer anecdotal evidence.[62] The slave narrative of Samuel Crowther, the famed Yoruba bishop, provides a particularly relevant and unique example. Crowther grew up in a province of Oyo but his father was a trader from Ketu. Perhaps because his mother was reputedly of royalty and a religious leader, Crowther emphasized his Oyo rather than Ketu background.[63] The specific stories of Crowther and others still raise questions about the identities of the millions of Africans who forcibly crossed the Atlantic. What range of experiences and backgrounds did enslaved Africans bring with them? Can we or should we go beyond theories of retentions and creolization?

It is not necessary to trace Iya Nasso from Ketu or Oyo-Ile and then across the Atlantic Ocean. Oyo-Ile's late eighteenth century push into the region south of Ketu explains references to Ketu and the prevalence of Oyo practices among enslaved Africans in the Americas. Oyo carried its titles and gods into new areas of expansion. Descriptions of Ketu's nineteenth century market noted traders from all regions from the far north, east, west, as well as the coast. The story of the three "mothers" of Ketu Candomblé is neither complete fact or fiction but an allegory or extended metaphor capturing Afro-Brazilian ideas about the Atlantic slave trade, religion, gender, and mobility. For me, retentions and creolization models imply an unconscious memory and haphazard mixing of practices and symbols. To use an allegory or metaphor involves a deliberate act that better characterizes the type of cultural production in the Americas. In the context on the Atlantic world, one cannot assume that Africans had little sense of a cultural identity or that African women had fewer ties to community or social groupings.[64] Regardless of how one analyzes the construction of black identities in the Americas, women participated in these historical and intellectual processes.

Eugenia Anna dos Santos or Mãe Aninha, *iyalorixa* or *mãe-de-santo* ("mother-in-saint") of the Ketu Candomblé house of Ile Axe Opo Afonja provides a provocative example of the complexity of identity and gender in an Atlantic world. During interviews with anthropologist Donald Pierson in the 1930s, Mãe Aninha boasted that she had "revived the African tradition that Engenho (Ile Iya Nasso*)* [had] forgotten."[65] Several scholars have pointed out that Mãe Aninha's parents identified as Grunchi, perhaps from Burkina Faso or northern Ghana. Dos Santos had been trained in Ketu Candomblé and adopted the practices and identity as her own.[66] Her experience was not simply an example of New World creolization or "Brazilianization," it also mirrored cultural exchange in the Bight of Benin before, during, and after the Atlantic slave trade. Perhaps, more importantly, dos Santos development of Ketu Candomblé during the early twentieth century was strategic. Matory argues that her partnership with diviner Martiniano do Bonfim allowed them both to redefine "pure" Ketu Candomblé practices in ways that continue to have ramifications today. Kim Butler emphasizes the agency of dos Santos in this period where Candomblé groups developed important connections to intellectuals and politicians.[67]

Linking West Africa and the African diaspora in this way does not impose a timeless African (or black) experience through time and space. Instead, by highlighting the historical nature of African identities during and after the trans-Atlantic slave trade, this chapter reorients the study of the African diaspora. African identities were not a "given" in the Americas. Africans who found themselves in the Americas chose, manipulated, politicized, and intellectualized identities that had very real meanings in West Africa and in the Americas. The story of the Ketu "mothers" of Bahian Candomblé shows that West Africans and their descendants integrated gender into their epistemology of an Atlantic world, as should scholars. Similarly, the story of "Brazilians" living in Ofia illustrates that West Africans continue to debate over identity and power as they engage the history of the Atlantic slave trade. By taking these stories seriously, we begin to rewrite Atlantic world history from the perspective of the women and men who lived it in Africa as well as in the Americas.

Notes

1. In 1993, a vodun festival called *Ouidah 92* was held in Ouidah, Porto Novo and Cotonou. For an overview of activities organized by UNESCO in Benin, see Slave Route Project: http://www.unesco.org/culture/dialogue/slave/html_eng/activity.shtml, Accessed October 19, 2005. The UNESCO Slave Route Project was inaugurated at Ouidah in 1994.

2. For a discussion comparing different West African conceptions of the "Slave Route" Project in Ghana and Benin, see Theresa Singleton, "The Slave Trade Remembered on the Former Gold and Slave Coasts," *Slavery and Abolition* 20, no. 1 (1999), 150-169. Recent studies in anthropology also challenge the idea that Africans communities have "forgotten" or are ambivalent about the Atlantic slave trade by highlighting how African communities have incorporated the slave trade into local religious and cultural practices. Robert Martin Baum, *Shrines of the Slave Trade: Diola Religion and Society in Precolonial Senegambia* (New York: Oxford University Press, 1999); Charles Piot, *Remotely Global: Village Modernity in West Africa* (Chicago: University of Chicago Press, 1999); Rosalind Shaw, *Memories of the Slave Trade: Ritual and the Historical Imagination in Sierra Leone* (Chicago: University of Chicago Press, 2002). Also see my book, *Mother Is Gold, Father Is Glass: Gender and Colonialism in a Yoruba Town* (Bloomington: Indiana University Press, 2010); parts of this chapter are drawn from my book.

3. "York/UNESCO Nigerian Hinterland Project Newsletter," no 1, (May 2000), 1. http://www.yorku.ca/nhp/newsletter/newsmay2.pdf, Accessed October 19, 2005.

4. Kristin Mann and Edna G. Bay, "Shifting Paradigms in the Study of the African Diaspora and of Atlantic History and Culture," in *Rethinking the African Diaspora: The Making of a Black Atlantic World in the Bight of Benin and Brazil*, ed. Kristin Mann and Edna G. Bay (London: Frank Cass, 2001), 7, 16.

5. For example, see Robin Law and Kristin Mann, "West Africa in the Atlantic Community: The Case of the Slave Coast," *The William and Mary Quarterly* 56, no. 2 (1999), 307-334; J. Lorand Matory, "The English Professors of Brazil: On the Diasporic Roots of the Yorùbá Nation," *Comparative Studies in Society and History* 41, no. 1 (1999), 72-103.

6. Ira Berlin, "From Creole to African: Atlantic Creoles and the Origins of African-American in Mainland North America," *William and Mary Quarterly* 53, no. 2 (1996), 251-288.

7. For overviews, see Sidney Lemelle and Robin D. G. Kelley, "Introduction: Imagining Home: Pan-Africanism Revisited," in *Imagining Home: Class, Culture and Nationalism in the African Diaspora*, ed. Sidney Lemelle and Robin D. G. Kelley (London and New York: Verso, 1994), 5-6; Sandra Gunning, Tera W. Hunter, and Michele Mitchell, "Gender, Sexuality, and African Diasporas," *Gender and History* 15, no. 3 (2003), 397-408. Also see Semley, *Mother is Gold, Father is Glass*.

8. Joseph C. Miller, "Retention, Reinvention, and Remembering: Restoring Identities through Enslavement in Africa and under Slavery in Brazil," in *Enslaving Connections: Changing Cultures of Africa and Brazil During the Era of Slavery*, ed. José C. Curto and Paul E. Lovejoy (Amherst, NY: Humanity Books, 2004), 81-121; J. Lorand Matory, *Black Atlantic Religion: Tradition, Transnationalism, and Matriarchy in the Afro-Brazilian Candomblé* (Princeton, NJ: Princeton University Press, 2005), 35.

9. See Melville J. Herskovits, *The Myth of the Negro Past* (New York: Harper & Brothers, 1941); Sidney Mintz and Richard Price, *The Birth of African-American Culture: An Anthropological Perspective*, 2nd ed. (Boston: Beacon Press, 1992 [1976]); John Thornton, *Africa and Africans in the Making of the Atlantic World, 1400-1800*, 2nd ed. (New York: Cambridge University Press, 1998); Philip D. Morgan, "The Cultural Implications of the Atlantic Slave Trade: African Regional Origins, American Destinations and New World Developments," in *Routes to Slavery: Direction, Ethnicity, and Mortality in the Transatlantic Slave Trade*, ed. David Eltis and David Richardson (London: Frank Cass, 1997), 122-145.

10. I contend that to speak of the "Yoruba" before the late nineteenth century is an anachronism. J.D.Y. Peel, "The Work of Cultural Ethnogenesis," in *History and Ethnicity*, ed. Elizabeth Tonkin (London: Routledge, 1989), 198-215.

11. Alaketu is the title for the king of Ketu that literally translates as "owner of Ketu."

12. Rev. Samuel Crowther, "Account of a Journey to Ketu," January 16, 1853, Church Missionary Society Archives (CMS), Birmingham, CA2/031/128.

13. Archibald Dalzel, *The History of Dahomy, an Inland Kingdom of Africa* (1793; reprint, London: Frank Cass, 1967), 199, 201-202; Thomas Moulero," Essai historique sur la ville de Kétou," *La Reconnaissance Africaine* 31 (15 décembre 1926), 4.

14. Edna G. Bay, *Wives of the Leopard: Gender, Politics, and Culture in the Kingdom of Dahomey* (Charlottesville: University of Virginia Press, 1998), 111.

15. J.D.Y. Peel, *Religious Encounter and the Making of the Yoruba* (Bloomington: Indiana University Press, 2000), 193-196.

16. Matory, *Black Atlantic Religion*, 79-89.

17. S. Goddard, "Town-Farm Relationship in Yorubaland: A Case Study from Oyo," *Africa* 35, no. 1 (January 1965), 21-29. Several outlying villages supposedly attempted to secede from Ketu in the late eighteenth century. Oral histories recorded during the French colonial period in the early twentieth century may have replicated disputes between Ketu and outlying villages. Dunglas, "Contribution à l'histoire de Moyen Dahomey," 70; and Direction des Archives Nationales du Bénin, "Rapport du Tournée dans le Cercle de Zagnanado (Holli-Kétou), *Mémoire du Bénin* 1 (1993): 86."

18. Hugh Clapperton, *Hugh Clapperton into the Interior of Africa: Records of the Second Expedition, 1825-1827*, ed. Jamie Bruce Lockhart and Paul E. Lovejoy (Leiden: Brill, 2005), 109; A.I. Asiwaju, *Western Yorubaland under European Rule 1889-1945: A Comparative Analysis of French and British Colonialism* (Atlantic Highlands, NJ: Humanities Press, 1976), 15; Robin Law, *The Oyo Empire, C.1600-C.1836: A West African Imperialism in the Era of the Atlantic Slave Trade* (Oxford: Clarendon Press, 1977), 93-96.

19. Law, *Oyo Empire*, 277.

20. Peel, *Making of the Yoruba*, chapter 3.

21. Thomas J. Bowen, *Adventures and Missionary Labours in Several Countries in the Interior of Africa from 1849 to 1856*, (1857; reprint, London: Frank Cass, 1968), 143; Jerry Michael Turner, "'Les Bresiliens': The Impact of Former Brazilian Slaves Upon Dahomey" (PhD diss., Boston University, 1975).

22. Bowen, *Adventures and Missionary Labours*, 149; Bay, *Wives of the Leopard*, 186-192.

23. Bowen, *Adventures and Missionary Labours*, 148.

24. Bowen, *Adventures and Missionary Labours*, 150.

25. Rev. Samuel Crowther, "Account of a Journey to Ketu," January 11, 1853, CMS, CA2/031/128.

26 Crowther, "Account of a Journey," January 15-16, 1853.

27 Crowther, "Account of a Journey," January 16, 1853. Crowther credited the absence of Egungun, Ogboni, and Oro for this freedom of movement for women. Oro specifically forbade women's appearance in public during Oro celebrations.

28. J. Lorand Matory, *Sex and the Empire That Is No More: Gender and the Politics of Metaphor in Oyo Yoruba Religion*, 2d ed. (New York: Berghahn, 1997), 8-13, chapter 2; Bay, *Wives of the Leopard,* chapters 2, 3.

29. James Barber, "Second Journey to Ketu," June 24, 1853, CMS 021/1-24. Barber visited with Alaketu Adebia once in April 1853 and then rushed back to express his condolences after the Alaketu died.

30. Barber, "Second Journey to Ketu," June 22-26, 1853.

31. Thomas Moulero, "Essai historique sur la ville de Kétou: Le Roi Adebede," *La Reconaissance Africaine* 33 (15 janvier 1927), 4-5.

32. Charles Andrew Gollmer, "Missionary Tour of the Ketu Country, Journal Extracts for the Half Year Ending September 25, 1859," August 15, 1859, CMS 043/132.

33. Gollmer, "Journal Extracts," August 18, 1859.

34. Biodun Adediran, "Islam and Political Crises in Kétu: A Case-Study of the Role of Muslims in a Nineteenth Century Yoruba Polity," *Ife Journal of Religions* III (1982-1989), 3-18.

35. Gollmer, "Journal Extracts," August 16, 1859.

36. Peel argues that women resisted conversion to Christianity because they linked religious worship with fertility and therefore remained more beholden to Orisha worship; Peel, *Making of the Yoruba*, 232-236.

37. Gollmer, "Journal Extracts," August 19, 1859.

38. Valentine Faulkner, August 8, 1875, in "Journal of Itinerary from Ebute Meta to the Kétu territory via Oyo, Badagry, Ado, Okeodan, and Ilaro, July - August 1875," CMS 037/1-146/128A.

39. Ketu may have allied with Oyo-Ile in the eighteenth century or recognized a blood pact with Dahomey in the nineteenth century. J.F.A. Ajayi and Robert Smith, *Yoruba Warfare in the Nineteenth Century* (Cambridge: Cambridge University Press, 1964), 4; Law,

Oyo Empire, 141-142; George Parrinder, *The Story of Ketu: An Ancient African Kingdom* (Ibadan: Ibadan University Press, 1967), 11; Forbes, *Dahomey and the Dahomans,* vol.1, 20; Johnson, *History of the Yorubas,* 455. Ketu may have also entered into a federation with the Yoruba communities of Ohori and Adja-Ouere against Dahomey at some point during the nineteenth century. Lt. Colonel Tereau and Dr. Huttel, "Monographie du Hollidge," *Études Dahoméennes* 2 (1949), 64-65; Paul Mercier, "Notice sur le peuplement Yoruba au Dahomey-Togo," *Études Dahoméennes* 4 (1950), 36. Despite the ongoing strife between Ketu and Meko, particularly after an Alaketu fled there, Ketu may have assisted Meko during Egba attacks in the 1860s. Parrinder, *Story of Ketu,* 56-58.

40. Révérend Père Pied, "De Porto-Novo à Oyo—Févier-Mars 1891," *Les Missions Catholiques* 1197 (1892), 231-236. Fehetona also is cited in early French colonial documents; see Lieutenant H. Aube, Rapport sur la mission accomplie dans la région Kétou-Savé du 18 janvier au 20 février 1894, à Archives Nationale du Bénin (ANB).

41. Pied, "De Porto-Novo à Oyo," no. 1204 (1 July 1892), 324.

42. A. I. Asiwaju, "The Alaketu of Ketu and the Onimeko of Meko," in *West African Chiefs: Their Changing Status under Colonial Rule in Africa,* ed. Michael Crowder and Obaro Ikime (New York: Africana Publishing, 1970), 134-161.

43. Anonymous, "The Story and the Biography of Abidogun Adebi Osundade Adebeji Family" (Ofia, Benin: n.d.), 1-8.

44. In the manuscript of the town's history, when the town's ancestor arrived at Ofia, the word "Ketu" is crossed out and "Ofia" is handwritten in its place.

45. The story of Iya Abiya's sacrifice is represented in a separate site called "The Jigbala Cowrie Shell." Anonymous, "Les Sites Touristiques - Village Ofia (Sous-Préfecture de Kétou)" (Ofia, Bénin: n.d.).

46. Compare with Edna G. Bay's discussion of Gbe-speaking deities Mawu and Lisa as contrasting pairs or twins rather than husband and wife; see Bay, *Wives of the Leopard,* 95-96.

47. Henry John Drewal and Margaret Thompson Drewal, *Gelede: Art and Female Power among the Yoruba* (Bloomington: Indiana University Press, 1983); Babatunde Lawal, *The Gèlèdè Spectacle: Art, Gender, and Social Harmony in an African Culture* (Seattle: University of Washington Press, 1996); Benedict M. Ibitokun,

Dance as Ritual Drama and Entertainment in the Gèlèdè of the Kétu-Yorùbá Subgroup in West Africa (Ilé-Ife: Obàfemi Awólowo University Press, 1993).

48. Lawal, Gèlèdè Spectacle, 262-268; Emmanuel D. Babatunde, "The Gelede Masked Dance and Ketu Society: The Role of the Transvestite Masquerade in Placating Powerful Women While Maintaining the Patrilineal Ideology," in West African Masks and Cultural Systems, ed. Sidney L. Kasfir (Tervuren: Musée Royal d'Afrique Centrale, 1988), 45-64.

49. Asiwaju, Western Yorubaland, 271-275.

50. Anonymous, "Les Sites Touristiques - Village Ofia," 1-8.

51. Bay, Wives of the Leopard, 255-259.

52. Sandra Barnes, ed. Africa's Ogun: Old World and New (Bloomington: Indiana University Press, 1997); Matory, Gender and the Politics of Metaphor, 13-17.

53. N. A. Fadipe, The Sociology of the Yoruba (Ibadan: University of Ibadan Press, 1970), 249-250.

54. Rachel E. Harding, A Refuge in Thunder: Candomblé and Alternative Spaces of Blackness (Bloomington: Indiana University Press, 2000), 44-51.

55. Edison Carneiro, Candomblés da Bahia (Salvador: Brasil Secretaria de Educação e Saúde, 1948), 31. For the different versions of Ketu Candomblé origins, see Kim D. Butler, Freedoms Given, Freedoms Won: Afro-Brazilians in Post-Abolition São Paulo and Salvador (New Brunswick, NJ: Rutgers University Press, 1998), 193-195.

56. The group claims that it was founded by a nine-year old girl named Otampê Ojarô who together with her twin sister was kidnapped by Dahomey from the Aro royal family in the late nineteenth century. An orisha in the form of a man immediately freed the girls upon their arrival in Bahia. Several years later the young girl traveled back to her home in Ketu before returning to Bahia to found Alaketu. Vivaldo da Costa Lima, "Nações-de-Candomblé," in Encontro de Nações de Candomblé: Salvador-Bahia, 1-6-81 a 5-6-81, ed. Vivaldo da Costa Lima (Salvador: Universidade Federal da Bahia Centro de Estudos Afro-Orientais, 1984), 24-26. Pierre Verger also took the connections between Ketu and Bahia literally; see Orisha: Les Dieux Yorouba en Afrique et au Nouveau Monde (Paris: Métailié, 1982), 26-27.

57. Robin Law, "Ethnicity and the Slave Trade: Lucumi and Nago as Ethnonyms in West Africa," *History in Africa* 24 (1997), 205-219, 212-215. One Brazilian author traces the origins to Ketu Candomblé to a Dahomey raid in Ketu in 1789. Juana Elbein dos Santos, *Os Nàgo e a Morte: Pàde, Asèsè, e o culto Egun na Bahia* (Petrópolis: Vozes, 1976), 29. Also see Edouard Dunglas, "Contribution à l'histoire du Moyen-Dahomey: Royaumes d'Abomey, de Kétou et de Ouidah," *Études Dahoméennes* 19 (1957), 69; and A. Le Herissé, *L'Ancien Royaume de Dahomey* (Paris: La Rose, 1911), 307-308.

58. Johnson, *History of the Yorubas*, 64.

59. Harding, *Candomblé and Alternative Spaces of Blackness*, 100-101.

60. Andrew Apter, "Herskovits's Heritage: Rethinking Syncretism in the African Diaspora," *Diaspora* 1, no. 3 (1991): 235-259.

61. Claire C. Robertson and Martin A. Klein, ed. *Women and Slavery in Africa* (Madison, WI: University of Wisconsin Press, 1983).

62. Robin Law and Paul E. Lovejoy, *The Biography of Mahommah Gardo Baquaqua: His Passage from Slavery to Freedom in Africa and America* (Princeton, NJ: Markus Wiener Publishers, 2001); Ivor Wilks, "Abu Bakr Al-Siddiq of Timbuktu," in *Africa Remembered: Narratives by West Africans from the Era of the Slave Trade*, ed. Philip D. Curtin (Madison: University of Wisconsin Press, 1967), 158.

63. J.F. Ade Ajayi, "Samuel Ajayi Crowther of Oyo," in *Africa Remembered: Narratives by West Africans from the Era of the Slave Trade*, ed. Philip Curtin (Madison: University of Wisconsin, 1967), 292.

64. Morgan, "Cultural Implications of the Slave Trade," 134; Miller, "Retention, Reinvention," 86.

65. Donald Pierson, *Negroes in Brazil, a Study of Race Contact at Bahia* (Chicago: University of Chicago Press, 1942), 292. For an astute critique of these narratives of "purity," see Matory, "Diasporic Roots of the Yoruba," 72-103.

66. Luís Filipe de Lima Muniz Sodré. *Um Vento Sagrado: História de Vida de um Adivinho da Tradição Nagô-Kêtu Brasileira* (Rio de Janeiro: Mauad, 1996), 26.

67. Matory, *Black Atlantic Religion*, 120-121; Butler, *Afro-Brazilians in Post-Abolition, São Paulo and Salvador*, 194-207.

Chapter 4

Competition over "Sites of Memory": Le Morne Brabant and Creole Identity in Mauritius[1]

Sandra Carmignani

On February 1st 2005, the 170th anniversary of the abolition of slavery, Le Morne Brabant became an official commemoration site for the first time in Mauritian history. Situated in the extreme south west of the island, a symbol of slavery and maroonage in the Mauritian collective memory, this mountain has acquired today the status of a unique cynosure. The formal recognition of this "site of memory" has come about at a crucial period that marks the Mauritian endeavour to re-engage with the colonial past.[2] This development echoes the global call for the acknowledgment of slavery and slave trade as a crime against humanity, paramount among which was the UNESCO decision to proclaim the year 2004 as the International Year to commemorate the Struggle against Slavery and its Abolition.

Yet, the recognition of Le Morne as a heritage site was contested because of the complex background of the Mauritian population and competing claims for recognition. Through an analysis of how this "site of memory," emerged in the local political context, this study examines the power struggle at work in the construction of Creole identity and in the establishment of its political legitimization. In the course of my stay on the island, I identified a number of social and institutional actors revolving around Le Morne. An analysis of this mountain as an object of memory enables us to distinguish a process of what I call the "ethnicization" of the category of actors involved, a process which mirrors Mauritian political and social structure. By "ethnicization" I am referring to the process of essentializing the meaning of identity in which Creoles had to Africanize their "community" to legitimize their citizenship.

The past has become more and more at stake in an identity struggle among peoples of diverse origins, especially in this island with no native population. Mauritian national identity finds its legitimization through claims of descent to the wave of peoples who arrived progressively in Mauritius since the end of the sixteenth century. The diversity of origins (colonizers, slaves, migrants) and the multiculturalism of this society constitute one of the many challenges that confront political leaders today. The institutionalization of Le Morne reveals contradictions in the politics of Mauritian national heritage that tend towards an essentialized perspective of ancestral origins, recognized on the social and political plane as communities distinct from each other.

In this context, establishing a connection with ancestral origins takes undeniably the Mauritian Creole to an unclear and diverse relation brought about by the undermining and violent nature of the institution of slavery. In the Mauritian context, the term Creole refers to an individual of mixed African, Malagasy, South Asian and/or European origin. The so-called African phenotype is an important factor in this categorization model. The term Creole does not refer, unlike on other islands, to all the Mauritian inhabitants. However, it does refer to cultural elements such as language, music and cuisine. Le Morne is a prime reference in this on-going process of redefining Creole identity. The handling of the institutionalization of this site, on one hand, bears witness to the present day appropriation of the memory of slavery, and on the other hand, also reveals the power struggle associated with the construction of Creole identity in Mauritius.

Le Morne: National Legitimacy and International Hallmark

Le Morne has served as a source of inspiration for many Mauritian artists. This can be seen in Assonne's poem, "Against the venom of the electric serpent" (2002).

> Against the venom of the electric cableway serpent that they want to inject into you, O Morne, I have the antidote! I offer you transfusion. I offer you the gift of my black blood so that their poison cannot creep into your veins, O Morne, land of the runaway slave! Despite the invasion of their ridiculous pyramids that the sand will swallow sooner or later, you will be forever, the eternal Sphinx the immutable witness standing before the horizon like a big No to their shady plans![3]

The poem epitomizes vibrantly the complex and symbolic stance of this mountain as a place of memory and attraction. It constitutes an indisputable asset for Franco-Mauritian property developers, who are the descendants of the former masters now promoting tourism and economic development. Le Morne represents a product in addition to "sun, sea and sand," as one of them pointed out to me. However, reducing Le Morne to a profitable tourist product is far from the unanimous trend. The poem expresses adequately this reality. Le Morne is for the descendants of slaves a historical symbol pregnant with sacredness.

When the Mauritian poet speaks about offering his blood to the mountain, he is referring to a very specific narrative. Le Morne is known for harboring maroons who had fled from their servile conditions during colonization. The story, transmitted through oral history, recounts how some fugitive slaves, fearing capture, jumped off the cliffs. Ever since, Le Morne has been a symbol of the struggle against slavery and the icon of maroon culture. While some may dispute the authenticity of this oral tradition, archaeological findings in the caves of the mountain show evidence of human occupation.[4] Further research is needed to confirm whether these caves were indeed maroon hideouts. Such validation would undoubtedly transform myth into history. However, validating the oral narrative is less important for this analysis than its role as a rallying point to make Le Morne a memorial site. The real estate developers who have questioned the oral tradition do not refrain, however, from exploiting the tradition for proposes of various tourism projects ranging from a maroon village to a temple consecrated to the memory of maroons and slaves and even a museum. These business persons are aware of the symbolic significance of this site for the descendants of slaves, which is why they have to convince them to sanction the development projects in the region.[5]

Evoked as the "immutable witness" in the poem cited above, Le Morne bore the brunt of property developers wanting to install a cableway in 1999. The counter rebuttal was rapid; a handful of opponents vowed to stop the project at any cost and succeeded after invoking historical, symbolic and ecological reasons in support of their argument. Although a resolution was adopted during a colloquium at the Mahatma Gandhi Institute in 1998 that declared Le Morne as a "site of memory," it was only after the cableway episode that the steps to make this site part of the cultural heritage actually got under way. Before this episode, the myth and the site were part of the collective memory without inciting any precise claims, covetousness or any projects for the conservation of the site.[6]

The promotion of Le Morne to the status of "site of memory" was a national affair and henceforth an international one as well, for, Mauritius was pursuing the procedure to include this site among the UNESCO World Heritage sites at the time of writing this paper. The developers who had promoted the cableway project were first to consult UNESCO expertise. They expected to garner the support of UNESCO for their project under the aegis of the Slave Route Project.[7] adhering to the framework of the commemoration of the memory of slavery and slave trade, this project aimed at developing economically selected sites by combining in equal measure, elements of cultural heritage, tourism and education. Nonetheless, as the brain behind the tourism project lamented, "it turned against us." The project did not conform to the criteria of conservation for a site classified as "World Heritage" and the verdict was delivered in favour of those who opposed the project.

This outcome illustrates the ambiguousness in the definition of "world heritage." Without examining the details of the debate, which would go beyond the context of this paper, one can, nevertheless, comprehend the essential paradox which, in one respect, motivates property developers to seek an international hallmark and on the other, induces the proponents for the protection of Le Morne to find an ally for the defence of their cause to conserve the site. UNESCO, confronted by local stakes which echoed the fragile political and social situation in Mauritius, found itself embroiled in the conflict in the role of protector of Le Morne, as an expert witness, and even as an economic partner.

The issue was politicized because a second memorial site that recognized immigration from India was submitted for international recognition. The site was Aapravasi Ghat, where the first Indian immigrants landed in 1834. The site has been part of the national heritage since 1985, and in the past few years, it has been subject to extensive excavations and restoration work. The Aapravasi Ghat Trust Fund submitted its application for international recognition of the site in spring 2005, that is, before that of Le Morne. After the cableway episode, the State did not made clear its position on the question of heritage management. The State initially proposed to present the project Le Morne to UNESCO; later, it was decided to nominate both sites simultaneously, and finally the Aapravasi Ghat dossier was selected to be first. Politics in this matter remain ambiguous at best. Subsequently, Le Morne only became a national heritage site in February 2006 and was not designated a World Heritage site until July 2008.

This tactic of pitching one "site of memory" against the other exemplifies the peculiar relationship that the Mauritian bureaucracy maintains with cultural referents to the different communities of the island. No matter how simplistic, it may appear, the formula "a Creole memorial site versus an Indian memorial site" embodies the terms of a process prone to essentialize the past and homogenize the origins of Mauritians. Political decisions and their vagueness only contribute to an interpretation of the debate along ethnic terms. Some persons I met, irrespective of their origins, accentuated this dichotomy through their discourse, either approving of it or rejecting it. "Not offending people's sensibilities" seems to be the only explanation shared by those who describe the indecision and the lack of transparency of political choices in relation to the two sites in question. In this inextricable position, the Mauritian government seems to relieve itself of this daunting task by delegating its responsibilities to UNESCO to resolve the issue between the two heritage sites.

Mauritius: Colonial Heritage and Multiculturalism

Mauritius attained independence in 1968, after having endured three colonial regimes. Slavery formed part of the settlement history of the island since the early Dutch colonial period (1598-1711) and continued under French colonization (1715-1810). The British period began in 1810 and was marked by the end of a regime based on the enslavement and trade of Africans with the abolition of slavery in 1835. The British colonial government introduced a system known as "apprenticeship" for former slaves and the indenture system that relied on migrants from India. The Mauritian social fabric is a society of settlers, constituted of descendants of European colonists and people from the Asian subcontinent mainly of indentured Indians, and African and Malagasy slaves.

This diversity is an integral component of the harmonious and peaceful image that the Republic upholds at the international as well as the national level. Popular slogans of Mauritian politics like "unity in diversity," "rainbow nation" and "one people, one nation" refer to the multicultural ideology characteristic of the political discourse of the island.[8] The unity professed in these slogans also portends a delicate situation. Mauritius "remains inter- and intra-ethnically divided but these divisions do not result in violent conflict, at least while economic progress continues to be made." To Bunwaree, the argument accentuates the absence of a national ethos. "Decolonization did not make a nation."[9] Intercommunity discord surfaced even during the negotiations to attain independence, contributing to the creation and the consolidation of ethnic frontiers.[10] At the time of independence, 44 percent of the Mauritian population voted against the latter.

In political practice, the management of multiculturalism of the island is typified by a perpetual oscillation between the promotion and protection of diversity and a nationalistic discourse that urges people to transcend their differences. Numerous researchers have pointed out the flaws of this discourse aimed at pigeonholing and isolating the island's different communities.[11] One of the priorities of the Mauritian political and social administration consists of maintaining the balance between these categories. The metaphor of the boat, employed by a politician in his inaugural speech at the conference[12] on memory of slavery, evoked this idea of equilibrium, reminding Mauritians that they were all sailing in the same boat, "since we all have to live in the same country"! Besides, this discourse on social and political stability recurs frequently in Mauritians description of their country. It is "indispensable to maintain this balance" said one of them, emphasising the non-violent nature of cohabitation in Mauritius.

When one speaks to a Mauritian about balance, one refers essentially to that among communities. A study of the sociopolitical structure and the stratification of the island reveals the paradoxes of this discourse.[13] Mauritians are divided into four principal groups: Indo-Mauritian, Muslim, Sino-Mauritian and the general population. Franco-Mauritians and Creoles (descendants of the former masters and descendants of their former slaves) curiouslycomprisethe last category. Although the basic logic behind this categorization is debatable, given that religious, ethnic and-cultural mixed together, do not in themselves adequately represent categories of comparable divisions, the most problematic in this respect is the general population. The existence of a category so vague that it does not confer any visibility or legitimate recognition of the Creole population is indeed astonishing. Furthermore, the Creoles who claim their slave ancestry have demanded the dissolution of this arbitrary category. In this regard, the colloquium, which benefited from the political speech that I have cited before, also provided a journalist with a forum in which to express his disillusionment on seeing that "Creoles were still associated with Whites" and to stipulate the dissolution of the category "General Population." Unfortunately, the politician left soon after delivering his speech and the question was shelved. Although the question triggered unsolicited embarrassment, this man had asked a fundamental question which, when articulated in the context of this conference, resurrects the problematic of political reparation for the insidious effects of slavery and of colonial heritage in general. What is the place of Creoles in Mauritian society? Social actors concerned by this state of affairs, denounced the State's intention to obliterate Creole identity. This analysis takes us back to the complex situation of "being Creole" in a society which has an ambiguous rapport with its African heritage and its cross-cultural identities, which encourages the polarization of communities between each other.

An uninhabited island before the arrival of the first Dutch colonisers Mauritius, unlike other nations, does not possess its unique myth of origin. As Chazan-Gillig argues, "Mauritius was a settlement colony and therefore, did not produce indigenous myths which could have been used in the institutionalization and production of a nation state."[14] Mauritian identity symbols can be retraced to the countries from which the different diasporas originated like India, China or Europe. In comparison, this link is more complex for the Creoles. Reflecting back to the violence of slavery and the denial of creolization, their origins are perceived as repressed, forgotten and uncertain. In the ambient discourse, the history and the culture of the descendants of slaves are characterized by this lack of "ancestral capital" as compared to communities whose cultural, social, economic and religious resources are seen as superior and who are thought to have preserved their memory and history. The following comment made by a Mauritian illustrates this paradox: "The Creoles have no roots, they have nothing concrete. They were converted to Christianity but were not educated. This is the reason why they never evolved." This cultural and social inadequacy combined with discrimination and persistent racial stereotypes, led to the portrayal of Creoles in negative light.[15]

The recognition of Le Morne and its identity stakes should be viewed in this context which contributes to the ethnicization of social and political relationships, because history and heritage also follow this logic. The Mauritian communities find in the management of the state, a significant echo of the necessity to uphold tenaciously these cultural, religious and economic links and to confer upon them, an undeniable social and political legitimacy. This approach is visible in the creation of several cultural centres devoted to each ethnic community. Created in the image of the first centre of this type, the Gandhi Institute, these institutions dedicated to the promotion and the conservation of the culture and of the language of origin, and at times, of the religion, have multiplied. In 1986, the Nelson Mandela Centre for African Culture was created with the aim of promoting culture and relations with Africa. The creation of this institution is in contradiction with the absence of African links which supposedly represents the provenance of the descendants of slaves, a cultural link often reduced to the *séga* (the traditional dance of the slaves). Moreover, the promotion of Creole culture, added much later to its scheme of service in 2002, only reinforced the uncertain nature of this political creation. Finally, the picture would not be complete without a Mauritian Cultural Centre supposedly embodying the ethnic diversity of all Mauritian communities.

This cultural repartition reflects the contradictions of the island: not only the incongruous persistence of compartmentalization and unifying national discourse, but also the invisibility of the Creole community. The staging and the process of commemoration of the cultural heritage and the past of the island should be read in this context. From then on, the stakes are high for the Creoles who seek today, their place and their legitimacy in this complex social and political landscape. The rivalry between Le Morne and Aapravasi Ghat is an indication of this conflict. Historical legitimacy, and, the occupation of Mauritian space, comprises part of the elements indispensable to attain political legitimacy.[16]

Le Morne: A Mauritian or Creole Heritage Site?

Since the 1980s, Mauritian politics have endeavoured to establish a new cultural order intended to rehabilitate the cultural diversity of the island. However, as Bunwaree notes, "this cultural order which is often heard of is simply a strong endeavour to revalorise ancestral languages and cultures, very often for political reasons. This simply leads to a compartmentalization or a collage rather than the formulation of unifying principles."[17] It is with this focus that one has to pay particular attention to the measures adopted by the State to restore the memory of slavery and indenture, and hence, the stakes involving Aapravasi Ghat and Le Morne. Nonetheless, the perspective of classifying the latter as "World Heritage" implied that the State considered it a Mauritian cultural heritage site, thus aiming at national and universal criteria (ecology, history, memory). The bestowal of a national identity on Le Morne provoked and continues to incite numerous reservations. "Why call the Aapravasi Ghat a site of Indian heritage and Le Morne a site of Mauritian heritage? No, Le Morne is part of Creole heritage!" This is the primary objection raised by many involved in the protection and commemoration of the site. In the opinion of another person, "The Grand Bassin (Ganga Talao) is sacred. For the last 100 years, it has represented the Hindu faith! Le Morne is not sacred. The mountain is not linked in any way to a lake in Africa!"[18]

Conflicting discourses further reveal the politics of differentiation deeply embedded in a game of national alignment in which the Indo-Mauritian model always becomes the point of reference. The dialectic of this rapport consists of maintaining a balance, of seeking and constructing Creole social and political legitimacy according to the Indo-Mauritian model. This is the case with the Gandhi Institute, which has today an "African" counterpart, the Mandela Centre. Political decisions also follow this logic. The decision to declare the 1st of February as the day of commemoration of the abolition of slavery, a triumph anticipated by every Creole activist, was also embroiled in controversy. It could not be made official until the 2nd of November was declared a public holiday to commemorate the disembarking of the first indentured immigrants, although initially, it was debated whether both events should be commemorated on one date. Finally, this reasoning has taken another angle; a Mauritian project called "Indentured Route," conceptualized on the same grounds as the Slave Route Project, is currently under consideration.

This dialectic process determines the emphasis accorded to the past and to the sites attached to it. The discourse tends to get reduced to a simplification of history and of the past for both memorial sites. The fact that numerous Africans or Indian Catholics also disembarked at Aapravasi Ghat does not prevent the site from being identified as part of the Indo-Mauritian (Hindu) patrimony. Similarly, Le Morne must have also sheltered Indian slaves. Some of my informants seemed opposed to this process of simplifying the past, but that did not preclude them from subscribing to the same ethnic bias. A few individuals consider Aapravasi Ghat a Creole heritage site since it was formerly a prison for slaves. One of them expressed himself as follows: "Aapravasi Ghat will loose its historical value if it becomes a Hindu site. One must remember who constructed this site, it was the slaves who constructed it; it is a Creole site!"

These circumstances reinforce the reasons why Le Morne cannot become a national reference point or "a Mauritian heritage site," at least for the moment. The quest for political legitimacy and a rightful Creole identity is marked by a refusal to accept a Creole identity that "dilutes" the Mauritian definition and which provides neither visibility nor recognition. "Dilutes" was a term that kept recurring in interviews. My interlocutors frequently used it to describe Creole identity and its place in Mauritian society. In this power struggle, supporters of the Creole heritage were "restrained" and compelled to play according to the rules imposed by the State system and to engage in a process of ethnicization of their African origins, often resulting in the reductionist formula: "Creole means African."

The process of declaring Le Morne a cultural heritage site demonstrates the same progression; the mountain has become a space and a medium for an identity struggle which operates through the exacerbation of links with African origins and the reappropriation of the slavery discourse. Le Morne has acquired a new symbolic meaning, for, sites bearing reference to slavery are rare, and those which do exist, like the Pointe Canon monument in honour of Mauritian slaves, do not possess the aura of the "sacred mountain." Remarkably, as a referent of identity, this mountain has acquired recognition as a prominent cultural heritage site, at a precise and crucial moment in Mauritian history. The present era is defined as an epoch of redefinition of the Creole community.[19] What Father Cerveaux denoted in 1993 as the "Malaise Créole" (Creole discontent) or an admission of the exclusion and poverty of the Creole population, has given way to the creation of secular and religious organizations to denounce the inequity of the Mauritian system, and to demand a political and social recognition. Some of these socio-cultural associations were part of the lobby that campaigned for the protection of Le Morne and the commemoration of the abolition of slavery at the site.

The principal stake in the claim process is undoubtedly "reparations" that are historical, moral, symbolic, political and financial. The commemoration on the 1st of February 2005 was a battle won; however, issues like the dissolution of the category "General Population" and official status for the Creole language remain part of the war, still to be fought. The theme of reparation also brings to the fore, the socially and economically marginalized condition of the Creole Mauritians. Thus, the declaration of Le Morne as cultural heritage and this commemoration cannot be disregarded as a means of settling scores, legitimized by a return to the past.

The commemorative discourse surrounding Le Morne actually has gone beyond the memory of slavery to make reference to the present lifestyle of the descendants of slaves. The implications of this vary, ranging from demands for financial aid from the Verts fraternels party (Organization Fraternelle /Les Verts),[20] to charges from the Rastafari Socio-Cultural Association of the alarming situation in working class housing developments. It was also an opportune moment to debate the conservation of the site in the wake of projects to promote tourism in Mauritius. None of these concerns have been settled, thus epitomising the symbolic conflict between the Creoles and property developers, many of whom are Franco-Mauritians.

The commemoration of Le Morne is an occasion for the enunciation of a subtle melange of political messages, claims and expressions of memory. For the spokespersons of the descendants of slaves, this "site of memory" is an important venue to evaluate the present. Everyone agrees for the need to recognize Creole identity and its transformation as something positive rather than just an acknowledgement of victimhood. This task of awakening consciousness is not only important but timely, for it has occurred at a moment when, unlike on other islands and in some diasporas, it cannot but gain momentum.[21]

Creole Does Not Mean African
•••

Commemorative discourses convey the power struggle characterising the construction of Creole identity in Mauritius. In the context of their strategies of redefinition, the Creoles claim their links to Africa and to slavery and strive to reappropriate, progressively, their "slave" identity. The commemoration on the 1st of February 2005 became a privileged space for the verbalization of claims for entitlements and for political discourse. Le Morne and its surroundings hosted not one but several celebrations, each honoring this date in its own way. Geographically and temporally, these festive manifestations were held independently from one another. The Rastafari Socio-Cultural Association, the Mandela Centre, the Prime Minister, Paul Berenger and the Verts Fraternels Party as well, were the principal participants of these commemorations.

A comparison of different discourses uncovers several notions associated with the experience of slavery and maroon culture, including sacredness, resistance, sacrifice and suffering. This ideological climate in a way has idealized the character of the heroic fugitive slave. One of my interlocutors told me that "the fugitive slaves and their rebellion is what we need to emulate today." The character of the maroon has been present in the discourse of certain parties, such as the Mouvement Militant Mauricien and the Verts Fraternels Party since the 1970s. After having incarnated a symbol of resistance, this figure offers the concerned social actors today, with the possibility to identify themselves with not only the maroon but also with the slave who now is no longer a victim but a handsome and active hero, thus emphasising the contribution of slavery to the construction of the country.[22] The choice of symbolic figures depends upon the intentions of the social and institutional actors. Thus, the Rastafari Socio-Cultural Association, which regularly makes pilgrimages to Le Morne, adopted Barbe-Blanche, the fierce chief of fugitive slaves, who had occupied the site, as its hero. Others relate themselves to Ratsitatane, the Malagasy prince often represented as a resistance figure. Even the speech of the Prime Minister underlined the sacred and mystic nature of the mountain by paying homage to African ancestors.

The plurality of evocations nullifies the discourse of deprivation associated with the past and with the origins of Creoles. Even though these references are derived from popular legends and accounts of travellers, they have, all the same, become identity markers for the Creoles. The multiplicity of the latter permits us to question the discourse of deprivation of "ancestral capital" associated with the Creoles. Deprivation in comparison to whom and to what, one may ask. This discourse has become part of the process of differentiation which operates on lines of the Indo-Mauritian model.[23] Trade in Africans, slavery and Christianization feature among the factors which have constrained a direct relationship with the cultures and languages of origin, or even the task of conservation, thus making way to cultural mixing and creolization. This peculiarity in the process of construction of Creole identity and culture contributed and continues to contribute to the diversity of bonds with Africa and slavery.[24]

The Mauritian example is closely akin to what Chivallon elaborates on in describing the specificity of the African Diaspora in the Caribbean, in that it is a community defined fundamentally by the absence of a meta-narrative.[25] If a single unifying narrative does not exist, it is nonetheless striking in the least to encounter so many modes of relating, constructing and identifying with one's roots. Young Mauritians of the same generation or the same family can have different identification models. Some oscillate between idealization and denial. Occasionally, the link is so removed that it is completely overlooked. Various elements, such as the colonial heritage or the tenacity of prejudices and racial stereotypes, contribute to this plethora of identifications. To call oneself a descendant of slaves is not easy. Creoles are not unanimous in their acceptance of the past. One of my Rasta interlocutors commented the following about the category "General Population," which includes "a large number of Creoles [who] do not want to be acknowledged as descendants of slaves." The memory of slavery and its commemoration confirm this difficulty in accepting the past and the "slave" origin. The division that exists within the Creole community provides an example of the consequences of submitting to an ever-powerful "whitening ideology."[26] This stratification exposes the strong tendency exhibited by certain Creoles to distance themselves (through education, color and social status) from their African origins and their slave ancestry. Others, quite the reverse, consciously nurture their relationship to Africa and the

Black diaspora in general. The emergence of the Rasta community in Mauritius also bears witness to the existence of a bond with the African continent, which defines itself beyond the confines of the island, in transnational terms. This multiplicity is a constituent feature of the African diaspora.[27] The plurality of narratives and of discourses of origins (or their rejection) has become part of the construction of the Creole identity in Mauritius.

According to Chivallon, these "de-multiplied" community types are produced in response to a compelling historical environment marked by long term social relationships unfavorable to equitable integration.[28] The analysis of the process of patrimonialization of Le Morne exposes the existence of a power struggle in the quest of political and social legitimacy. For Creoles to identify themselves exclusively with Africa entails re-engaging with the multicultural and ethnic game of the State and relinquishing their Creole heritage and cross-cultural identity, encapsulated in the French meaning of "*métissage.*" Although Creole activists proudly advocate this mixed identity in certain occasions, they are undeniably limited on the political terrain in the multicultural Mauritian landscape. Many researchers define the bond with Africa as something that has been "reinvented" or "retrieved."[29] Generally, Creoles are defined by their lack of culture and ancestry. It is therefore tempting to create a link that was lost. The formation of the Mandela Centre corroborates this political will to institutionalize a link with Africa. Le Morne as a "site of memory" becomes, a part of this ethnicization process of the Creoles in the framework of a cult ideology of ancestral origins.

The essentialization of ancestry undermines the acknowledgement of the cross-cultural dimensions of Creole and Mauritian identity. For many, the bond with Africa does not make any sense. If some Creoles can identify with these commemorations, it is not only because of their slave ancestry but also because of the fact that they are Mauritians. As Laville points out, instead of aspiring to reconstitute a cultural identity, it is vital to recognize continuity and to identify links without over emphasizing these. Bearing this in mind, one must not construe diversity of identifications (or non-identifications) with Africa as a sign of weakness, deprivation or invention but as an aspect unique of the expression of identity of the Creole "community."

Conclusion
··················

The recognition of Le Morne as cultural heritage evinces the importance of identity stakes in the appropriation of signs and symbols of the past in post-colonial Mauritius. As an exercise in national positioning, this site of memory proved to be a medium, furnishing space for expression and tangibility, for Creole Mauritians. The performative value of heritage is represented by the range of commemorations and social actors involved in the celebration of the abolition of slavery. The commemoration of cultural heritage of Le Morne highlights the way in which in people of slave descent have cast themselves in narratives referring to slavery and Africa as a strategy in the struggle to establish citizenship in Mauritius, which has resulted in the ethnicization of their identity. It bears witness to the political and strategic limitations which determine the means of appropriating Africa and slavery. The process of ethnicization of Creoles at work in the Le Morne case institutionalizes the link to the origins in Africa as authority, resulting in a reductionist definition of Creole identity. Creole identity symbols are numerous, perhaps as numerous as the means of tracing or denying one's ancestry to Africa and the slave past. Ultimately, the patrimonialization of Le Morne is evidence of a process of construction of a Creole identity which can be compared to similar experiences elsewhere in the African diaspora. The Mauritian example comes within the scope of a larger field of research on the question of the plurality of Creole identity, its understanding and formulation in diaspora, its references to the land, to myth and to memory, as well as its capacity of resistance in a historical context marked by social and political inequities.

Notes

1.   An earlier version of this chapter was published as "Figures identitaires créoles et patrimoine à l'Ile Maurice, une montagne en jeu," *Le Journal des Anthropologues* 104-105 (2006), 265-286, and a slightly different version published in *Legacies of Slavery: Comparative Studies,* ed. Maria-Suzette Fernandes Dias (Newcastle: Cambridge Scholars Publishing, 2007). I would like to thank Maria-Suzette Fernandes Dias for her translation and also Joyce S.

Fortuné for her review and suggestions. We wish to thank Maria-Suzette Fernandes Dias and Cambridge Scholars Publishing for permission to publish a revised and expanded version.

2. Pierre Nora, ed. *Les Lieux de mémoire* (Paris: Gallimard, 1984), Vol. 1.

3. "Contre le venin du serpent électrique téléphérique qu'ils veulent injecter en toi le Morne j'ai l'antidote ! je t'offre la transfusion je te fais le don de mon sang noir pour que leur poison ne puisse s'insinuer dans tes veines le Morne, territoire marron ! malgré l'invasion de leurs ridicules pyramides que le sable engloutira tôt ou tard tu seras toujours là sphinx éternel témoin immuable debout en face de l'horizon comme un grand non à leurs sombres desseins !" Sedley Assone, "Contre le Venin du Serpent Électrique," *Le Morne, territoire marron !* (Port-Louis: Éditions de la Tour, 2002).

4. The Maroon Slave Archaeological Project (2002-2003) was directed by the University of Mauritius. It consisted of a study conducted to identify the sites associated with fugitive slaves in Mauritius. By combining historical, archaeological and ethnographical aspects of maroon culture, the study proposed several recommendations for the preservation of this heritage and for eventual scientific research on this subject.

5. The attention accorded to the cultural heritage of Le Morne reflects a quite paternalistic and strategic attitude toward the Creole population, particularly the villagers and the fishermen of the surrounding areas who hope to improve their quality of life with tourism.

6. See Jean-Clément Cangy, Jocelyn Chan Low and Mayila Paroomal, ed. *L'esclavage et ses séquelles: mémoire et vécu d'hier et d'aujourd'hui. Actes du Colloque international UOM* (1998) (Port-Louis: Presses de l'Université de Maurice, 2002). Le Morne is private property and public access to the site is prohibited.

7. "In a bid to retrace slave trade routes, the [UNESCO] Slave Route Project, launched, a cultural tourism program for Africa, in 1995, with the International Organization for Tourism, whose mission is to identify, rehabilitate, restore and promote sites, buildings and sites of memory of the African slave trade. This economic, historical and ethical conception of tourism is at the same time a stake in collective memory." (http://www/aidh/org/esclav/unes-program.htm)

8. Sheila Bunwaree, "Elusive Multiculturalism in Post-gatt Mauritius," in *Towards the Making of a Multi-cultural Society*, ed. S. Nirsimloo-Gayan (Moka, Mauritius: MGI Press, 2000), 238-249.

9. Bunwaree, "Elusive Multiculturalism," 239-240.

10. Jocelyn Chan Low, "Esclaves, exclus, citoyens?" in *L'esclavage et ses séquelles*, ed. Cangy, Chan Low and Paroomal, 237-267.

11. Chan Low, "Esclaves, exclus, citoyens?" and Suzanne Chazan-Gillig, "The Roots of Mauritian Multiculturalism and the Birth of a New Social Contract: Being *Autochtone*, Being Creole," *Journal of Mauritian Studies*, New Series, 2-1 (2003), 64-84; and Vijaya Teelock, "Questioning the Link between Slavery and Exclusion: the Experience of Plantation Slavery," in *L'esclavage et ses séquelles*, ed. Cangy, Chan Low and Paroomal, 279-288.

12. International conference, "Slavery: Resistance, Abolition and Memory," organized by the Mauritian Cultural Centre, the Gandhi Institute and the Nelson Mandela Centre, 17 February 2004.

13. Chazan-Gillig, "Roots of Mauritian Multiculturalism;" and Chan Low, "Esclaves, exclus, citoyens?"

14. Suzanne Chazan-Gillig, "Insularité et mondialization, diasporas et créolization de la société mauricienne contemporaine," *Journal des Anthropologues* 96-97 (2004), 321. Jocelyn Chan Low, "Les enjeux actuels des débats sur la mémoire et la réparation pour l'esclavage à l'île Maurice," *Cahiers d'études africaines* 44, no. 1-2 (2004), 401-418.

15. In Mauritian context, stereotypes associated with Creoles are often those of laziness, senseless spending and of "eating, drinking and merry making." R. Laville, "Prospects for Creole Identity Beyond 2000: An Anthropological Perspective," in *L'esclavage et ses séquelles,* ed. Cangy, Chan Low and Paroomal, 289-301.

16. The question of Creole language, as well as education, historiography of slavery, and land rights, which are important to Creole associations and activists in their identity struggle, is not discussed here.

17. Bunwaree, "Elusive Multiculturalism in Post-gatt Mauritius," 244.

18. The "Grand Bassin" is a sacred place for Hinduism in Mauritius. The history of this religious site claims a direct link to the Ganges in India.

19. Chan Low, "Les débats sur la mémoire et la réparation pour l'esclavage à l'île Maurice," 401-418.

20. The Organization Fraternelle was a sociocultural association that became a political party, which is known in Mauritius as OF/Les Verts.

21. Although certain Mauritian intellectuals have individually tried to position themselves with international movements like *négritude* or the Afro-American movements, these efforts have not consolidated into any recognized collective endeavor.

22. Slavery in Mauritius metamorphosed into plantation slavery only much later. Slaves initially worked mainly in naval construction and the building of the ports, in logging and in the construction of the city of Port-Louis and its fortifications.

23. The conservation of Indian origins is the fruit of a concerted and consistent effort backed by the bureaucracy. But cross-cultural experience undoubtedly favored a "creolization" of Indo-Mauritian practices and lifestyles as well.

24. The diversity of these relationships also includes all the general cultural influences of the island.

25. Christine Chivallon, *La diaspora noire des Amériques, expériences et théories à partir de la Caraïbe* (Paris: CNRS Éditions, 2004), 231.

26. Chan Low, "Esclaves, exclus, citoyens?" 257.

27. Chivallon, *Diaspora noire des Amériques*, 214.

28. Chivallon, *Diaspora noire des Amériques*, 214.

29. Jocelyn Chan Low, "De l'Afrique rejetée à l'Afrique retrouvée ? Les Créoles de l'île Maurice et l'Africanité," *Revi Kiltir Kreol* 3 (2003), 39-50; and Jean-Luc Alber, "Les ressorts d'une africanité réinventée à Maurice," in *Fabrication des traditions, inventions de la modernité*, ed. Dejan Dimitrijevic (Paris: MSH, 2004), 99-118.

Chapter 5

Forgetting and Remembering the Atlantic Slave Trade: The Legacy of Brazilian Slave Merchant Francisco Félix de Souza

Ana Lucia Araujo

Brazilian slave merchant Francisco Félix de Souza (1754-1849) plied his trade between Brazil and the west African kingdom of Dahomey, now the Republic of Benin. Since the 1960s, de Souza's biography has been the object of numerous studies.[1] However, most scholars have not yet considered the visibility he acquired as a result of official projects to promote the memory of slavery in the Republic of Benin. Of greater significance than the bare facts, de Souza's biography offers us a methodological example of how to deal with the old opposition between oral tradition and written sources. It questions the relationship between memory and the writing of history.

In recent years, Robin Law has questioned the key political and economic role usually assigned to de Souza in the history of Benin.[2] De Souza's image seems disproportionate to his real place in the slave trade in the Bight of Benin. Even if new evidence indicates that many other merchants were more prosperous, de Souza continues to occupy a central place in the memory of the slave trade, not only in Benin but in the whole South Atlantic region. What elements allowed the merchant's memory to survive? Why and how did Francisco Félix de Souza become a symbol of the exchanges between Bahia and the Bight of Benin? How did his identity become mythologized as a founder and reference point for the Afro-Luso-Brazilian community in Benin? How can collective memory and family memory reconcile his dual roles as slave merchant and philanthropist? What role does Brazil have in the reconstruction of de Souza's myth? By analyzing historical documents, interviewing members of the de Souza family, and examining the memorial of Francisco Félix de Souza at the de Souza family compound of Singbomey in the Benin coastal city of Ouidah, I attempt to answer these questions.

Trans-National Memories of Slavery

At the beginning of the 1990s, the memorialization of slavery and the transatlantic slave trade came to constitute a transnational movement that reached beyond the Americas and Europe. In Benin, the emergence of a debate about the slave past was followed by the development of a number of official projects, carried out by the Benin government and by international agencies including UNESCO and non-governmental organizations. Even local elites, connected to some extent to the slave trade of the past, were part of this new movement. Many descendants of Brazilian and Portuguese slave merchants, along with the descendants of former slaves who returned to West Africa from Brazil, started promoting their past in the public space, contributing to the success of the memorialization phenomenon.

The emergence of the memory of slavery in Benin is associated with the commemoration of the 500th anniversary of Columbus's arrival in the Americas. At the time, it was argued that little attention was being given to the Atlantic slave trade and the contribution of Africans to the construction of the Americas. This debate gave rise to two distinct initiatives: a transnational scientific venture entitled "The Slave Route" project, and a Vodun festival entitled *Ouidah 92*, which focused on religion and aimed in part to increase tourism. The two projects were to some extent combined, and both received the support of UNESCO and of Benin's new government.[3]

In 1991, after more than twenty years of Marxist-Leninist military dictatorship, democratic elections had been held and Nicéphore Soglo elected president of Benin. The new government sought not only to promote religious freedom but also to develop the national economy by attracting tourists. In this context, both the Vodun religion and the transatlantic slave trade became the focus of programs aimed at developing cultural tourism.[4] The new projects emphasized the material and non-material heritage of the slave trade through forms of commemoration, the construction of monuments, and the creation of family museums. These projects were controversial,[5] resulting in a widespread debate covered in the local newspapers.[6] In Ouidah, it is possible to grasp the multiple dimensions of the memory of slavery, expressed on the one hand by the descendants of slaves, and on the other by the descendants of those who were responsible for the slave trade. The memory of slavery is inscribed in the physical and political landscape, which is divided by conflicts that are not always perceived by visitors and tourists. In this context, the family of the Brazilian slave merchant Francisco Félix de Souza, which still occupies an important position within Ouidah society, has been playing a crucial role in this memorialization movement.

Francisco Félix de Souza's biography sheds light on the existence of plural memories of slavery. Though they sometimes converge, these multiple memories very often present dissonant elements. In the Republic of Benin, a specific memory is visible in the discourses of the descendants of former slaves and slave traders. Because these individuals did not live the experience of their ancestors, however, studying their memories entails dealing with mediators: the witness no longer exists.

As Marianne Hirsch has stated, "postmemory characterizes the experience of those who grow up dominated by narratives that preceded their birth, whose own belated stories are evacuated by the stories of the previous generation shaped by traumatic events that can be neither understood nor recreated."[7] In this context of mediated memory, the notion of heritage, material or non-material, is unavoidable, because heritage is an inheritance that actively participates in the transmission of identity.[8] For the heirs of slavery (those who claim to be, directly or indirectly, the descendants of slaves), the memory is marked by rupture and gaps. Among the descendants of the perpetrators of slavery (masters, slave merchants, and other collaborators), memory is rather characterized by continuity. The families of the slave merchants of American or European origin who established themselves on the West African coasts during the period of the slave trade have been able to preserve their bonds with the cities where their ancestors settled while also preserving ties with the other side of the Atlantic Ocean. These ongoing connections and the wealth these families accumulated via the transatlantic slave trade have allowed them to perpetuate their personal and family possessions: houses, furniture, objects, photographs, and so forth. The stability of their elite position in the local society has helped them to preserve cultural and religious practices associated with their Brazilian or Portuguese community of origin, by means of incorporating indigenous customs into these practices. This deep South Atlantic identity, largely based on Luso-Brazilian traditions associating paternalism and Catholicism, is solid but at the same time flexible and mixed because of its openness to reciprocal exchanges.[9]

The Brazilian Slave Trade and Slavery

The Portuguese were the first Europeans to arrive in the Gulf of Guinea. In 1721, they founded the fort São João Batista da Ajuda in Ouidah. In 1727, the kingdom of Dahomey conquered the kingdom of Hueda, seized Ouidah, and gained direct access to the coast. During the period of the slave trade, Ouidah became, after Luanda, the most important African slave port.[10]

The enslaved Africans sent to Brazil came from different regions commercially controlled by the Portuguese. The majority of them were captured in West Central Africa (mainly Angola), though some came from the Gulf of Guinea (including the Bight of Benin); by the end of the eighteenth century, they also came from Mozambique in East Africa.[11] In the South Atlantic region, especially between Angola and Brazil, slave voyages were direct instead of following the traditional triangular model.

Starting at the end of the seventeenth century, the Brazilian slave system relied on the one hand on the importation of large numbers of slaves, and on the other hand on a large number of manumissions.[12] Recent estimations indicate that between 1550 and 1850, Brazil imported more than 5 million enslaved Africans, the largest number in all the Americas.[13] In cities like Rio de Janeiro and Salvador, slaves constituted almost half of the population. They performed many different kinds of activities: they were domestic servants, merchants, shoemakers, surgeons, barbers, carriers, artisans, artists, tailors, and so on.

In 1835, Africans in Bahia numbered 21,940 out of a total population of 65,000, of whom 17,325 (26.5 percent) were slaves and 4,615 (7.1 percent) were freed former slaves.[14] During the first three decades of the nineteenth century, most of the 7,000 Africans who arrived each year in Bahia were Yoruba-speaking people from the regions that now form Nigeria and the Republic of Benin.[15] These Yoruba and, in much smaller proportion, Hausa populations were captured during the wars between the Fulani and the states dominated by the kingdom of Oyo.

Muslims were a minority in Bahia but had religious freedom to some extent and were able to organize themselves into various groups. Although they belonged to many distinct ethnic groups, African Muslims were all referred to as Malês. The origin of this term derives from the Yoruba word *imale,* meaning Muslim. The large Yoruba population, and the Hausa presence, played a role in the Malês uprising of 1835 in Bahia.[16] Many participants in the uprising were familiar with the Qu'ran. They carried amulets, they were able read and write in Arabic, and many wore long white robes called *abadas.* After the rebellion's defeat in 1835, deportation to the Bight of Benin was the most common penalty imposed on free Africans alleged to have participated in the rebellion but against whom the Bahian government had no evidence.[17] Former slaves continued this movement of return throughout the nineteenth century until the very beginning of the twentieth century.

The Formation of an Afro-Luso-Brazilian Community

Between 3,000 and 8,000 former slaves returned to the Bight of Benin. Once in West Africa, they settled in the coastal towns in what is now the Republic of Benin (Petit Popo, Grand Popo, Agoué, Ouidah, Cotonou, and Porto-Novo) as well as in the cities of what is now Nigeria (Badagry and Lagos). Here, they joined Portuguese and Brazilian slave merchants already established in the region, forming a community that came to be called Aguda. In Ouidah, Francisco Félix de Souza supported former slaves and helped them to settle in several neighborhoods of Ouidah: Maro, Brazil, Quénum, Zomaï, and Boya.[18]

In Benin, the Aguda represent 5-10 percent of the current population.[19] However, they are not a homogeneous community: among them are descendants of former returned slaves, descendants of Brazilian and Portuguese slave merchants, and descendants of the slaves kept by these two groups, who were later assimilated by them. These assimilated descendants carry the Portuguese names of their old Brazilian masters, and they share Brazilian customs and culture.[20] The Aguda are Catholic, but among the former returned slaves were also Muslims and adherents of traditional religions such as Vodun and Orisha worship.[21] African-born former slaves belonged to various ethnic groups and had several different native languages, but spoke mainly Yoruba or one of Gbe languages.

Despite these distinctions, all the former slaves had a common past marked by enslavement and their experiences in Brazil. Unlike the indigenous population, they were baptized, carried Portuguese names such as Silva, Reis, Assunção, Almeida, Santos, Cruz, Paraíso, Oliveira, and Souza, dressed in European fashion, and had so-called white manners. In the early days, the Aguda often chose to marry within their community, in order to preserve its cohesion. These former slaves brought from Brazil a particular cuisine, including dishes such as *feijoada* (beans and several kinds of pork, similar to the French *cassoulet*), *cozido* (boiled meat and vegetables), and *acará* (deep-fried dough made with white beans). The Aguda community also marked its presence in the public space through the development of a vernacular architecture inspired by Luso-Brazilian houses. In Benin, the construction of these "Brazilian" houses, which typically had two storeys and a veranda, exerted an influence on the local community, which adopted some decorative elements of this style.[22]

Once settled in the Bight of Benin, these former slaves attempted to continue following the model of the Brazilian slave society, and not only in customs and culture; many former slaves became slave merchants. Even if they were not able to amass great fortunes, as other slave merchants of the region did, some became prosperous. By 1850, several former returned slaves were actively involved in the slave trade at Ouidah, Agoué, and Porto-Novo.[23]

The former slaves also brought to the region Catholic brotherhoods such as the Nosso Senhor do Bom Fim, which had helped to free numerous slaves in Bahia. They also reproduced on African soil the *bouryan,* a masquerade popular in the Brazilian northeast and very similar to the *bumba-meu-boi.* Today, by preparing dishes inspired by Bahian cuisine, singing songs in an approximation of Portuguese,[24] and dancing the samba, the Aguda keep alive an Atlantic memory.

The indigenous population perceived the Aguda as a more educated and civilized group because of their different manners. Their Westernization was seen as assimilation and denial of their African origins, and this apparent "superiority" was not always well accepted by the local population. As being an Aguda meant belonging to a modern bourgeoisie, some indigenous families sought to follow or even imitate the Aguda way of life, sometimes by adopting Portuguese names.

In 1892, the regions constituting the kingdom of Dahomey and the kingdom of Porto-Novo were conquered and became part of the French colony of Dahomey. The end of the slave trade had led to a decrease in prosperity in the Aguda community. However, they were now able to forge a new place in the colonial society. Still connected to a Brazilian culture, they perceived the European presence as an advantage.[25] Many of their descendants continued to perform the professional activities their ancestors had in Brazil (as carpenters, tailors, and masons) and others occupied administrative positions (as clerks, interpreters, and traders).[26] They collaborated with the French regime and received favors in exchange, consolidating their privileged place in the colonial society. The pages of the *Journal officiel de la colonie du Dahomey* not only identify the names of several members of the Aguda community who held administrative positions during the colonial period but also thus reveal the extent to which they endorsed the colonial regime.[27]

After the independence of Dahomey in August 1960, the Aguda definitely lost their influence. With the emergence of national sentiment, they were perceived as having collaborated with the French regime. When General Mathieu Kérékou became president of the country in 1972 and established a Marxist-Leninist dictatorship, the economic and social changes had a negative effect on the most prosperous Aguda families. Those who opposed the new regime, such as Francisca Patterson (born Medeiros), were sent to prison,[28] while other businessmen, such as Urbain-Karim-Elisio da Silva, considered leaving the country.[29]

In 1990, several distinguished members of the Aguda community, including Monsignor Isidore de Souza (1934-1999), archbishop of Cotonou, actively participated in the organization of the National Conference of the Living Forces of the Nation, which established the means for a democratic transition of power and prepared the schedule for presidential elections.[30] With the end of the dictatorship and the development of projects to promote Vodun cultures and religions and to memorialize slavery, some members of the Aguda community regained prestige and visibility on the political scene. This was true of Vieyra family, whose ancestor Sabino Vieyra was a former slave who had "returned" from Rio de Janeiro. Rosine Vieyra Soglo, the wife of President Nicéphore Soglo, was elected a deputy in the 1990s and participated in her husband's government, while during the same period her brother, Désiré Vieyra, was appointed minister of culture.

The international attention Benin received over projects to promote Vodun and African cultures and to recuperate the memory of slavery and the slave trade played a large part in creating the opportunity for some Aguda to gain back political prestige following the National Conference. By claiming their Brazilian identity, the Aguda were encouraged to talk publicly about slavery, formerly a difficult subject. However, in emphasizing the slave past the Aguda did not insist on the elements they shared with the descendants of slave merchants but rather on their differences. From this perspective, conceiving a common Brazilian memory is sometimes a complicated task because it means erasing the plurality of the memories of slavery.[31]

Embracing the memorialization movement, the Aguda promoted their history and their heritage. American tourists and Brazilian authorities traveling to Porto-Novo and Ouidah visit the most important Aguda families. The Aguda continue to emphasize the centrality of their connections with Brazil, but this is no longer a naïve enterprise. Brazil is now a new power, different from the old French colonizer. It represents not only a link with the past but also a promise of a future, a horizon of hope.

The Brazilian Slave Merchant

Francisco Félix de Souza is considered the founder of the Aguda community in Benin. He may have been born in 1754 in Salvador, Bahia,[32] but we know very little about the period prior to his settlement in Ouidah. Family tradition represents him as a typical Brazilian rich man. He is described as white, with Portuguese ancestors on his father's side but native Amazonian heritage from his mother. Although Amazonia was almost unknown territory at the end of the eighteenth century and the beginning of the nineteenth, the rainforest is often present in the family discourse as the symbol of an imagined Brazil, rich in natural resources. Simone de Souza, a historian who is member of Souza family, for example, describes Francisco Félix de Souza as a member of a noble family composed mainly of military and administration employees. According to her, the Brazilian merchant was an eighth generation descendant of the Portuguese officer Tomé de Souza (1503–1573 or 1579), the first governor general of Brazil and the founder of Salvador.[33] Today, this version has been slightly modified by the family and Francisco Félix de Souza is said to be the grandson of Tomé de Souza, even though this claim is incompatible with the death of the governor almost two hundred years before de Souza's birth.[34] This revision is an attempt to fill in the lack of information about de Souza's early life, thus contributing to the reconstruction of his memory.

De Souza came to the coast of Western Africa for the first time in 1792.[35] He spent three years in the region, returned to Brazil, and then came back to settle permanently in Africa by 1800. In Ouidah, he may have served as governor of the Portuguese fort, a post left vacant by the death of his brother, Jacinto José de Souza.[36]

Some years later, he left this position to become a private slave merchant.[37] According to travelers who met de Souza, he was so poor when he first arrived in Africa that he was obliged to steal the cowries given as offerings at Vodun shrines.[38]

Once in Ouidah, de Souza clashed with Adandozan (r. 1797-1818), the king of Dahomey, probably because of a debt that Adandozan owed him. The tradition says that de Souza went to Abomey, the capital of Dahomey, to claim the money, but the king sent him to prison.[39] According to tradition, to punish de Souza the jailers plunged him in a large jar of indigo. This operation was repeated several times over many weeks.[40] In prison, de Souza is said to have met Prince Gakpé, one of the sons of King Agonglo (r. 1789-1797), who had been murdered in 1797. Gakpé visited de Souza in prison and together they decided to gather their forces to fight Adandozan. To confirm their alliance, the tradition states they made a blood pact, a well-known practice in the old kingdom of Dahomey.[41]

De Souza escaped from prison and probably settled in Little Popo (modern-day Anécho). From there, he supplied Prince Gakpé with guns and goods, allowing him to prepare the *coup d'état*.[42] Adandozan was deposed in 1818, and Prince Gakpé became King Gezo (r. 1818-1850). The new king invited de Souza to settle in Ouidah and take charge of the kingdom's commercial affairs. De Souza adopted the title "chacha," an honorific title associated with the nickname he had received when he escaped from prison with the help of his allies.[43] According to tradition, the Dahomean guards asked de Souza's men what they were carrying out of the prison. They replied that it was a *chacha*, meaning "mat."[44] However, this version of the story is unlikely, as in the Fon language spoken in the kingdom of Dahomey, the word for "mat" is *zàn*. In the Fon language the word *chacha* (written *cacà*) actually means "quickly done."[45] It is probably an adaptation of *já já*, a Portuguese expression meaning "quick, quick," that de Souza used to repeat. Eventually, chacha came to be a hereditary title given to the highest-ranking representative of the Souza family. After the death of the first chacha, the king of Dahomey nominated his successor.

The position occupied by Francisco Félix de Souza is commonly equated with that of viceroy.[46] In recent years, however, local tradition, which usually designates de Souza as the chief of the whites, has been questioned by Robin Law, who reminds us that this position, also known as the *yovogan,* was always filled by a native.[47] The exaggeration of de Souza's status can be attributed in part to British travelers who described him as a rich and powerful man. However, these same travel accounts indicate that when European visitors arrived in Ouidah, they first met the yovogan, and only after this first meeting visited the chacha. Thus, de Souza was in fact a local chief, or *caboceer.*[48] Even if the term viceroy does not accurately define de Souza's function, Alberto da Costa e Silva has observed that in the context of an autocracy, "being the king's commercial agent was a political function."[49] Thus, it is not surprising that de Souza was perceived as an actor of great importance in Dahomean society.

The period of Gezo's rule and de Souza's appointment as his agent coincided with the slow decline of the transatlantic slave trade and a transition to the palm oil trade. Until the 1830s, de Souza was a very prosperous man who owned several slave ships.[50] However, in the 1840s, his activities considerably decreased, partly because of his advanced age and partly because of repressive measures against the slave trade imposed by the British navy, which confiscated twenty-two of his slave ships.[51] At the time of his death in 1849, de Souza had significant debts with King Gezo as well as with Brazilian and Cuban merchants. According to some members of the family, when de Souza died, the king of Dahomey sent his agents to his residence to seize his possessions.

The Memorial at Singbomey

Singbomey, the de Souza family compound, is located in the Brazil neighborhood of Ouidah, where de Souza and some Aguda families settled during the first half of the nineteenth century. At the end of the courtyard are two large houses painted in reddish-orange inspired by the Brazilian vernacular architecture of the eighteenth and nineteenth centuries. Inside the two single-storey buildings, formerly part of de Souza's residence, is a memorial. Although it has existed for many years, it became accessible to the public only in the 1990s, when Honoré Feliciano Julião de Souza was appointed Chacha VIII.

When I visited the memorial in the company of Christian de Souza and David de Souza[52] they were evidently trying to rehabilitate the memory of their ancestor, framing him not as a slave trader but as a great entrepreneur.[53] They emphasized the family's bonds with Brazil, and justified the merchant's activities by insisting that slave trading was a legal activity at the time. According to the family's point of view, de Souza contributed to the development of Africa by introducing new goods and new crops to the region, including the oil palm tree.

The various accounts I collected during my interviews indicate that the history of Francisco Félix de Souza's family includes betrayal of each other, and collaboration with the Europeans in exchange for political power. The existence of different interest groups within the family often created serious conflicts; some episodes involve suspicious deaths, probably the result of poisoning. Disagreements with the royalty of Dahomey also deeply mark the family's memory. There is still a belief that marriage between a de Souza and a Fon from Abomey will be unsuccessful and may have serious consequences such as illness and divorce. One older woman in the de Souza family told me that her daughter was deeply depressed because of her marriage to a Fon from Abomey.[54]According to the various accounts circulating, those who did not listen to the family warnings regretted it later. It seems that even if the blood pact with King Gezo was profitable, its price was very high.

While visiting the memorial, one sees the intersection among several memories related not only to slavery and Dahomean royalty but also to the exchange between Dahomey and Brazil. Christian de Souza noted that the official history stresses the opposition between King Gezo "the builder" and Francisco Félix de Souza "the slave merchant," but Christian de Souza himself minimizes the conflicts between the family and the royalty of Dahomey, instead putting the accent on the collaboration between them.

According to the family, de Souza rescued Na Agontimé,[55] a wife of King Agonglo and reputedly the mother of King Gezo, from slavery. After the murder of her husband, Na Agontimé is said to have been sold as a slave and sent to Brazil by King Adandozan. Although there is a lack of written evidence confirming this event, several deities of the kings of Dahomey are present in the Vodun practiced at the temple Casa das Minas in the Brazilian state of Maranhão.[56] These deities existed prior to King Agonglo and were not "borrowed" from the neighboring states during the wars.[57] According to the story accepted by some scholars such as Melville Herskovits and Pierre Verger, Na Agontimé introduced the Vodun of Abomey to Brazil.[58] By allegedly liberating the king's mother, Francisco Félix de Souza transformed the rupture provoked by the transatlantic slave trade into a fruitful connection with Brazil.

Despite this tradition, no evidence confirms that de Souza actually travelled to Brazil to search for Na Agontimé. In 1821, he obtained a passport allowing him to visit his homeland, but he did not embark to Brazil and it is hard to explain why he did not attempt the trip later.[59] There are two possibilities: either King Gezo prevented de Souza from leaving Dahomey, or the slave merchant had legal problems that prevented him from entering Brazil. King Gezo probably sent one of de Souza's employees, Dossou-Yovo, one of the men who may have helped de Souza escape from Abomey's prison.[60]

Christian de Souza and David de Souza reinforce the idea that their ancestor was a virile man. According to them, Francisco Félix de Souza had 201 children: 106 daughters and 95 sons. They ascribe this remarkable progeny not to his wealth or the great number of slaves he owned but to his extraordinary physical force. Because of his reputation as a prosperous man, many people living in Ouidah today claim to be his descendants. Physical strength and seductive qualities are traits assigned to him not only in the family discourse but also in works of fiction such as Bruce Chatwin's novel *The Viceroy of Ouidah* (1980) and Werner Herzog's film adaptation *Cobra Verde* (1987). In the film, the Brazilian merchant terrifies other men and attracts beautiful women without having to say a single word.

At the end of the nineteenth century, when the Dahomean monarchy was abolished under French rule, the de Souza family as an assembly became responsible for choosing the chacha. By this time the family had lost much of its influence and its internal divisions had increased. The difficulty in electing the highest representative of the family led to long periods of vacancy.

The Healer Ancestor

Inside the memorial, Francisco Félix de Souza's old bedroom is still intact. In it one finds not only his original Brazilian wood bed, freshly made each day as if he were alive, but also his tomb. The room reinforces the idea that he remains among his family members. According to David de Souza, when his ancestor died, the king of Dahomey "sent a dozen slaves, a dozen men to be buried alive at the same time as the merchant, but his children said 'there is no question, we do not support this kind of thing,'... and the men were freed."[61] Despite family opposition, de Souza received all the honors related to the funeral of a great Dahomean chief: four individuals were sacrificed, two on the beach and two others on his tomb.[62] The account of this episode presents a Westernized and humane image of the family, which rejected both local religious practices and the cruelty practiced against the slaves.

The de Souzas are said to be Catholic, but when their ancestor settled in Ouidah, King Gezo ordered the installation of several Vodun shrines in the city to protect him. Close to the tomb of Francisco Félix de Souza is a large ceramic jar that may have been brought by him from Brazil. This jar contains water, used in libation rituals aimed at healing members of the family.[63] In this context, the ancestor himself becomes a sort of vodun, a divinity who is able to heal. In the Vodun religion, the spirit or divinity must be located in a precise physical space. The presence of Francisco Félix de Souza in his former room is ensured by his tomb, while water from the earthenware jar produces the cure. This room has become a major symbol of the original bond with Brazil as well as the political influence still exerted by the de Souza family over the Aguda community and other communities in Ouidah. This sanctification of Francisco Félix de Souza increases the family's authority, which reaches beyond the political, economic, and family arenas to also gain a religious dimension.

Like other elite families of Ouidah, the de Souzas owned slaves brought from the neighboring areas and used in the local economy. They were employed in agricultural and household activities. Those who were initiated into the Fa or Egungun and Zangbeto forms of worship were given religious roles. For example, an ancestor of the Olougoudou family who belonged to the royal family of Abeokuta was brought to Ouidah in 1830, at the time of the illegal export slave trade. According to the historian and professor, Emile Olougoudou, his ancestor was in a slave ship whose final destination was the Americas. While skirting the West African coast, the ship ran into difficulties and went to Ouidah. According to Olougoudou, de Souza bought all six hundred slaves who were on board, thereby "saving" them from being sent into slavery in the Americas.[64]

Olougoudou's account suggests that far from being perceived negatively by his slaves, de Souza was rather seen as helping them. This image is similar to the one presented in British travelogues of the time. According to Frederick Forbes, de Souza's values differed from those of the indigenous population; for example, he was opposed to human sacrifice.[65] The de Souza family perpetuates this aspect of his reputation, as evidenced in David de Souza's words:

> When the slaves were brought to Ouidah to be sold, some families recognized their members. They used to ask Chacha to help them recover the captive who was to be sold and sent overseas. In the praise names [the panegyrics] there is a particular word hailing Dom Francisco Félix de Souza. We say, the one who re-buys the slave and gives him back to his family [...] is the one who saves the slave.[66]

Indeed, David de Souza referred to *é plé vi plé nò,* which means "he used to buy the child and the child's mother." However, by the 1990s, when Honoré Feliciano Julião de Souza was appointed Chacha VIII, this portion of the praise name has been suppressed because it clearly referred to commerce in human beings. Although buying the child and its mother can be interpreted as an attempt to prevent family members from being separated, it can also be understood as a demonstration of how rich the Brazilian merchant was; he could buy many members of the same family. The memory of Chacha I is thus reconstructed according to moral values belonging to the present. He is depicted as concerned with human rights and disposed to liberate his slaves. However, it seems this idea is not new. In his account of his travels, John Duncan reported that de Souza was benevolent to his slaves.[67] Indeed, some travelers who met him mentioned that de Souza considered himself a great philanthropist, "on the grounds of having saved the lives of the slaves whom he purchased for export" and consequently prevented them from being sacrificed.[68]

About one hundred meters from Singbomey, on the road towards the beach, is the temple of Dagoun, the vodun of Francisco Félix de Souza. Although he was Catholic, the merchant was the only Aguda who had his own vodun. According to the most reliable version of Dagoun's origin, when King Gezo invited de Souza to settle in Ouidah, he gave him two voduns to protect the city; the first was installed at the entrance to the city, and the second was placed at the exit. He was ultimately awarded a third vodun for his personal protection: Dagoun.[69]

Today, the descendants of the religious chiefs sent to Ouidah during Gezo's reign still remain close to the de Souza family.[70] The relationship between the merchant's family and Dahomean royalty was not always positive, and the presence of the traditional chiefs sent by the king of Dahomey was part of this combative relationship. Through them the king was able to exert his control over the family. The current chacha conserves his authority over the traditional shrines overseen by the religious chiefs of the Brazilian quarter. Unlike the chiefs of other shrines, the chief of Dagoun's shrine is chosen by the council of the de Souza family, and not by the Vodun's supreme leader.

Updating the Memory of Francisco Félix de Souza

The rehabilitation of the memory of Francisco Félix de Souza started about fifteen years ago, when Chacha VIII was nominated. Today, the family members openly discuss the slave trade. Many of them believe that de Souza and his children cannot be condemned for the past involvement of the family in the slave trade. They think one should not judge the past through the eyes of the present and note that the slave trade was a legal form of commerce at the time, although Francisco Félix de Souza and his children are known to have continued their slave trading activities until the 1850s, when it had become illegal. In spite of these justifications, in order to rebuild the memory of their ancestor and to gain political capital it has been necessary for family members to obscure the slave trading aspect of de Souza's biography.

In recent years, probably because of the repercussions of "Ouidah 92" and the launch of The Slave Route project by UNESCO, discussing the slave past is no longer taboo in Benin. However, slavery within Africa and the Muslim slave trade are absent from this public memorialization. Slavery on African soil is still seen as more humane and benevolent, and thus more acceptable, than the Atlantic slave trade and slavery. However, we know that with the intensification of the transatlantic slave trade the nature of slavery in Africa changed, and slavery became a central institution in many African societies.[71]

Robin Law claims that during the first half of the nineteenth century Francisco Félix de Souza was not the only important merchant in Ouidah. Several other successful slave traders established themselves in the town, including Joaquim Teles de Menezes, Juan José Zangronis, Joaquim d'Almeida, and Domingos José Martins. Although his examination of Ouidah slave trade networks is a detailed one, Law neglected an essential dimension related to memory rather than to history, specifically how Francisco Félix de Souza became a mythical figure in the history of Ouidah and of the kingdom of Dahomey despite being only one of many actors in the region's slave trade. Élisée Soumonni and Alberto da Costa e Silva have put forth some important points with respect to this issue. They note that de Souza played a central role during the transition to the palm oil trade, which contributed to the establishment of his reputation. For a long time, he was perceived as the "protector" of the Aguda community. The local population considered him Westernized and more evolved than the indigenous population. He was able to exercise this role thanks to the appointment conferred on him by King Gezo. This position contributed to the construction of his reputation as a generous and benevolent man. In spite of his Brazilian ancestry, Francisco Félix de Souza became a perfect African chief.[72]

The myth around him is based on the bonds and exchanges between Brazil and the kingdom of Dahomey. In the framework of the construction of a South Atlantic zone, marked by the disruption provoked by the Atlantic slave trade, de Souza is no longer the slave trader who became rich by buying and selling human beings but the benevolent patron who preserved a flexible Brazilian identity and who allowed the community of former Brazilian "returned" slaves to find their native Africa.

Although de Souza was not the only active and prosperous merchant in the territory of the old kingdom of Dahomey, he made his mark on the history of the slave trade in the area by becoming an important reference for the Aguda community and also a genuine myth. Today, the reconstruction of his memory is based on the reconstitution of the region's connections with Brazil. The evolution of the myth of Francisco Félix de Souza is also the result of the work of historians and anthropologists, who have privileged the study of relations between Bahia and the Bight of Benin even though the majority of the slaves brought to Brazil came from West Central Africa.

Even though de Souza and his descendants have been having children with African women since the merchant first arrived in Africa, there seems to persist among the family members an idea of "biological" authenticity. This idea is not associated with racial purity but rather with a certain "Brazilianity," which here refers to hybridity and miscegenation. The de Souza myth borrows from the Brazilian founder myth of the three races: the origin of the family is based on the encounter of a white Brazilian of Portuguese origin and an Amerindian woman, who gave birth to a genuine Brazilian individual, who then perfectly adapted himself to the African context. "Smoothed by the oil of the deep miscegenation,"[73] this hybridity allowed de Souza to forge an idealized "Brazilian" identity which combined Catholicism, paternalism, polygamy, and African religions, and therefore incorporated different cultures and traditions.

The construction of this myth was possible thanks to several political and economic factors, including de Souza's wealth and his position during a crucial period of the involvement of Dahomey in the Atlantic slave trade. Over the years, the religious aspect of this myth has played an important role in consolidating de Souza's position as a kind of viceroy. De Souza introduced Catholicism to Dahomey but also inserted himself into local religious practices. The most important representative of the Afro-Luso-Brazilian community in Ouidah, Francisco Félix de Souza was gradually Africanized. He symbolizes the idea of mixed identity based on bonds with an imaginary or imagined Brazil. These elements, which form the basis of the myth, are reinforced by the present wave of memorialization and the new importance being accorded to local chiefs, allowing the de Souza family to regain political power lost since the decolonization of Benin.[74]

In a globalized world, in which slavery and the slave trade are considered crimes against humanity, the de Souza family has succeeded in reinforcing its position of legitimacy, although not necessarily at the economic and political levels. Its new symbolic position relies on its Brazilian origins and on the celebration of "miscegenation" and the encounter of cultures. Paradoxically, the official projects of UNESCO have helped to commemorate not only the victims of slave trade but also those who enslaved and sold them. Through a process of reconstructing the memory of the ancestor, endorsed by these official projects, the de Souza family is slowly recovering its political capital. If celebrating a slave trader is inconceivable from a Western point of view, in the African context it is better accepted because the Atlantic slave trade and slavery in the Americas are not perceived also as an African problem. Moreover, slave trade and slavery on African soil are part of a recent history in which multiple actors were involved, making difficult distinguish victims and perpetrators.

The valorization of the memory of Francisco Félix de Souza, relying on the idea that he was not only the most important slave merchant of the region but also a protector of the weak, is a relatively successful enterprise among the local population. Nevertheless, certain tourists, in particular African Americans and those whose populations that provided a great number of captives to the slave trade, such as the Ketu and Savalu, strongly contest this historical reconstruction.

Notes

1. See David Ross, "The First Chacha of Whydah: Francisco Félix de Souza," *Odu* 2 (1969), 19-28; Robin Law, "A carreira de Francisco Félix de Souza na África Ocidental (1800-1849)," *Topoi* (2001),

9-39; Alberto da Costa e Silva, *Francisco Félix de Souza, mercador de escravos* (Rio de Janeiro: Nova Fronteira, 2004).

2. See Law, "A carreira de Francisco Félix de Souza;" Law, "The Atlantic Slave Trade in Local History Writing in Ouidah," in *Africa and Trans-Atlantic Memories: Literary and Aesthetic Manifestations of Diaspora and History,* ed. Naana Opoku-Agyemang, Paul E. Lovejoy and David V. Trotman (Trenton, NJ: Africa World Press, 2008); and Robin Law, *Ouidah, The Social History of a West African Slaving "Port," 1727-1892* (Athens: Ohio University Press, 2004).

3. See Emmanuelle Kadya Tall, "De la démocratie et des cultes voduns au Bénin," *Cahiers d'études africaines* 137 (1995), 195-208; Ana Lucia Araujo, "Mémoires de l'esclavage et de la traite des esclaves dans l'Atlantique Sud: enjeux de la patrimonialisation au Brésil et au Bénin" (PhD diss., Université Laval, 2007), and Ana Lucia Araujo, *Public Memory of Slavery: Victims and Perpetrators in the South Atlantic* (Amherst, NY: Cambria Press, 2010).

4. Vodun religion comprises different deities who personalize the forces of nature. The word *vodun* also means "deity." According to Suzanne Preston Blier, *vodun* are "mysterious forces or powers that govern the world and the lives of those who reside within it;" see *African Vodun: Art, Psychology, and Power* (Chicago: University of Chicago Press, 1995), 4.

5. See Tall, "De la démocratie et des cultes voduns au Bénin" and Nassirou Bako-Arifari, "La mémoire de la traite négrière dans le débat politique au Bénin dans les années 1990," *Journal des Africanistes* 70, no. 1-2 (2000), 221-231.

6. Araujo, "Mémoires de l'esclavage et de la traite des esclaves dans l'Atlantique Sud," 156.

7. Marianne Hirsch, *Family Frames, Photography Narrative and Postmemory* (Cambridge: Harvard University Press, 1997), 22.

8. Bogumil Jewsiewicki, "Patrimonialiser les mémoires pour accorder à la souffrance la reconnaissance qu'elle mérite" in *Traumatisme collectif pour patrimoine: Regards croisés sur un mouvement transnational*, ed. Bogumil Jewsiewicki and Vincent Auzas (Quebec: Presses de l'Université Laval, 2008), 7.

9. Gilberto Freyre was one of the first scholars to insist on this particular feature of the Portuguese colonization in the South Atlantic.

See Freyre, *Casa Grande & Senzala* (São Paulo: Global Editora, 2003 [1933]).

10. See Law, *Ouidah,* 2 and Paul E. Lovejoy, "The Context of Enslavement in West Africa: Ahmad Bābā and the Ethics of Slavery," in *Slaves, Subjects and Subversives: Blacks in Colonial Latin America,* ed. Jane Landers and Barry M. Robinson (Albuquerque: University of New Mexico Press, 2007), 25.

11. Herbert Klein, "Tráfico de escravos," in *Estatísticas Históricas do Brasil, Séries econômicas, demográficas e sociais de 1500 a 1985* (Rio de Janeiro: IBGE, 1987), 53.

12. Rafael de Bivar Marquese, "A dinâmica da escravidão no Brasil: resistência, tráfico negreiro e alforrias, séculos XVII a XIX," *Novos Estudos* 74 (2006), 109.

13. See *The Trans-Atlantic Slave Trade Database,* http://www.slave-voyages.com.

14. João José Reis, *Slave Rebellion in Brazil: The Muslim Uprising of 1835 in Bahia* (Baltimore: Johns Hopkins University Press, 1993), 6.

15. Reis, *Slave Rebellion in Brazil,* 93-94.

16. Reis, *Slave Rebellion in Brazil,* 96-97.

17. Reis, *Slave Rebellion in Brazil,* 207.

18. See Law, *Ouidah,* 181.

19. The population of Benin in 2005 was 8,294,941 inhabitants.

20. Milton Guran, *Agudás: Os "Brasileiros" do Benim* (Rio de Janeiro: Editora Nova Fronteira 1999), 88.

21. Júlio Santana Braga, "Notas sobre o 'Quartier Brésil' no Daomé," *Afro-Ásia,* no. 6-7 (1968), 189; Guran, *Agudás,* 15; and Manuela Carneiro da Cunha, *Negros, estrangeiros: os escravos libertos e sua volta à África* (São Paulo: Brasiliense, 1985), 189.

22. Alain Sinou, "La Valorisation du patrimoine architectural et urbain: l'exemple de la ville de Ouidah au Bénin," *Cahiers des Sciences Humaines* 29, no. 1 (1993), 36.

23. See Cunha, *Negros, Estrangeiros,* 109.

24. Today the Aguda do not speak Portuguese, however they preserve some words and expressions, such as: *cama* ("bed"), *chavi* ("key"), *camisa* ("shirt"), *gafu* ("fork"), *Bondyé Senhor* ("good morning sir"), etc. See Dohou Codjo Denis, "Influences brésiliennes à Ouidah," *Afro-Ásia* 12 (1976), 198-199.

25. Catherine Coquery-Vidrovitch, *L'Afrique occidentale au temps des Français : colonisateurs et colonisés (c.1860-1969)* (Paris: La Découverte, 1992), 373.

26. Bako-Arifari, "La mémoire de la traite négrière," 222.

27. Araujo, "Mémoires de l'esclavage et de la traite des esclaves dans l'Atlantique Sud," 135-136.

28. Interview with Francisca Patterson (born Medeiros), Porto-Novo, August 2, 2005.

29. Interview with Urbain-Karim Elisio da Silva, Porto-Novo, July 22, 2005.

30. See Tall, "De la démocratie et des cultes voduns au Bénin."

31. See Bako-Arifari, "La mémoire de la traite négrière," 223.

32. See Costa e Silva, *Francisco Félix de Souza*, 12; and Law, "A carreira de Francisco Félix de Souza," 5.

33. Simone de Souza, *La Famille de Souza du Bénin-Togo* (Cotonou: Les éditions du Bénin, 1992).

34. "Discours de bienvenue du porte-parole de son Excellence Mito Honoré Feliciano Julião de Souza, Chacha 8 à la délégation de l'Université de Rutgers (État du New Jersey)," Ouidah, July 24, 2005.

35. See Law, "A carreira de Francisco Félix de Souza," 13-14; Law, *Ouidah*, 165 and Costa e Silva, *Francisco Félix de Souza*, 12.

36. Law, *Ouidah*, 165.

37. See Pierre Verger, *Flux et reflux de la traite des nègres entre le Golfe de Bénin et Bahia de Todos os Santos, du XVIIᵉ au XIXᵉ siècle* (Paris: Mouton, 1969), 638; Law, "A carreira de Francisco Félix de Souza," 16 ; and Law, *Ouidah*, 165.

38. See Costa e Silva, *Francisco Félix de Souza,* 14; Law, "A carreira de Francisco Félix de Souza," 11.

39. Paul Hazoumé, *Le Pacte de Sang au Dahomey* (Paris: Institut d'Ethnologie, 1956), 28.

40. Hazoumé, *Pacte de Sang au Dahomey*, 29.

41. Hazoumé, *Pacte de Sang au Dahomey*, 29.

42. Costa e Silva, *Francisco Félix de Souza,* 86.

43. See Ana Lucia Araujo, "Enjeux politiques de la mémoire de l'esclavage dans l'Atlantique Sud: La reconstruction de la biographie de Francisco Félix de Souza," *Lusotopie* XVI, no. 2 (2009): 107-131.

44. Costa e Silva, *Francisco Félix de Souza*, 89.

45. Basilio Segurola and Jean Rassinoux, *Dictionnaire Fon-Français* (Madrid: Société des missions africaines, 2000).

46. The inaccurate information stating that de Souza received the title of viceroy was disseminated mainly via Bruce Chatwin's novel, *The Viceroy of Ouidah*. See Law, "A carreira de Francisco Félix de Souza," 18; and Law, *Ouidah*, 167-168. Guran (*Agudás*, 22) also states that de Souza received the title of viceroy.

47. After 1823, a man whose last name was Dagba occupied this position.

48. Law, *Ouidah*, 168.

49. Costa e Silva, *Francisco Félix de Souza*, 90.

50. See Law, "A carreira de Francisco Félix de Souza," 23.

51. John Duncan, *Travels in Western Africa in 1845 and 1846: Comprising a Journey from Whydah, through the Kingdom of Dahomey, to Adofoodia in the Interior* (London: Frank Cass, 1968 [1847]), vol. 1, 204; and Law, "A carreira de Francisco Félix de Souza," 28.

52. Christian de Souza, during the visit of Francisco Félix de Souza's memorial, Singbomey (Ouidah), June 19, 2005.

53. See Ana Lucia Araujo, "Renouer avec le passé brésilien: la reconstruction du patrimoine post-traumatique chez la famille De Souza au Bénin" in *Traumatisme collectif pour patrimoine*, ed. Jewsiewicki and Auzas, 305-330.

54. Interview with Marie de Souza (fictitious name) and David de Souza, Cotonou, July 23, 2005.

55. Edna Bay, *Wives of the Leopard: Gender, Politics and Culture in the Kingdom of Dahomey* (Charlottesville, VA: University of Virginia Press, 1998), 180; and Edna Bay, "Protection, Political Exile, and the Atlantic Slave Trade: History and Collective Memory in Dahomey," *Slavery and Abolition* 22, no. 1 (2001), 16-18.

56. See Luis Nicolau Pares, "The Jeje in the Tambor de Mina of Maranhão and in the Candomblé of Bahia," *Slavery and Abolition* 22, no. 1 (2001), 91-115.

57. See Pierre Verger, "Le culte des vodoun d'Abomey aurait-il été apporté à Saint Louis de Maranhão par la mère du roi Ghèzo?" *Études Dahoméennes* 8 (1952), 22-23; Edna Bay, "Protection, Political Exile and the Atlantic Slave-Trade: History and Collective Memory in Dahomey," in *Rethinking the African Diaspora: The Making of a Black Atlantic World in the Bight of Benin and Brazil*, ed. Kristin Mann and Edna G. Bay (London: Frank Cass, 2001), 57 and Judith Gleason, *Agotime: Her Legend* (New York: Grossman, 1970).

58. Pierre Verger, *Os Libertos: Sete caminhos na liberdade de escravos da bahia no século XIX* (Salvador: Corrupio, 1992), 71-72.

59. Law, *Ouidah*, 166.

60. Law, *Ouidah*, 177 and Bay, *Wives of the Leopard*, 179.

61. Filmed interview with Christian de Souza and David de Souza, during the visit of Francisco Félix de Souza's memorial, Singbomey (Ouidah), June 19 2005.

62. Law, *Ouidah*, 215.

63. Filmed interview with David de Souza, during the visit of Francisco Félix de Souza's memorial, Singbomey (Ouidah), June 19, 2005.

64. Interview with Emile Olougoudou, Ouidah, July 24, 2005.

65. Frederick E. Forbes, *Dahomey and the Dahomans. Being the journals of Two Missions to the King of Dahomey and Residence at his Capital in the Years 1849 and 1850* (London: Frank Cass. 1966 [1851]), vol. I, 106-108.

66. David de Souza, during the interview with Honoré Félicien Julião de Souza (Chacha VIII) and David de Souza, Singbomey, Ouidah, June 19, 2005.

67. Duncan, *Travels in Western Africa in 1845 and 1846*, vol I, 114.

68. Law, "The Atlantic Slave Trade in Local History Writing in Ouidah," 274 n20.

69. Guran, *Agudás*, 203-204.

70. Interview with Honoré Félicien Julião de Souza (Chacha VIII) and David de Souza, Singbomey, Ouidah, June 19, 2005.

71. Paul E. Lovejoy, *Transformations in Slavery: A History of Slavery in Africa* 2nd ed. (Cambridge: Cambridge University Press, 2000), 21.

72. Élisée Soumonni, *Daomé e o mundo atlântico* (SEPHIS, South-South Exchange Programme for Research on the History of Development, Centro de Estudos Afro-Asiáticos, 2, 2001), 13.

73. As Freyre stated this Brazilian identity "suavizou-as aqui o óleo lúbrico da profunda miscigenação," *Casa-Grande & Senzala*, 231.

74. See Tall, "De la démocratie et des cultes voduns au Bénin," and Emmanuelle Kadya Tall, "Dinamique des cultes voduns et du Christianisme céleste au Sud-Bénin," *Cahiers des Sciences Humaines* 31, no. 4 (1995), 797-823 and Guran, *Agudás*, 274-275.

Chapter 6

Scattered Memories: The Intra-Caribbean Slave Trade to Spanish America, 1700-1750[1]

Nadine Hunt

> Our vessel being ready to sail for the Musquito shore, I went with the Doctor on board a Guinea-man to purchase some slaves to carry with us, and cultivate a plantation; and I chose them all of my own countrymen, some of whom came from Libya.... All my poor countrymen, the slaves, when they heard of my leaving them, were very sorry, as I had always treated them with care and affection, and did everything I could to comfort the poor creatures, and render their condition easy.
>
> – Gustavus Vassa, also known as Olaudah Equiano[2]

On February 12, 1776, Gustavus Vassa sailed from Jamaica to Central America with Dr. Charles Irving, several Miskitu from the Mosquito Shore, and "some" enslaved Africans who were destined for plantation labor. Vassa sailed back to Jamaica on June 18th leaving "that spot of the world" never to return. In effect, Vassa documented his personal involvement in an intra-Caribbean slave trade via Jamaica – an entrepôt colony – to the coast of Central America.[3] Since Vassa claimed to have been born in Africa, the epigraph to this chapter provides an insightful perspective and a rare written account of the intra-Caribbean slave trade as seen through the eyes of an African. Although Vassa wrote this exceptional description in the late eighteenth century, the same pattern of trade prevailed for earlier periods when African communities were still in their formative stages in Spanish America. The term "intra-Caribbean" highlights the forced and continued movement of enslaved people between Caribbean islands or to other destinations in the Caribbean basin; hence "intra." The circum-Caribbean is defined here to include the islands in the Caribbean, but also the northern littoral of South America, Central America and indeed the Gulf of Mexico. My focus is on trade within this region, which often crossed colonial boundaries.

Comparatively, "inter-colonial" typically refers to economic exchange of commercial and material goods such as sugar, rum, tobacco, indigo, cocoa or livestock among Caribbean colonies.[4] "Middle Passage" is typically used to describe the arduous and horrendous transatlantic crossing endured by millions of enslaved Africans. However, the intra-Caribbean slave trade can be considered a continuation of the Middle Passage. "Entrepôt" is a term used to describe places where transatlantic ships temporarily unloaded their human cargo after the transatlantic crossing before moving them to other destinations in the Americas. Entrepôt islands in the Caribbean generally functioned as a resting stop sometimes to restore the health of the people after the brutal transatlantic crossing or sometimes as a seasoning period to introduce newly landed Africans to the toil of plantation labor. The intra-Caribbean movement also included enslaved peoples who were born on a Caribbean island or who had lived for long periods but were nonetheless sold into the intra-Caribbean slave trade.[5] The focus of this paper is on the enslaved peoples who were moved between islands and the mainland, whether they originated in West Africa and temporarily resided in Jamaica or elsewhere before being sold on. The study will focus on Jamaica, especially Kingston, and to a lesser extent on Curaçao, which served as two of the most important trans-shipment points in the Caribbean.

The intra-Caribbean slave trade has received some attention by historians studying the British Caribbean. In the 1920s and 1930s, historians began examining the involvement of the British

South Sea Company and a contraband trade within the Caribbean.[6] Moreover, Elizabeth Donnan examined the Company's involvement in the slave trade in 1929 and printed several slave contracts in *Documents Illustrative of the History of the Slave Trade to America* in 1931.[7] Colin Palmer and others have also highlighted the Company's part in selling enslaved Africans within the Caribbean.[8] More recently, Gregory O'Malley has examined the wider intra-American slave trade via English-speaking islands with a focus on the trade in African peoples to North America.[9] Much of the historical interest in the South Sea Company, however, has been on the financial crisis, the South Sea Bubble, which erupted in the 1720s, rather than on the destinations of enslaved Africans.[10]

Both the First and Second Dutch West India Company (West-Indische Compagnie) were involved in human trafficking to Spanish America. Curaçao was the main headquarters of the Dutch in the Caribbean and their center for their intra-Caribbean trade. After the liquidation of the first West-Indische Compagnie in 1674, the Dutch lost control of the *asiento* to the Portuguese, the French and then the British. Nevertheless, the Dutch had established trading networks with Spanish America. After the second West-Indische Compagnie was formed, the Dutch continued to trade, even if it was considered "illegal." When the second Dutch company went into decline after 1730, the trade was opened to private entrepreneurs.[11] Moreover, other scholars have focused their investigations on private entrepreneurs and the second company's involvement in contraband trade. More recently, Dutch scholars are re-examining Dutch Caribbean entrepôts by focusing on Curaçao and St. Eustatius as entrepôt islands and their role in the trade in African peoples.[12]

Despite this earlier work, we still do not know much about those Africans trafficked via Jamaica and Curaçao into the intra-Caribbean slave trade to Spanish America in the first half of the eighteenth century and hence we are dealing with scattered memories. According to Maurice Halbawchs, "the most painful aspects of yesterday's society are forgotten because constraints are felt only so long as they operate and because, by definition, a past constraint has ceased to be operative."[13] The forced movement of Africans via the intra-Caribbean slave trade validates

Halbawchs's observation because the memories of these people are rarely acknowledged in the historiography. Understanding the journey of enslaved peoples and cross-cultural interactions is central to comprehending the forced movement of Africans in the intra-Caribbean trade. Furthermore, it is important to discuss the lives of enslaved women and men who were not part of the primary narrative that speaks of forced migration within the Americas. Reconstructing the memory of Africans transported within the Caribbean during the era of the transatlantic slave trade is difficult due to availability of documented evidence. Much of the trade was contraband. To make matters worse, the traffic in enslaved people around the Caribbean has all but disappeared from the living memory of African descendents. Between 1713 and 1748, English and Dutch traders were the main contenders in the intra-Caribbean slave trade.

This chapter examines the transport of Africans via two major Caribbean entrepôts, Jamaica and Curaçao, by analyzing the South Sea Company, which under its Asientistas was contracted to sell enslaved Africans in Spanish America, and the Second West-Indische Compagnie and Dutch interlopers.[14] Based on available evidence taken from shipping records related to the intra-Caribbean trade from Jamaica and Curaçao, it is possible to determine how Afro-communities in Spanish mainland America formed. Whether or not the Spanish Crown feared British and Dutch influence via the transatlantic and intra-Caribbean slave trades, Africans sold into the intra-Caribbean slave trade only experienced temporary contact with the traders who sold them. It is likely that Africans found persons of similar ethnic backgrounds, as evidence from *The Trans-Atlantic Slave Trade Database* shows that people arriving in South Sea Company and Dutch vessels departed from similar embarkation points along the coast of West Africa. Thus, the ability to interact with peoples of similar African heritage would have helped to shape the formation of African descended communities in Spanish America. Although there is limited documentary evidence and the living memory of passing through an entrepôt colony is almost forgotten, the history of these people contributes to a deeper understanding of the African diaspora in the Americas.

Remembering West Africans in the
Intra-Caribbean Slave Trade
••

The levels of contact with West Africa by the British and Dutch companies were different, because of the charters granted to the companies. The South Sea Company's charter restricted trade to "the east coast of South America from the River Orinoco to south of Tierra del Fuego and along the whole west coast."[15] Consequently, the British Parliament instructed the Company to purchase enslaved Africans on Jamaica or Barbados from the Royal African Company.[16] According to Palmer, in some instances, ships sailed directly from West-Central African ports to the Viceroyalty of Buenos Aires.[17] In its earliest contracts, the Company agreed that "forty eight thousand Negroes of both Sexes and of all ages which shall be neither of Mina nor Cape de Verd" were to be transported to Spanish America.[18] It is unclear whether they did send Mina or Cape Verde peoples, because the Company had little control over their affairs on the West African coast. The Company established factories on the Spanish American Caribbean mainland at Vera Cruz, Cartagena, and Porto Bello and on Jamaica and Barbados.[19]

Unlike the South Sea Company, the West-Indische Compagnie had geographic claims that "included Africa south of the tropic of Cancer, all of America, and the Atlantic and Pacific islands between the two meridians drawn across the Cape of Good Hope and the eastern extremities of New Guinea."[20] The Dutch advantage in trafficking Africans was its ability to control European, African, and American commercial trade via Dutch ports. Thus, enslaved people embarked in West Africa at Elmina, for example, were sent to Curaçao or St. Eustatius, thereby, enabling Asientistas to purchase enslaved Africans and subsequently to hire West-Indische Compagnie ships to transport these people to Spanish American ports, including Vera Cruz, Porto Bello, Cartagena, and Havana. New Granada was the ideal place to transport Africans, because of its proximity to Curaçao. The British and Dutch Atlantic systems facilitated the steady arrival of enslaved peoples from West Africa to Spanish America from 1640 through 1730.

The *Trans-Atlantic Slave Trade Database* shows where Africans embarked in West Africa and establishes where ships landed in the Americas. As the contributors to *The Trans-Atlantic Slave Trade Database* acknowledge, many ship captains and owners did not leave information relating to their human cargo upon arriving in the Americas, let alone on intra-Caribbean exchange.[21] As Gwendolyn Midlo Hall has argued, "studies based entirely on transatlantic slave trade voyages need to be supplemented by studies of the trans-shipment slave trade as well as other types of documents generated over time in various places in the Americas. These studies can help us discover which Africans from which regions, ethnicities, and genders found themselves where, when, and in what proportions."[22] Many Africans experienced multiple port movements after their initial arrival in the Americas and those born into slavery in the Caribbean were also moved.

The regional origins of people leaving West Africa enable an exploration of the "dimensions of ethnicity" in the context of the intra-Caribbean slave trade.[23] The numbers suggest that many of the persons arriving at Jamaica and Curaçao were embarked in similar West African regions, specifically the Bight of Benin, the Gold Coast and West Central Africa. Hence the concentrations of Africans leaving similar embarkation ports probably allowed some enslaved peoples to seek out or form alliances with persons of similar heritage, language, or religious background.

The *Trans-Atlantic Slave Trade Database* shows that the South Sea Company embarked 13,083 enslaved Africans on forty-one British ships but only 11,203 enslaved Africans disembarked at Jamaica from 1713 through 1729, which means that 1,880 Africans died in the Atlantic passage. As can be seen in table 6.1, 46 percent of the enslaved came from the Bight of Benin, 36 percent came from the Gold Coast, 13 percent left from West Central Africa, while 3 percent came from Senegambia and 2 percent from the Windward Coast.[24] While the proportions of these arrivals subsequently sent to Spanish America is not known, it can be reasonably assumed that most would have come from those parts of Africa from where the most people came. Table 6.1 illustrates some voyages sailing from West Africa that belonged to the South Sea Company.

TABLE 6.1: ENSLAVED AFRICANS DISEMBARKED AT JAMAICA BY THE SOUTH SEA COMPANY, 1713-1729

YEAR	SOUTH SEA COMPANY
1713	0
1714	454
1715	0
1716	0
1717	1,222
1718	323
1719	201
1720	0
1721	0
1722	1,077
1723	1,321
1724	723
1725	1,331
1726	3,499
1727	675
1728	0
1729	377
Number of Africans Disembarked	11,203

Source:*The Trans-Atlantic Slave Trade Database*,http://www.slavevoyages.org. Query: Years = 1700-1800. Principal place of slave landing = Jamaica. Vessel Owners = South Sea Company.

These vessels appear to have been under contract to the South Sea Company, because many of the enslaved Africans sold by the Company were bought on Jamaica. Without detailed disembarkation records for Jamaica, it is extremely difficult to know the origins and accurate figures of many of the enslaved Africans purchased by the Company.

In 1716, the Jamaica Assembly introduced a head tax of £1 on enslaved Africans leaving the island.[25] According to Richard Sheridan, between 1711 and 1750 100,870 enslaved Africans who arrived in Jamaica were subsequently sold elsewhere, which represented 37.1 percent of the total number of enslaved arriving from Africa (271,968) (see table 6.2). Even though it is possible to calculate the number of persons embarked on Jamaica as a result of an enforced head tax, as Sheridan notes, the estimates of arrivals and departures must be considered as conservative because "numerous slaves were reportedly smuggled into and out of Jamaica in order to avoid the duties."[26] While the South Sea Company did not transport all the people recorded in the table, the Company did transport a significant number of people to Spanish America. Overall, the majority of newly landed enslaved Africans remained on Jamaica, while the Company and its agents, as well as interlopers, transported more than a third of all captives arriving in Jamaica to other places. However, the process of determining who remained in Jamaica and who was sent to Spanish America is not carefully documented.

TABLE 6.2: JAMAICA'S SLAVE TRADE, 1711-1750

Decade	Slave Ships	Arrivals from Africa	Number Exported	Number Retained	% Retained	% Leaving
1711-20	222	53,740	24,991	28,749	53.5	46.5
1721-30	324	77,689	33,179	44,510	57.3	42.7
1731-40	315	73,217	27,148	46,069	62.9	37.1
1741-50	254	67,322	15,552	51,770	76.9	23.1
Total	1,115	271,968	100,870	171,098	62.9	37.1

Source: R. B. Sheridan, "The Slave Trade to Jamaica," 2-3.

By 1703, Dutch participation in the intra-Caribbean slave trade declined, since an asiento with Spain had not been granted to Dutch traders or the West-Indische Compagnie. Therefore, Spanish officials viewed the trade in Africans with Dutch traders as contraband. Four factors explain why there was a decline. First, Queen Anne's War (1702-1713), which involved Dutch, French, Spanish and British forces, disrupted inter-colonial trade.[27] Secondly, the French Guinea Company obtained the asiento between 1702 and 1712.[28] Thirdly, as victors of the War, Britain obtained the asiento and awarded the contract to the South Sea Company. Finally, Dutch merchants, especially those from Zeeland, sought to challenge the West-Indische Compagnie's monopoly, arguing that private traders had the right to enter the West India trade.[29] Nevertheless, the West-Indische Compagnie loaded 7,442 captives on sixteen ships in West Africa and disembarked 6,123

Africans on Curaçao between 1713 and 1729. Regrettably, 1,319 people died in the Atlantic's Middle Passage. Of these Africans, 44 percent came from the Bight of Benin, 28 percent from the Gold Coast, and 28 percent from West-Central Africa. Because the Dutch controlled the fort at Elmina, the West-Indische Compagnie and private Dutch vessels concentrated on moving Africans from the Gold Coast and the neighboring Bight of Benin to Curaçao and other American colonies, which accounted for 72 percent of the total.[30]

TABLE 6.3: ENSLAVED AFRICANS DISEMBARKED ON CURAÇAO
BY THE DUTCH WEST INDIA COMPANY, 1713-1729

YEAR	DUTCH WEST INDIA COMPANY
1713	0
1714	1,105
1715	911
1716	1,226
1717	0
1718	449
1719	0
1720	0
1721	0
1722	0
1723	0
1724	331
1725	0
1726	225
1727	0
1728	672
1729	1,204
Africans Disembarked	6,123

Source:*The Trans-Atlantic Slave Trade Database,*http://www.slavevoyages.org. Query: Years = 1700-1800. Principal place of slave landing = Curaçao. Vessel owners = West-Indische Compagnie.

Table 6.4 compares the region of embarkation of Africans disembarked on Jamaica by the South Sea Company and on Curaçao by the Dutch Company. Consequently, it reveals that a significant number of these people were embarked at similar regions in West Africa. The Bight of Benin was the primary port of embarkation with 7,637 enslaved Africans landed on Jamaica and Curaçao. Embarking at the Gold Coast was 6,320 captives, in West-Central Africa 2,854 Africans, while 341 Africans left from Senegambia and 174 from the Windward Coast. Since, the Dutch company and the South Sea Company primarily embarked enslaved Africans in three regions, understanding the African experience in West Africa is quintessential. Joseph Miller argues, that "rather than beginning with the struggle of the slaves against their masters, one must therefore start the quest for the strategies of the enslaved by looking at their formative experiences in Africa, what they had lost, and how they sought to recover from the experience."[31]

TABLE 6.4: ENSLAVED AFRICANS DISEMBARKED BY THE SOUTH SEA COMPANY AND THE DUTCH WEST INDIA COMPANY ON JAMAICA AND CURAÇAO: EMBARKATION ORIGINS IN WEST AFRICA, 1701-1751

AFRICAN REGION	SOUTH SEA COMPANY	DUTCH WEST INDIA COMPANY
Bight of Benin	5,022	2,615
Gold Coast	4,117	2,203
West-Central Africa	1,549	1,305
Senegambia	341	0
Windward Coast	174	0
Total	11,023	6,123

Source: Tables 6.1 and 6.3.

Heretics in Colonial Spanish America

African captives had contact with Dutch and English groups upon embarking slaving vessels in West Africa, during the "Middle Passage," on the respective Caribbean slave entrepôt, and finally during the intra-Caribbean voyage. The degree of contact, of course, varied depending on the number of people, the length of contact, and the circumstances that allowed for cultural and religious interaction. Furthermore, Protestant Dutch and English crews were not the only persons in contact with enslaved Africans, but also Jews. According to Eli Faber, in 1737, a South Sea Company Agent wrote that "the Jews with us know very well how to land goods at our wharfes in the night time, without any Notice being taken of them."[32] According to Faber, Jewish merchants understood several languages, including English, Portuguese and Spanish, which contributed to their commercial success.[33] Furthermore, Faber suggests that the Jewish firm of Lamego & Furtado "perhaps...purchased sickly slaves for export to Spain's colonies, for merchants in Jamaica after 1730 purchased 'refuse' slaves for that purpose."[34] Subsequently, the Spanish Crown believed that Dutch and English heretics corrupted Africans.[35] According to Leslie Rout,

> since the slaves to be shipped often spent long periods under Dutch control on islands like Curacao or Aruba, they might become infected with the germs of heretical doctrine; naturally heretics could not be allowed in the Indies.... The Spanish government was in an extremely uncomfortable position because it could not publicly admit what had been going on without acknowledging that many "Protestant" *bozales* [Africans] had already been allowed to enter the Indies.[36]

It appears that during periods of contact with British and Dutch groups, enslaved peoples underwent a process of creolization by adopting these Europeans' language, food preference, clothing, and religious beliefs.[37] While living in Spanish America, did enslaved Africans transported via Caribbean colonies display their knowledge about the entrepôt's inhabitants, the European seamen, or other enslaved Africans encountered? It is a difficult question to answer, however, further research might demonstrate the short-term memory of enslaved Africans and their cross-cultural contact with Dutch and English groups in the Atlantic world.

In the earlier phase of Jamaica's slave trade, a Spanish agent of the *asiento*, James Castillo, a devote Roman Catholic, held service initially at his home, which was later relocated to a chapel at Old King's House in Port Royal.[38] Castillo was responsible for selling enslaved peoples to Dutch and British factors in the 1680s. It is likely that Castillo or someone of divine importance performed baptismal ceremonies for newly landed Africans on Jamaica. Subsequently, enslaved peoples landing in Spanish America would become members of the Catholic Church shortly after their arrival in Spanish America. However, it is puzzling to understand why the Spanish crown and colonial administrators were concerned with Dutch and British merchants influencing enslaved Africans, because the limited contact did not mean that Africans learned the language skills to communicate with their captors. However, it might be to the advantage of enslaved Africans to learn about and possibly exploit European rivalries in Spanish America. Hence, the means to escape slavery after their arrival may have been far greater, if they understood and recalled Spaniards ills or deficiencies, as discussed and mocked by English and Dutch seamen. Combining this knowledge with other Africans, who experienced a similar fate, may have improved their chances for survival in colonial Spanish society in the Americas.

Many of the enslaved were destined for similar ports in Spanish America, so did these people unite or reconnect with their family, friends, ethnic groups, or former community in colonial Spanish American society? It is conceivable that these groups found or reunited with their former community in Spanish America. Palmer reinforces this notion by highlighting a case from 1633 where

> Juan, a male slave from "Angola," reported that he had known Angelina, who was about to be married, "ever since he could remember since she is his sister and the travelled together to this country about six years ago." Although they belonged to different masters in Mexico City, they had found each other and preserved their bond as brother and sister.[39]

If ethnic and community reformation was a reality of the enslaved Africans under investigation, how did their common social, political, and economic views influence colonial Spanish American society? Furthermore, how much of an influence did Dutch and British sailors, company agents, and other West African groups have on captives? If British and Dutch traders did not keep accurate records of persons embarking on ships destined for Spanish America via Jamaica or Curaçao, it means that they probably did not inform Spanish Americans that Africans were arriving from similar embarkation ports in West Africa. Moreover, whether Dutch and British traders were aware that they were trafficking Africans from similar areas is unknown. Subsequently, it appears that there was a far greater chance of African cultural retentions in Spanish America than captives being influenced by European heretics.

The Intra-Caribbean Slave Trade via Jamaica

Pierre Nora maintains that "*Lieux de mémoire* originate with the sense that there is no spontaneous memory, that we must deliberately create archives, maintain anniversaries, organize celebrations, pronounce eulogies, and notarize bills because such activities no longer occur naturally."[40] Jamaica needs to be remembered as a place that transported enslaved Africans to other parts of the Americas. It is important to highlight these enslaved women and men, who are not a part of the typical narrative of plantation life on Jamaica. Their stories present a different perspective, which requires a broader examination of Atlantic movement of Africans and their descendants within the Americas.

Frustrated Jamaican planters relentlessly argued that Spanish Americans acquired the "best" slaves, because of their ability to pay in silver *pesos* and pieces of eight.[41] Possibly, there was some truth in their claim, since Spanish buyers used an awkward system called *pieza de Indias*, which meant that the slave trader received payment based on the health condition of the enslaved, seeking persons with no major illness, no missing teeth, arms, and fingers, and taking age and gender into consideration. For example, a healthy "man or woman between the age of eighteen and thirty and at least seven Spanish *palmos* tall" with no imperfections would be considered a whole *pieza de Indias*.[42] As a result, it appears that health, age, and gender were determining factors of who was sold to Spanish America.

Jamaican planters suggested that the "best" slaves were sold into the intra-Caribbean slave trade, but it cannot be entirely true, since many colonial Spanish American economies did not always have access to silver or gold mines. For example, in Costa Rica a product such as cocoa was exchanged for slaves.[43] In 1744 and 1748, Jamaica imported a substantial amount of cocoa, which probably came to Jamaica either directly from Costa Rica or via Panama, but Caracas was also a regional supplier.[44] In 1719, a summary of various items reflected payment for 2,901 slaves transported to Jamaica. Naval officers at Kingston recorded the following items exported on behalf of the Royal African Company, South Sea Company, and Separate Traders: sugar, indigo, ginger, pimento, cotton, molasses, rum, lime juice, cocoa, logwood, Nicaragua wood, Brazillia, lignum vitæ, juniper plank, tortoise shells, elephant teeth, tanned leather, sarsaparilla, and two unknown items.[45] Consequently, these items suggest that a barter system in tropical products was another means by which the South Sea Company received payment for enslaved Africans and not exclusively in precious metals, as some Jamaican planters had thought.

According to Palmer, "in the unusual event that the slaves were in good physical condition, they were sent on to Spanish America without delay, either on the original ship or aboard company sloops or packet boats."[46] From December 5, 1716 to August 3, 1717, the South Sea Company transported 1,248 enslaved Africans to Spanish American destinations without landing or transferring to a sloop in Jamaica.[47] The enslaved who could not endure another voyage were sent to "rudely constructed houses and huts within enclosures or 'pens' which the company owned or rented. The agents hired local whites and free blacks to care for the slaves, and a physician was on call. To speed their recovery."[48]

On June 13, 1710, Thomas Morgan sailed to Kingston from the Spanish Coast with fifty-four mules, four horses and two tons of stock wood. He left the same day to return to the Spanish Coast with fifty-eight "Negroes" and "Sundry dry Goods."[49] Two months later, August 11, 1710 Morgan landed at Kingston with "26 Negroes and Sundry dry Goods Returned." A few weeks later, he sailed to the Spanish Coast with eighty-five "Negroes" and "Sundry dry Goods."[50] Based on the entry, it seems that Morgan returned to Jamaica with the enslaved Africans transported in June. It is not clear why these slaves were returned, possibly, they were in ill condition and Morgan could not find a buyer willing to nurse them on the Spanish Coast. Han Jordaan notes in Curaçao, "once they were sold and delivered, any risk associated with them belonged to the new owner. Only in the case of 'hidden defects,' could the purchaser return a slave to the West-Indische Compagnie."[51] However, buying and returning enslaved Africans in regional American slave trades is mind-boggling and should raise serious questions about the process of buying and selling enslaved people in the Americas.

The arrival of enslaved African women on Jamaica is curious and the intra-Caribbean slave trade possibly hints at the dynamics of a slave entrepôt, operating within the Caribbean. As David Eltis and Stanley Engerman suggest, historians of the Atlantic slave trade have not adequately explored the demographic issues pertaining togender.[52] For example, Jordaan finds from 1700 through 1730, major and minor asiento Dutch buyers purchased mainly women at Curaçao and sold them to Spanish slave traders, responding to Spanish demands for enslaved women.[53] Seemingly, the South Sea Company in Jamaica was designed to compete with its rival at Curaçao. In 1717, the Company's committee of correspondence queried "the prices also of the Angola negroes nb the women as near as possible to be all virgins."[54] Whether the pristine status of women indicated their age or potential to bear children, as a determining factor of a *pieza de Indias*, was a likely explanation. Furthermore, in 1736, John Merewether, a Company agent reported to Peter Burell that

> A brigantine arrived last Friday called the *post boy* of Bristol with 350 negroes. These are proper for Havanas and Cuba. As we want girls we shall take those who are too much on the yellow cast, to which these country slaves are subject.[55]

What did women and girls represent to Caribbean slave traders and slave markets? Did the gender of an enslaved African matter in established colonial societies such as Spanish America? Eltis and Engerman write that

> The new world arguments rest in part on letters of instruction to slave traders, but are buttressed by arguments suggesting that females had limited capability to handle field labour on the sugar plantations, to

which most were sent, and implying a markedly lower value for female slaves than for male slaves there. Yet recent research on plantations has determined both that a higher percentage of females than of males were involved in field labour, and that price differentials were relatively small.[56]

A substantial number of women may have been sold into the intra-Caribbean slave trade, "according to the ancient code of Alfonso the wise, 'children born of a free mother and a father who is a slave are free because they always follow the condition of the-mother.'"[57] In colonial Spanish America, a child inherited their mother's social status, possibly explaining a desire for female slaves. Through the continuous purchase of enslaved Africans; it is possible that a trend in buying enslaved women with an expectation that they would produce and maintain the slave population was possibly a long-term labor solution for Spanish Americans. As it has been argued, when Jamaica was emerging as a sugar colony, it required a large number of men to make this transformation, so it is possible that Jamaican planters did not pay attention to the amounts of women sold into the intra-Caribbean slave trade.

Importantly, Jamaica has to be interrogated as place with slave ports and contrasted with West African ports such as Ouidah, for example. It is necessary to learn more about the experiences of enslaved Africans embarking and disembarking on its shores.[58] The first half of the eighteenth century marked Jamaica's rapid transformation into a sugar colony, and like many pioneer sugar colonies, Jamaica had to sustain a steady and predominantly male labor force in order to develop its widespread plantation society. Ultimately, Jamaica's eighteenth century economic, political, and social function as an emerging sugar colony makes the slave entrepôt experience highly unique, distinguishing it from established Caribbean slave entrepôts, for example, Curaçao, where the number of plantations was limited to unfavorable agriculture conditions due to the lack of natural water sources, moreover, the size of the island also determined the potential scale of production.

Conclusion

It is the aim of this chapter to understand the lives of extraordinary people, who resiliently lived in the first half of the eighteenth century, enduring wars, multiple sea voyages, and finding themselves in unknown places. Collecting the scattered memories of enslaved Africans experiencing intra-Caribbean movement is one piece of the puzzle in unearthing the complex historical processes of the African diaspora in the era of the Atlantic slave trade. Understanding the transport from and accommodation in a Caribbean entrepôt for enslaved peoples will reveal their cross-cultural interactions, which is central to comprehending the traffic in African peoples. Vassa's "interesting narrative" describes a number of places in the Caribbean Atlantic world, especially the British-speaking areas such as the Mosquito Shore and Jamaica. Vassa's entry on February 12, 1776 sheds light on the process of obtaining enslaved peoples on Jamaica.[59]

The Africans arriving on Spanish America after 1640 were culturally and religiously complex. Interacting with friends, family and strangers, the forced movement of Africans across the Atlantic Ocean and Caribbean Sea allowed enslaved peoples to participate in African and European institutions and to see places where dynamic cultural and religious exchanges would occur. Despite the fears of Spain that English and Dutch heretics corrupted some Africans during the voyage to the Americas, it is the aim of this chapter to make a strong case that Africans were embarked in similar regions on the West African coast. Furthermore, research on Caribbean entrepôts and their impact on the Africans trafficked into the intra-Caribbean slave trade has to be investigated. Remembering who they and their descendents were and would become, will demonstrate their involvement and contribution to colonial life in the Americas.

Notes

1. I wish to thank Paul Lovejoy, David Trotman, Ismael Montana, and Henry Lovejoy for reading and commenting on earlier drafts. I thank Rina Cáceres Gómez for her explanation of colonial Spanish

terms. I also kindly acknowledge Greg O'Malley for clarifying his contribution to the *Trans-Atlantic Slave Trade Database*. Versions of this paper were presented at *Crossing Memories: Slavery and African Diaspora*, Quebec City, Canada, May, 2-3, 2005, *Caribbean Migrations: Negotiating Borders*, Toronto, Canada, July, 18-22, 2005, and *Cahuita Symposium: Slavery, Culture, and Religion*, Cahuita, Costa Rica, February, 11-14, 2006. I thank all participants for their comments and discussion.

2. See Vincent Carretta, ed., *Olaudah Equiano: The Interesting Narrative and Other Writings* (New York: Penguin, 1995), 205-11.

3. For Vassa's account, see Carretta, *Interesting Narrative*, 32-45; Paul E. Lovejoy, "Las ambiciones imperiales británicas en la Costa de la Mosquitia y la abolición de la esclavitud indígena, 1773-1781," in *Haití: revolución y emancipación,* ed. Rina Cáceres and Paul E. Lovejoy (San José: Universidad de Costa Rica, 2008), 98-118; Lovejoy, "Equiano, Empire and Slavery: the Scottish Connection," paper presented at the Scotland, Slavery and Abolition Conference, University of Edinburgh, 10 November 2007; and Lovejoy, "Autobiography and Memory: Gustavus Vassa, alias Olaudah Equiano, the African," *Slavery and Abolition* 27, no. 3 (2006), 317-47.

4. Shalini Puri, ed., *Marginal Migrations: The Circulation of Cultures in the Caribbean* (Oxford: Warwick University, 2003), 1-16.

5. See the case of Michael Kendall in Woodes Rogers, *A Cruising Voyage round the world; first to the South Seas; thence to the East-Indies, and homeward by the Cape of Good Hope; begun in 1708, and finished in 1711* (London: A. Bell and B. Lintot, 1712), 225. I am thankful to Kris Lane for bringing Kendall's story to my attention.

6. Curtis Nettels, "England and the Spanish American Trade, 1680-1715," *The Journal of Modern History* 3, no. 1 (1931), 1-32; Vera L. Brown, "Contraband Trade: A Factor in the Decline of Spain's Empire in America," *Hispanic American Historical Review* 8, 2 (1928), 178-189; Vera L. Brown, "The South Sea Company and Contraband Trade," *American Historical Review* 31, No. 4 (1926), 662-678. Also see, George H. Nelson, "Contraband Trade under the Asiento, 1730-1739," *American Historical Review* 51, no. 1 (1945), 55-67.

7. Elizabeth Donnan, ed., *Documents Illustrative of the History of the Slave Trade to America: Volume II, The Eighteenth Century* (New York: Octagon Books Inc., [1931] 1965); Elizabeth Donnan, "The

Early Days of the South Sea Company, 1711-1718," *Economic and Business History* 2 (1929), 419-450.

8. Colin A. Palmer, "The Company Trade and the Numerical Distribution of Slaves to Spanish America, 1703-1739," in *Africans in Bondage: Studies in Slavery and the Slave Trade*, ed. Paul E. Lovejoy (Madison: University of Wisconsin, 1986), 27-42; Colin A. Palmer, *Human Cargoes: The British Slave Trade to Spanish America, 1700-1739* (Illinois: Illinois University Press, 1981); Leslie I. Rudnyanszky, "The Caribbean Slave Trade: Jamaica and Barbados, 1680-1770" (PhD diss., Notre Dame University, 1973); Philip D. Curtin, *The Atlantic Slave Trade: A Census* (Madison: University of Wisconsin Press, 1969), 21-26.

9. Gregory O'Malley, "Beyond the Middle Passage: Slave Migration from the Caribbean to North America, 1619-1807," *William and Mary Quarterly* 66, no. 1 (2009), 125-172; Gregory O'Malley, "Final Passages: The British Inter-Colonial Slave Trade, 1619-1807" (PhD diss., Johns Hopkins University, 2006).

10. John Carswell, *The South Sea Bubble* (Stroud, Gloucestershire: Sutton Publishing Ltd., [1960] 2001); John G. Sperling, *The South Sea Company: An Historical Essay and Bibliographical Finding List* (Boston: Harvard University Printing Office, 1962), 25-38.

11. Johannes M. Postma, "A Reassessment of the Dutch Atlantic Slave Trade," in *Riches from Atlantic Commerce: Dutch Transatlantic Trade and Shipping, 1585-1817,* ed. Johannes M. Postma and Victor Enthoven, (Leiden: Koninklijke Brill, 2003), 115-138; Johannes Postma, "The Dutch and the Asiento Slave Trade: African Slaves to the Spanish American Colonies, 1662-1715," in *De la traite à l'esclavage: actes du colloque international sur la traite des Noirs, Nantes: Ve-XVIIIe siécles*, ed. Serge Daget (Nantes-Paris: Centre de recherche sur l'histoire du monde atlantique, Société française d'histoire d'outre-mer, L'Harmattan, 1988), 299-324.

12. Henk den Heijer, "The Dutch West India Company, 1621-1791," in *Riches from Atlantic Commerce*, ed. Johannes M. Postma and Victor Enthoven, 77-112; Postma, "Reassessment," in *Riches from Atlantic Commerce*, ed. Johannes M. Postma and Victor Enthoven, 115-138; Wim Klooster, "An Overview of Dutch Trade with the Americas, 1600-1800," in *Riches from Atlantic Commerce*, 365-383; Victor Enthoven, "An Assessment of Dutch Transatlantic Commerce, 1585-1817," in *Riches from Atlantic Commerce*, ed. Johannes M. Postma and Victor Enthoven, 385-445. Also see,

Linda M. Rupert, "Inter-imperial trade and local identity: Curaçao in the colonial Atlantic worlds" (PhD diss., Duke University, 2006).

13. Maurice Halbawchs, *On Collective Memory* (Chicago: University of Chicago Press, 1992), 51.

14. Individuals who the Spanish Crown (*Casa de Contratación*) awarded *asiento de negros* included Domingo Grillo, Ambrosio and Agustín Lomelín in 1662, García Siliceo in 1672, Juan Barroso del Pozo in 1682, Baltazar Coymans in 1685, Nicolás Porcio in 1689, and Marín de Guzmán in 1694. Although not necessarily Dutch in origin, these men secured licenses either through Dutch contacts in Spain or used Curaçao and St. Eustatius as commercial hubs to transport Africans and trade goods to Spanish America. See Gonzalo Aguirre Beltrán, *Obra antropológica II: la población negra de México estudio ethnhistórico* (Mexico, D.F.: Fondo de Cultura Económica, [1946] 1989), 55-66; I. A. Wright, "The Coymans Asiento, 1685-1689," *Bijdragen voor de Vaderlandse Geschiedenis en Oudheidjunde* 6, no. 1 (1924), 23-62.

15. Sperling, *The South Sea Company*, 11.

16. Donnan, *Documents Illustrative*, Vol. II, 159-168.

17. Palmer, *Human Cargoes*, 71-73.

18. Donnan, "Introduction," in *Documents Illustrative*, Vol. II, 16-17.

19. Donnan, "The Early Days," 430-431.

20. den Heijer, "The Dutch West India Company," 80; Cornelius Ch. Goslinga, *The Dutch in the Caribbean and the Guianas, 1680-1791*, ed. Maria J. L. van Yperen (Assen: Van Gorcum & Company, 1985), 1-2.

21. See David Eltis et al. *The Trans-Atlantic Slave Trade Database: Voyages*, http://www.slavevoyages.org. See "History of the Project;" and David Eltis and David Richardson, "Routes to Slavery and the Numbers Game," *Slavery and Abolition* 18, no. 1, special issue "Routes to Slavery: Direction, Ethnicity and Mortality in the Transatlantic Slave Trade" (1997), 1-15.

22. Gwendolyn Midlo Hall, *Slavery and African Ethnicities in the Americas: Restoring the Links* (Chapel Hill: University of North Carolina Press, 2005), 25-26.

23. Paul E. Lovejoy, "Ethnic Designations of the Slave Trade and the Reconstruction of the History of Trans-Atlantic Slavery," in *Trans-Atlantic Dimensions of Ethnicity in the African Diaspora,* ed. Paul

E. Lovejoy and David V. Trotman (London: Continuum, 2003), 9-42.

24. According to *The Trans-Atlantic Slave Trade Database*, the enslaved embarked at the Bight of Benin did so at the port of Ouidah; Gold Coast ports are Anomabu, Cape Coast Castle, and unspecified locations; West Central Africa ports were Cabinda and unspecified locations; Senegambia was essentially Gambia; and the Windward Coast referred to unspecified locations west of the Gold Coast.

25. Palmer, *Human Cargoes*, 66.

26. Richard B. Sheridan, "The Slave Trade to Jamaica, 1702-1808," in *Essays Presented to Douglas Hall: Trade Government and Society in Caribbean History, 1700-1920*, ed. B. W. Higman (Kingston: Heinemann Educational Books (Caribbean) Ltd., 1983), 2-3.

27. Cornelius Ch. Goslinga, "Curaçao as a Slave-Trading Centre during the War of the Spanish Succession (1702-1714)," *Nieuwe West-Indische gids (New West Indian Guide)* 52 (1977), 1-50.

28. While France held the Spanish *asiento* between 1702 and 1713, they did not fulfill their contractual obligations. Moreover, they appear to have vanished from the intra-Caribbean slave trade after 1713. See, Georges Scelle, "The Slave-Trade in the Spanish Colonies of America: The Assiento," *American Journal of International Law* 4, no. 3 (1910): 612-661; Georges Scelle, *La traite négrière aux Indes de Castile, contrats et traités d'assiento* (Paris: L. Larose & L. Tenin, 1905).

29. den Heijer, "The Dutch West India Company," 101-102.

30. Christopher DeCorse, *An Archaeology of Elmina: Africans and Europeans on the Gold Coast, 1400-1900* (Washington: Smithsonian Institution Press, 2001).

31. Joseph C. Miller, "Retention, Reinvention, and Remembering: Restoring Identities through Enslavement in Africa under Slavery in Brazil," in *Enslaving Connections: Western Africa and Brazil During the Era of Slavery*, ed. José C. Curto and Paul E. Lovejoy (Amherst, New York: Humanities/Prometheus, 2003), 85.

32. Eli Faber, *Jews, Slaves, and the Slave Trade: Setting the Record Straight* (New York: New York University Press, 1996), 63.

33. Faber, *Jews*, 69.

34. Faber, *Jews*, 80-81.

35. Wright, "The Coymans Asiento," 62.

36. Leslie Rout, *The African Experience in Spanish America: 1502 to the Present Day* (Cambridge: Cambridge University Press, 1976), 34-35.

37. Kamau Brathwaite, *The Development of Creole Society in Jamaica, 1770-1820* (Kingston: Ian Randle Publishers, [1971] 2005), 296-305.

38. Francis J. Osborne, *History of the Catholic Church in Jamaica* (Aylesbury, Bucks: Ginn and Company, Caribbean Universities Press, 1977), 53-56.

39. Colin A. Palmer, "From Africa to the Americas: Ethnicity in the Early Black Communities of the Americas," *Journal of World History* 6, no. 2 (1995), 230.

40. Pierre Nora, "Between Memory and History: Les Lieux de Mémoire," *Representations* 26 (1989), 12.

41. Rudnyanszky, "The Caribbean Slave Trade," 84 and 94-98.

42. Bowser, see note 4 in *African in Colonial Peru*, 39; also see Palmer, "Numerical Distribution," 29-30.

43. Juan Carlos Solórzano, "El comercio de Costa Rica durante el declive del comercio Española y el desarrollo del contrabando Ingles: periodo 1690-1750," *Anuario de Estudios Centroamericanos* (Costa Rica) 20, no. 2 (1996), 71-119; María E. Brenes Castillo, "Matina, Bastión del contrabando en Costa Rica," *Anuario de Estudios Centroamericanos* (Costa Rica) 4 (1978), 416-418.

44. Yu Wu, "Jamaican Trade: 1688-1769 A Quantitative Study," (PhD diss., Johns Hopkins University, 1995), 145.

45. National Archives (NA), Kew, Colonial Office (CO) 142/14/96, "An Account of Goods Exported from the island of Jamaica from the 29th of June 1719 of the 25th of December following; and of Negroes Imported by the African and South Sea Company, and Separate Traders."

46. Palmer, *Human Cargo*, 61.

47. Donnan, *Documents Illustrative,* Vol. II, 211-212.

48. Palmer, *Human Cargoes*, 61.

49. NA, CO 142/14/20, "Naval Office Shipping Lists of Jamaica."

50. NA, CO 142/14/21.

51. Han Jordaan, "The Curaçao Slave Market: From *Asiento* Trade to Free Trade, 1700-1730," in *Riches from Atlantic Commerce*, ed. Johannes M. Postma and Victor Enthoven, 240.

52. David Eltis and Stanley L. Engerman, "Was the Slave Trade Dominated by Men?" *Economic History Review* 46, no. 2 (1993), 308-323.

53. Jordaan, "The Curaçao Slave Market," 250.

54. Donnan, *Documents Illustrative*, vol. II, 215.

55. Donnan, *Documents Illustrative*, vol. II, 459-460.

56. Eltis and Engerman, "Was the Slave Trade," 308.

57. E. F. Love, "Legal Restrictions on Afro-Indian Relations in Colonial Mexico," *Journal of Negro History* 55, no. 2 (1970), 135.

58. Robin Law, *Ouidah: The Social History of a West African Slaving Port, 1727-1892* (Athens: Ohio University Press, 2004); Robin Law, "Ouidah: A Pre-colonial Urban Centre in Coastal West Africa, 1727-1892," in *Africa's Urban Past*, ed. David M. Anderson and Richard Rathbone (London: James Currey, 2000), 85-97; Robin Law and Silke Strickrodt, ed. *Ports of the Slave Trade: Bights of Benin and Biafra* (Stirling: University of Stirling Press, 1999); Robin Law, *The Slave Coast of West Africa 1550-1750: The Impact of the Atlantic Slave Trade on an African Society* (Oxford: Clarendon Press, 1991).

59. Carretta, *Interesting Narrative*, 205.

Chapter 7

Voices of Those Who Testified on Slavery in Kano Emirate

Mohammed Bashir Salau

This essay relates to part of the resources available at the Harriet Tubman Institute for Research on the Global Migrations of African Peoples in Canada. The Tubman Institute houses a digitalized research facility that focuses on the history of the African diaspora and the movement of Africans to various parts of the world, particularly the Americas and the Islamic lands of North Africa and the Middle East. The Tubman Institute is a repository for archival documents, oral data on tapes, maps, and other primary materials.[1] The Tubman Institute has a large collection of oral data on Northern Nigeria, portions of which form the substance of this essay.

The resources at the Tubman Institute also consist of archival materials some of which are on Northern Nigeria.[2] Historians of slavery in Africa have considerably drawn upon such archival materials and other "external" sources of knowledge, such as diaries and notes of explorers who visited Africa prior to large scale European occupation, for their works.[3] Indeed, colonial records and travelers' accounts have been valuable for helping scholars comprehend more fully the precolonial African existence. However, explorers and colonial administrators did not always understand African social phenomena and their accounts reflect racial biases as well as their administrative and other related concerns. Hence they have presented a distorted picture of slavery. In recognition of the limitations of travelers' accounts and colonial records, scholars have increasingly looked within Africa for sources of knowledge concerning slavery in the continent.

Due to the primacy of oral narratives in African communities, many scholars have employed oral sources to particularly learn of local perceptions of slavery. The oral sources employed are of two main types, oral tradition and oral history. Oral traditions could be defined as the form in which man relates by word of mouth the past of his people, the rulers, and the ancestors, as far back in time as possible, or simply, a testimony about the past transmitted orally from one generation to another. Oral history, on the other hand, involves the collection of evidence through interviews in which informants speak of their own experience about the past whether as participants, eyewitnesses, or not.[4] On several issues, such participants or informants give more useful information, comments, and elucidations in oral interviews than a researcher would be able to glean from private published diaries, memoirs, and other papers, which persons publicize after they may have rationalized their roles, if any, in relevant events. On slavery in Western Sudan, however, Martin Klein, a leading authority on slavery in the region, argues that oral sources have not been very useful to historians.[5] In his view African "slaves are present in oral traditions only of the larger community, but only in passing"[6] while African slaves and their descendants, as compared with African-Americans, are ashamed of their background hence they "do not like to recognize their slave origins."[7] In justifying this assertion, Klein cited interviews conducted in the Western Sudan by himself and several other historians like Richard Roberts. Following that, he noted that the silence of servile informants on their origins is not only due to their "reticence."[8] Rather it is partly because experiences of enslavement have robbed them of their ability to meaningfully talk about their genealogy and also develop a tradition of their own slave community. One result of limited development of slave traditions, Klein further reasons, is that slaves are often invincible in historical records. For him, the problem is compounded by the fact that colonial administrations in Senegal and French Sudan also avoided discussing African slavery surviving during the colonial era, despite their practice of imposing taxes on slaves. Klein generally concludes that there is no significant amount of oral data out there to tap on slavery in Africa and that it is impossible to still tap that source for information on slavery.

Klein may be right in arguing that oral traditions of larger communities say little on slavery and that it may be impossible to still tap oral traditions for information on slavery. But it would be an exaggeration to conclude that there is no significant amount of oral data out there to tap on slavery in all parts of Africa. Partly to illustrate that considerable oral data on slavery in certain parts of Africa are available, this essay will consider the Hausa oral data collection at the Tubman Institute. I first came across the material in question when I started conducting research on my PhD dissertation some years ago. After working with the resources for about three years, I have come to realize that they have been largely ignored by historians in spite of their richness in information on several themes, especially slavery in the Central Sudan. Currently, I am committed to, among others, retranslating and retranscribing the Hausa oral data in question. Although the ultimate objective is to make the historical sources more widely available, in this essay my concern is to comment on select testimonies in the collection so as to give flavor of the kind of the issues the entire holding highlight in terms of slavery in Kano Emirate.

Kano Emirate was the commercial nerve center of the Sokoto Caliphate, the largest state in West Africa during the nineteenth century. A considerable number of scholars have thrown light on the character of slavery in this particular emirate. As with others who have written on the same theme in other parts of the Sokoto Caliphate, these scholars disagree on several issues. Put simply, there are conflicting views on the character of slavery and the slave trade in Kano Emirate. A major argument which many scholars still support is that slavery in the region in question was mild. Heinrich Barth first expressed that view in the nineteenth century thus, "The quiet course of domestic slavery has very little to offend the mind of the traveler; the slave is generally well treated, is not overworked, and is very often considered as a member of the family."[9] He also indicated, as other nineteenth century European travelers, that slavery was widespread in Kano

Emirate (specifically, that slaves constituted about half of the population in the region), and that slaves were marketed in this same space. As hinted, Barth's interpretations of slavery characterize many scholarly works subsequently written on Kano Emirate. Polly Hill, in her case study of the Dorayi district of Kano, for instance, revealed that unlike slaves in "ancient Greece and Rome, in the United States, and in Brazil and Haiti" those in Hausaland, including Kano, "enjoyed more rights"[10] and were better treated by their masters. She also marshaled evidence to show that small agricultural holdings using both free and slave labour were relatively more significant in Hausaland than plantations. For her, except for thirteen slave owners with holdings large enough to be identified as plantations, it was smallholdings that dominated the agricultural sector in Dorayi. Hill uses the term "farm slavery" and *gandu* to refer to this feature, which she perceived to have been relatively more widespread. She also argues that Fulani groups alone owned the few plantations that existed in Hausaland and that their holdings were mainly concentrated in the frontier emirates, such as Zaria.[11] Although Hill questioned the notion that second generation slaves could not be sold in Kano Emirate and that slavery was not widespread as Barth and other European travelers had suggested, her conclusion that slavery was mild in the region further popularized the view among scholars.

In recent times, however, the view that slavery in Kano Emirate was mild has increasingly been challenged. Perhaps the most ardent critic of that thesis is Paul E. Lovejoy.[12] He contends that although slavery in Kano Emirate, and indeed in other parts of the Sokoto Caliphate, had benevolent features, it was also characterized significantly by brutality. To Lovejoy, therefore, caliphate slavery was complex and sometimes contradictory and to properly grasp the phenomenon he partly urged scholars to shift their attention to exploring the ideology that underpinned the system.

All the testimonies in this essay provide information on the nature of slavery in Kano Emirate or reflect the issues and themes of current interest to researchers, and this partly indicates that the selection of the testimonies is not altogether arbitrary. But the analytical commentary provided below does not seek to justify the position of any of the camps involved in the above-mentioned dispute. That I leave to you. The informants whose testimonies are relied on in this study include Hamidu Galadiman Shamaki (70 years old in 1975, hence born in 1905). Yusuf Yunusa recorded his testimony on April 4, 1975 at Fanisau. As the chief overseer of the emir's estates in this settlement as well as a descendant of the slaves introduced there from the Ningi region, he [Shamaki] was knowledgeable about royal slavery and the affairs of the settlement mentioned above, especially as they related to plantations. Muhammadu Rabi'u (59 years in 1975, hence born in 1916) was interviewed by Yunusa on July 13, 1975 at Fanisau. At the time of the interview Rabi'u was an Islamic scholar as well as a farmer. He was very knowledgeable about the history of slavery in Kano Emirate. Alhaji Miko Hamshaki (97 years in 1969, hence born in 1872) was recorded by Lovejoy on September 8, 1969. He was the son of Madugu K'osai who owned one of the private estates in the vicinity of Fanisau. Kosai was a kolanut merchant and an established slave trader. Abdulrahman (65 years in 1975 hence born in 1910) was interviewed by Yunusa on July 28, 1975. At the time, Abdulrahman resided at Nassarawa ward in Kano city and it was in that same location that his parents and grand parents were born. He was, therefore, well informed on developments related to slavery in Kano Emirate.

Before underlining what the above named individuals reveal on slavery in Kano Emirate, it is pertinent to first provide some background information on how and why their testimonies, and those of others that form the broader Hausa oral data collection at the Tubman Institute, were collected. The collection of the Hausa oral data in question began in the 1960s. In that decade, the use of oral traditions to write African history became recognized and increasingly popularized. Initially, most African historians who collected oral traditions were mainly concerned with document-ing political topics. Of the few who were interested in economic topics, Lovejoy used reel-to-reel tapes to record oral data on commerce in pre-colonial Northern Nigeria. He mainly collected relevant information through structured interviews with kolanut traders and or their descendants in the region.[13] Today, this body of material constitutes the earliest among the Hausa oral data available at the Tubman Institute.

Lovejoy is however not the only person responsible for recording the Hausa oral data deposited at the Tubman Institute. Indeed, several scholars/researchers have been involved in the collection of the materials. In 1975, Lovejoy and Hogendorn were dissatisfied with "the use of notebooks as the primary means of recording information, in situations where tape recorders can be employed successfully," and wanted "to promote the collection of economic data for archival deposit and public use by other scholars." Consequently they initiated an expansive scheme for the collection of oral traditions on the economic history of the central savanna in 1975.[14] Many scholars/researchers were involved in this project. Ultimately, in line with a major aim of the scheme, the oral data they collected were deposited with the Northern History Research Scheme at Ahmadu Bello University, Zaria. However, Lovejoy also retained copies, which are now deposited at the Tubman Institute. Outside the oral data derived through the above stated means, other scholars (not connected with the Economic History Project, but who are closely associated with Lovejoy) have recorded interviews in Hausa during the course of their independent works, and have made their materials available at the Tubman Institute.[15]

Collectively, the Hausa oral data reflect the memories and voices of diverse people including former slaves, the sons and daughters of slaves, and the families of plantation owners and their assistants. The material is rich in information on agricultural production, craft specialization (dyeing, leather work, women's crafts), labour mobilization, commerce, slavery, family histories, salt mining, the 1913-14 drought, and other economic topics. Although most of the Hausa oral data were originally deposited on reel-to-reel tapes and in cassette tapes, translations and transcriptions of most of the materials have also been available. The latter seem to be the most ignored probably partly because of their inconsistent standard and due to the incomplete translation of the entire data. In the past few years, with the aid of Eugene Onutan, graduate students affiliated with the Tubman Institute (including myself) have transferred the collection from the original reel-to-reel and cassette tapes to CDs. The aim of all those involved in this exercise is to facilitate access to the Hausa materials. Thus the transfer of data into CDs has, among others, made the sound of some of the testimonies more audible, and this is useful for retranslation and related purposes.

In spite of the fact that the materials under consideration have been deposited first at the Northern History Research Scheme at Ahmadu Bello University and later at the Tubman Centre for public use, most scholars working on the Central Sudan have, as mentioned, ignored the collection. For instance, even though Nasiru Ibrahim Dantiye, Abdullahi Mahadi, Adamu Mahdi, Polly Hill and other more recent writers[16] (who studied different aspects of Kano Emirate) must have had access to the collection either at Ahmadu Bello University or the Tubman Institute (or even in both centers) there is no evidence of samples drawn from the collection in their works.

Neglect of the Collection is due to a number of factors. In the first place, this may be connected to strategic considerations since any in-depth analysis of the oral data, for instance, inevitably evokes evidence that may undermine the legitimacy or credibility of the Sokoto Caliphate leaders and that of their successors. This is something many scholars are uncomfortable with. Researchers preference for making use of mainly the oral materials they amassed during their own field interviews might have also discouraged the use of the Collection. Another important factor that caused the neglect of the Hausa oral data has been the collection's inaccessibility. Although few historians, (as those mentioned above) had access to the resources, the collection does not generally circulate. Few laymen are aware of its existence, and most scholars acquainted with it have not been interested in making the materials widely accessible. Indeed, most scholars who used the Collection do not even include excerpts and selections from it in their works.[17] Moreover, some of them also fail to fully exploit the materials. For instance, Ibrahim Hamza did not adequately draw upon the available testimonies on Dorayi in his study of plantation slavery in the region.[18]

Whatever the dominant disposition to ignore or inadequately use the Hausa oral data, the few historians who have increasing drawn attention to their significance have also impressively drawn from them. Thus, for instance, Sean Stilwell, Ibrahim Hamza and Paul E. Lovejoy have provided the translation and annotation of a particular testimony by a royal slave in Kano in their work entitled "The Oral History of Royal Slavery in Sokoto Caliphate: An Overview with Sallama Dako"[19] while in my PhD dissertation, I have partly followed this orientation by highlighting translations of excerpts from two testimonies.[20] Although I did not include any annotation in my own work, the relevant Hausa transcription inserted therein is instructive.

Several uses of the Hausa oral data are immediately apparent. In the case of testimonies that address the issue of slavery in Kano Emirate, the materials often bring into sharp focus information not found in colonial records. For instance, while no slave trading account by a Kano based slave trader is so far discovered in colonial sources, Hamshaki recollects that merchant's like his father, Madugu Kosai, often purchased slaves from Borno and Bargami and disposed them along the caravan route to Gonja. He also mentions how such merchants used slaves along caravan routes and as agents for the disposal of their kolanut within Kano Emirate. More importantly, Hamshaki said that he sold slaves when he accompanied his father to Gonja as a youth and that during the early colonial era British colonial administrators arrested him while he was attempting to import ten slaves into Kano. In his own words: "I was caught together with him (Madugu Shaho) by the Europeans when I bought ten slaves; I was given fifty strokes and the slaves were seized." To be sure, Hamshaki's account, as any other testimony on slavery and slave trade in Kano Emirate or elsewhere, raises several questions. What, for instance, did the British colonialists do with the slaves seized from Hamshaki and other slave traders? Was Madugu Shaho also arrested with slaves that he purchased on this occasion? Were fifty strokes the only punishment slave traders received for disregarding the colonial anti-slave trade policies? If not, what other forms of punishment did slave trading attract in early colonial Northern Nigeria? By raising such questions, the testimony of Hamshaki, and indeed others, partly serves to suggest new subjects for research. Unquestionably, this enhances their significance.

Beyond providing rare information on slave trading, other testimonies throw light on several issues such as the slave's daily life, resistance, and accommodation that are not found in colonial sources. In describing the slave's daily routine at the royal estates, for instance, Rabi'u provides a picturesque account of their early morning activities:

> *Ai su kan gaida gandu. Idan su, idan gari ya waye, shi gandu babban aikinsa in gari ya waye sai maza ya tafi gona sai yasa mai dauko ruwan da za'a sha; wane kazo da ruwa. Shi. Gandu yana nan yana zaune a gandu. Wanda yaje to wane ya zo, wanda bai zo bawane mai hana shi zuwa. Wanda rana tai mai be je ba, kai ko menene yasa rana tayi. A mar fada a mar fada a ce in kuna haka za ku bata gandun nan, za ku kashe gandun nan. Ku ne manya amma za ku kashe gandu, yaya bazo ku zo da wuri ba.*

Yes they do pay homage to the head slave. The primary duty of the head slave in the morning is to go to the farm and assign someone to get the day's drinking water, "you bring along water." The head slave will be seated in the farm and he will acknowledge the arrival of whoever was present. He would also inquire about anyone absent, "what has prevented such and such from coming." Whoever was late in arriving, "why are late in coming." Such a person will be scolded, "if you continue in this manner, you will destroy the estate, you are the senior ones but you will destroy the estate. Why don't you come much earlier?"[21]

Similarly, when Rabi'u is asked to explain whether or not slaves took estate produce without the permission of their master, he explained in the following colloquy with the interviewer with statements never encountered in written sources:

> *Q: Wato bayi ma su kan dan diba ba a basu izini ba su dauka ko*
> *A: Aay sai su diba mana*
> *Q: Sukan sata*
> *A: Sukan sata. Kamar da, Sarkin gida sai a hada baki sai a zo a sata aje aci. Galadima in ya zo ya tai fada.*
> *Q: To in an kamo mutum ya sata, me ake masa*
> *A: To me za ayi mar. Shi dama bawa ne, su suka noma, ci kuma yayi. Kamar wanda za'a kama yasayar to*

za'a iya masa duka, sai a bashi wahali ace in ka
kuma za a gayawa Sarki. Yayi ta tuba.

Q: Do slaves take estate produce without permission
of their master.
A: Of course they did
Q: Do they steal?
A: They do steal. For instance, in the past they will
connive with Sarkin Gida, and steal the produce for
food. When the Galadima finds out he may scold
them or punish them depending on his mood at that
moment.
Q: What happens to a slave who was caught stealing?
A: What do you expect to be done to him. After all
he is a slave and was among those who suffered
to produce the grain, and what he stole is to feed
himself. But any slave who stole and sold it, will
be beaten and tortured when caught. He will be
told, "If you repeat this, you will be reported to the
Emir." He may then be repentant.[22]

Although Rabi'u's account mainly relate to the slave's life in royal
estates, there are other testimonies that throw light on their experiences in urban areas and elsewhere. In addition to the diversity
of rare information on slavery in Kano emirate, Rabi'u's account
and other relevant testimonies unquestionably provide invaluable
reference source for testing historical and social scientific generalizations. Not only that, the fact that the translations and interpretations of the relevant testimonies can be crosschecked is an added
advantage in terms of research.

Although the Hausa oral testimonies have several merits,
many of them are also filled with internal contradictions. This can
be seen in the account of Rabi'u who commented extensively on
the life of slaves employed at Kano royal estates and concludes
that they were better treated than those used in private estates:

Bayin mai arziki sun fi shan wahala a aiki soboda su
bayin Sarki su aikin su kaman na ma'ana ne, yanada
sauki shi mai sauki ne aikin bayin Sarki. Sunansa yafi
yinsa. Sai su matsa ma talakawa ma suyi aikin. Idan
gandun yaki naumuwa za su iya zuwa su je wurin mai

mulki su ce to kai zaman banza kake za ka bar gandun Sarki ya, ka bamu mutane kaza za ayi noma. Ya bada mutane aje ayi noma a gama amma bayin sune sukayi noman.

Slaves engaged in private estates suffered more, because they worked indiscriminately. But emir's slaves performed fewer tasks and had more time for themselves. The emir's slaves can even force free men to do their task. If the farm work cannot be finished, the slaves could approach the authorities and say "of what value are you if you will allow the emir's farm to fallow; give us such number of men to farm." He would give such number as available and the work will be accomplished to the credit of the slaves.[23]

Following the above statement, the interviewer asked Rabi'u a related question:

Q: Bayin mai arziki kuwa su har abada a cikin shan wuya su ke.

A: Idan ka ga bawan mai arziki ya zauna to mai arzikin ne ya yarda da shi yasa shi ya bi shi ya dinga ganin sa kurum. Kuma har yau ya samu shekaru, an gan tsufa. Amma goninta sa in yana da karfi ya ta yin aiki nan dede da ransa. Yayi sammako ya je yayi na sa. Kamun karfe tara duk an hadu ana yin noma, idan azahar tayi to sanan a tashe su.

Q: What about the slaves of a wealthy individual?

A: The slaves of a wealthy individual are forever in suffering. If you find a wealthy man's slave resting, then it is because the man has trust in him and as such wants the slave to follow him and be close to him. Such slaves were the trusted ones, also the supervisors. Besides such slaves had aged or were old. A strong young slave normally worked as hard as possible at the expense of his life. Such slaves would go as early as possible to work in his farm and then leave for his master's before 9 o'clock. They would work until after 2 o'clock when they will be dismissed.[24]

Despite the characterization of the slave's life on royal estate as being better than on private estates, Rabi'u offers proof that slaves in the former also suffer extreme forms of maltreatment. Responding to a series of questions related to how slaves at royal estates were used he responded thus:

> *Q: To banda noma akwai wani aiki da bayin gandu sukan yi*
> *A: Sai de yaki, sai de yaki kurum*
> *Q: Wato akan zo nan gandun Fanisau a dibi bayi su je suyi yaki*
> *A: Sosai*
> *Q: Suyi wa Sarki yaki*
> *A: Aay idan zamanin yaki ya zo, dama shi shumaga-ban yaki dole shi Galadiman Shamaki da shi da mutunen sa, dole za su tafi yaki. In sunje yaki ba damar munafinci, Sarki na kalon su suna kalon Sarki ana yaki a gabansa. Tilas*
> *Q: Watau yanzu a zamanin yaki, a kulun yaki ya tashi Galadiman Shamaki na nan garin tilas sai ya je da shi da wa*
> *A: Tilas sai ya je*
> *Q: Da mutanen sa*
> *A: Da mutanen sa din*
> *Q: Duk bayin gandu koko*
> *A: A'a ba duk gandu ba. Bakin wanda yake yana da doki; wanda yake mai karfi mai doki to da shi za a tafi*

Q: Apart from farming, was there any other work which plantation slaves did?
A:. Except fighting wars, except going to war only.
Q: Were slaves taken from estates in Fanisau to fight wars?
A: Certainly.
Q: To fight for the emir?
A: Yes. During warfare, it is compulsory for the Gala-diman Shamaki to go to war with his men. In the war front, there was no room for hypocrisy since the emir would be watching them.

> Q: Whenever there was warfare, was it compulsory for the Galadiman Shamaki of this town to go to war with whomever?
>
> A: It is a must for him to go
>
> Q: Together with his men.
>
> A: Yes, together with his men.
>
> Q: All the estate slaves or what?
>
> A: No, not all the plantation slaves, but those sufficiently strong and who had horses could go.[25]

In addition to being forced to fight wars, slaves in the royal estates, especially those considered disobedient could be flogged or sold.[26] The emir, but not the fieldworkers, used most of the agricultural yield from his estates, while the royal slave's chances of securing freedom or enjoying more independence under slavery was relatively limited. Furthermore, when asked to explain the reasons why slaves were exempted from work at the royal estates, Rabi'u notes that, "the reasons that would make him free from work was only when he had physical problems" and this means, "If a slave was sick and could not work, he could be excused to take a rest. Secondly, if a slave was old and his children also worked at the estate with him, he would be instructed to rest since the children are around." Indeed we learn from him that "a strong slave was never excused from work." Rather he was required to constantly show his ability.

Beyond inherent contradictions, testimonies related to slavery and slave trade in Kano emirate were recorded very long after slavery was abolished that colonial and post-emancipation experiences obscured or shaped many of the accounts. To be sure, some of the testimonies were based on childhood experiences of individuals of various backgrounds including, as mentioned, descendants of slave owners and slaves. Other testimonies were even supplied by those born after the abolition of slavery, and who in turn derived knowledge of the events they described from their parents or ancestors. No wonder, recalling the history of slavery and slave trade in Kano Emirate, a few of those who offered testimony portrayed images that evidences from most of the recorded oral accounts and indeed other sources, do not support. For instance, while most sources agree that when on display all the slaves sold in Kano city market were rubbed with ashes, Abdulrahman contends that nothing like that was done to them. On another level, he could not also remember the name of any slave dealer in the Kano city even though he identified a number of slave markets therein.

Finally, in spite of the diverse background of individuals who were interviewed, the testimonies were mainly derived from men. Representatives of women are virtually absent. In addition, questions on child slavery were not seriously addressed. Due largely to this and other related factors; the testimonies examined herein only offer a partial picture of slavery and slave trade in Kano Emirate. All in all, therefore, they are as problematic as any other historical source materials. As such they should be critically tested as any other historical source.

In conclusion, this study indicates that a rich collection of oral data on slavery is currently deposited at the Tubman Institute for public use. In spite of past efforts to draw attention to these materials as well as improvement in the mode of preserving them, they are still ignored by historians. This essay attributes the disregard for the Hausa oral data to strategic and other consideration. It also notes the significance and limitations of the resources in questions. To this end, it indicates that on the one hand they are useful because they suggest new subjects for research, provide invaluable reference source for testing historical and social scientific generalizations, and provide rare information on slavery in Kano Emirate. On the other hand, the paper demonstrates that the testimonies on slavery in Kano Emirate are characterized by internal contradictions, they have been shaped by colonial and post emancipation experiences and they present only a partial picture of slavery in the society. As with other historical sources that have strengths and limitations, the importance of the oral data on slavery in Kano, and indeed the Hausa oral data, cannot be ignored. Therefore, for a better understanding of slavery in Kano Emirate, the data must be critically tested and also used hand in hand with other source materials.

Notes

1. For more information on the Tubman Institute visit its website: www.yorku.ca/tubman.

2. The archival materials on Northern Nigeria derive from several locations including the National Archives Kaduna, National Archives Ibadan, Jos Musuem, Katsina Musuem, Kano State History and Culture Bureau and Rhodes House Oxford.

3. Heinreich Barth, *Travels and Discoveries in North and Central Africa Being a Journal of an Expedition Undertaken Under the Auspices of H. B. M'S Government in the Years 1849-1855,* Vol. 1, (London: Cass, 1965). Hugh Clapperton, *Journal of a Second Expedition into the Interior of Africa fr the Bight of Benin to Socaccatoo* (London: Cass 1966). Charles H. Robinson, *Hausaland, or Fifteen Hundred Miles Through the Central Sudan* (London: Marston, 1897).

4. For more details on oral sources see Jan Vansina, *Oral Tradition: A Study in Historical Methodology* (Harmondsworth, Middlesex: Penguin Books, 1973).

5. Martin A. Klein, "Studying the History of Those Who Would Rather Forget: Oral History and the Experience of Slavery," *History in Africa* 16 (1989), 209-217.

6. Klein, "Studying the History of Those Who Would Rather Forget," 211.

7. Klein, "Studying the History of Those Who Would Rather Forget," 211.

8. Klein, "Studying the History of Those Who Would Rather Forget," 212.

9. Barth, *Travels and Discoveries:* vol. 1, 527.

10. Polly Hill, "From Slavery to Freedom: The Case of Farm Slavery in Nigerian Hausaland," *Comparative Studies in Society and History* 18, no. 3 (1976), 395-426; for the quotation, p. 397.

11. Polly Hill, *Population, Prosperity and Poverty: Rural Kano, 1900 and 1970* (New York: Cambridge University Press, 1977), 209. See also Hill, "From Slavery to Freedom," 406-407.

12. See, for instance, Paul E. Lovejoy, "Slavery in the Sokoto Caliphate," in *The Ideology of Slavery in Africa,* ed. Paul E. Lovejoy (Beverly Hills, London: Sage Publications, 1981), 201-243.

13. For details on the techniques Lovejoy used see Paul E. Lovejoy, *Caravans of Kola. A History of the Hausa Kola Trade (1700-1900)* (Zaria and Ibadan: Ahmadu Bello University Press, 1980), 5-9.

14. For details on the techniques used in this project see Paul E. Lovejoy and J. S. Hogendorn, "Oral Data Collection and the Economic History of the Central Savanna," *Savanna* 7, no. 1 (1978), 71-74.

15. For instance the Ibrahim Jumare's collection is also deposited at the Tubman Institute.

16. Nasiru Ibrahim Dantiye, "A Study of the Origins, Status and Defensive Role of Four Kano Frontier Strongholds (Ribats) in the Emirate Period (1809-1903)" (PhD diss., Indiana University, 1985), Abdullahi Mahadi, "The State and the Economy: The Sarauta System and its Roles in Shaping the Society and Economy of Kano with Particular Reference to the Eighteenth and Nineteenth Centuries" (PhD diss., Ahmadu Bello University Zaria, 1982), Adamu Mohammed Fika, *The Kano Civil War and British Overrule 1882-1940* (Ibadan: University Press, 1978); and Hill, *Rural Kano*. It is evident that these writers visited Zaria during the course of their research. However, the use of the NHRS oral data on Kano is not visible in their works.

17. For instance see Jan S. Hogendorn, "The Economics of Slave Use on Two 'Plantations' in the Zaria Emirate of the Sokoto Caliphate," *International Journal of African Historical Studies* 10 (1977), 369-383.

18. Ibrahim Hamza, "Slavery and Plantation Society at Dorayi in Kano Emirate," in *Slavery on the Frontiers of Islam,* ed. Paul E. Lovejoy (Princeton, NJ: Markus Wiener, 2004), 125-148.

19. Sean Stilwell, Ibrahim Hamza and Paul Lovejoy, "The Oral History of Royal Slavery in Sokoto Caliphate: An Overview with Sallama Dako," *History in Africa* 28 (2001), 273-291.

20. Mohammed Bashir Salau "The Growth of Plantation Economy in Sokoto Caliphate: Fanisau 1819-1903" (PhD diss., York University, 2005).

21. Testimony of Muhammadu Rabi'u interviewed at Fanisau, Kano Emirate, July 13, 1975 by Yusuf Yunusa. Interview translated by Mohammed Bashir Salau.

22. Testimony of Muhammadu Rabi'u.

23. Testimony of Muhammadu Rabi'u.

24. Testimony of Muhammadu Rabi'u.

25. Testimony of Muhammadu Rabi'u.

26. This fact is confirmed by several other testimonies in addition to that of Rabi'u discussed above. For instance, when Gwadabe was asked to describe the sought of punishment a "lazy" slave was given, he responded that, *"Kama shi ake a bashi kashi, gobe ba zai koma ba. Kaji yanda ake mar. Wani har daure shi akan yi"* (He is caught and beaten; tomorrow he will not repeat it. That is what is done to him. Some are even tied up first).

Chapter 8

Life Stories and Ancestor Debts: "Creole Malagasy" in Eighteenth-Century Virginia

Wendy Wilson-Fall

The intention of this essay is to discuss the family narrative as historical artifact and social process,[1] and to underscore the potential that oral texts have for inquiries into the history of the African diaspora in the United States. My particular interest is contemporary oral accounts regarding Malagasy slaves who arrived to Virginia between 1719 and 1721, thereby focusing on the "old" African diaspora in North America.[2] I am concerned with recording alternative views of history, in this case represented by descendents of slaves. Moreover, my intention is to provide a written record of oral testimonies shared with me through informal interviews and via email correspondence. This record, admittedly a first collection of many voices on a new theme, can provide material for future researchers on this and related topics.

All the families who have generously contributed to the collection of stories upon which my work is based, which I call the "Madagascar Narratives," are not socially marginalized today, though earlier generations were certainly so. More importantly, their view of who their ancestors were remains on the borders of historical and ethnographic scholarly concern. I learned of contemporary oral accounts and family narratives through oral interviews, email correspondence and written historical records.

All these forms of communication elicit, for scholars, the question of how to approach the problem of remembrances, opinions and hearsay. These forms of communication were and still are used to share messages[3] about what Malagasy slaves and their descendents experienced and thought about the period of slavery in eighteenth and nineteenth century America. The subject fits well with the approach of historical anthropology as a conceptual tool. In terms of method, unorthodox approaches to data collection such as email correspondence allowed me to cover a wide field of informants, and to create new documentation on the topic.

Methodological and Conceptual Issues: The Specificity of Oral Tradition

Whether memory changes or not, culture is reproduced by remembrance put into words and deeds. Oral traditions are documents of the present, because they are told in the present. Yet they also embody a message from the past, so they are expressions of the past at the same time. They are the representation of the past in the present.[4] The specificity of the oral tradition is this quality of being both of the past and of the present. Indeed, it is the present which continues to have need for the past, and it is this living need which ensures the life of the inherited message. The goal of this essay is to elucidate and explain what some of these needs might have been for successive generations of Americans who claim to descend from Malagasy slaves. I have found that the *problématique* of the oral tradition as described by Vansina best describes the principle of oral tradition as history for my purposes, and his views have been critical to the work of assessing the apparent meaning and the intended meaning in the family narratives discussed here.[5]

Vansina tells us that oral tradition as history need not be seen as a substitute or a poor excuse for written histories or primary archival materials. Rather, he argues that though there is special concern with which we approach the problem of "truth" and reliability in the oral narrative, nevertheless, this genre offers an opportunity to compliment or question existing written materials that cannot be had otherwise.[6] Anthropologist Michel-Rolph Trouillot states that "Narratives are occasionally evoked as illustrations or, at best, deciphered as texts, but the process of their production rarely constitutes the object of study."[7] I began to collect and study oral traditions because I saw in them both documentation and process; memorized messages that both described past conditions and conditioned the present.[8]

Using Diverse Data Sources

As I followed social networks that were brought to my attention through personal contacts in the African American community, I learned several things. One is that there was a certain unity in the messages as I will discuss later in this essay, just as there were definite particularities to each family narrative. I learned that as is typical of oral narratives, generations were often conflated, such that there was confusion between the terms of grandfather, great-grandfather, great-great-grandfather and so forth. As Americans are a very mobile people, it was soon apparent that in order to collect various family member testimonies, the internet would have to do. As it turned out, the internet was in fact a wonderful tool because of the relative autonomy, anonymity, immediacy, and control that it offered to email interviewees. I learned that this topic, throughout all the families, was normally reserved for family visits or intimate friends, hence there was a certain reticence that was apparent in all contexts. The internet allowed those who felt most secretive, it seemed, to speak through the veil of a computer screen.

I established categories of families and testimonies. These categories were based on geographic and chronological criteria. Through this it became apparent that one group, or generation of messages, recalled an era before the Civil War. This realization sent me to the archives, where I eventually found, through the help of colleagues,[9] the work of Virginia Bever Platt.[10] Platt describes the arrival of more than a thousand slaves from Madagascar within a three-year period, mostly women and children. I found that Lorena Walsh's application of the "group biography" approach to the slaves of the Carter plantations in and around Williamsburg, Virginia was also extremely useful. Walsh has tracked families and kin networks through various permutations of sales, inheritances, loans and gifts among Virginia planters.[11] This concept proved to be critical to my understanding of what conditions led to the repetition and remodeling of the Madagascar oral traditions in Virginia. It was necessary to constantly compare data between the archives, secondary biographical sources, web-based correspondence, and oral narratives.

It eventually became clear that among the accounts collected were family narratives which probably did not originate with a slave/captive ancestor, but with someone who appeared to be a mariner, or trader, or both. I thus have divided my efforts among the various categories of slave/captive, mariner/trader, and missionary supported/immigrant. All of these categories pertain to families who claim arrival to the U.S. before the end of the nineteenth century, and one person may have passed through more than one of these categories. This essay is concerned with the first category, that of the oral traditions of self-defined descendents of Malagasy slaves.

Web-Based Interviewing

Even a brief foray into the web-based genealogy forums of today reveals a plethora of exchanges focused on family origins in Africa, both imagined and inherited.[12] These narratives present a meta-text based on a re-reading of family histories and oral traditions by the inheritors of such material. Where, one rightly queries, is this coming from? Where are these family histories, why have they not come under study in the scholarly community, and how and why have they been maintained?

The relative anonymity of the internet provides a good environment for people who are unused to having their stories taken seriously, as most of the people I worked with were. They say that in recounting narratives outside of intimate circles they are not taken seriously, or that their audiences had little investment in the subject of Madagascar as homeland or as exotic geographic site. Consequently, stories had been shared on genealogical websites in the course of searching for new information regarding ancestors. The web also provided opportunities for recognition and commentary on having "a place that they knew they came from" besides the plantations, mines and urban grottos where slaves had lived before emancipation.

Where potential conflict in the web-based method existed was quite clear. The first, in the internet context, had to do with the potential of exposure that storytellers felt regarding a narrative that had a quality that I would name as "familial sanctity." It appears that this exposure is more directly related to protecting the dignity of the family than that of the individual relating the family narrative. The second potential conflict has to do with the possibility of the narrative being discounted as historically impossible, or the possibility of identifying and going deeply into vaguely remembered or suspected situations that obtained in Madagascar related to the capture of the interviewee's ancestor. Variables in this latter category would include regional origins, social status imagined versus probable social status based on historical fact (in Madagascar), and suspicions that the exchange would result in the demonstrated unlikelihood that the family had any Malagasy origins at all.

Initially, I found that there were obvious advantages and disadvantages to the initiation process via internet. The disadvantage, for me as researcher, was that people could "disappear" at any time that they felt the exchange was too time consuming, not interesting, or risky in terms of their emotional investment in the subject. Some interviewees disappeared after a few weeks of exchanges only to show up a year or so later. This anonymity was also an advantage because it depersonalized the context of the exchange to some extent. Since this group was characterized by people who were self-selected (those posing a query about Madagascar) there was no conflict concerning the topic itself, but on how much any interviewee was willing to discuss it in a new context.

The internet provides a rich environment for "observing" contemporary interest in African pasts as demonstrated by slave and freedman descendents in the U.S. Further, consistent study of queries of African Americans on internet sites devoted to African American history shows that family oral histories are more often assigned importance than, say, genetic analysis, although this is also an increasingly popular topic. Although cost is admittedly a factor (tests may range from $300 to $700 for a genetic reading of mitochondrial histories or even combined-gender genetic histories) it is obvious that inherited histories regarding ancestor origins are of particular importance to this population. It is in these texts that we find reference to Mandingo great-great grandfathers (a great uncle named "Prince") and queries on names such as "Sukey" and "Pullo."

Many of the genealogical inquiries which I found regarding Madagascar were not posted on African American focused sites such as *afrigeneas.com*, but rather on surname sites. This almost gives the impression that the authors assumed that the Malagasy were as memorable (to their captors) as they have been to their descendents; that the whites of these families might likely remember someone from Madagascar as they had – as unusual and exotic denizens of the colonial world. It may also be that they feel that the history which their family believes also is assumed by others.

Data collected from internet sites[13] reveals that carriers of these histories refer to their family experience as a rare, special and unique history. Among those claiming Malagasy descent there are many people whose surnames are those of the well-off planters of Virginia. Among the surnames I have collected, there are many names which match the list of officers and members of the House of Burgesses from the years 1715 to 1722. This runs counter to the current understanding of African American slave post-emancipation behavior, which was to cast off the name of their masters and to create or adopt new ones. Perhaps in the world of eighteenth century Virginia where families owned several plantations in diverse regions of Virginia, using the "Master's" surname was a way of being recognized by lost relatives following emancipation.[14] The names Randolph, Lee, Merriweather and Botts, for example, are all surnames of African Americans who have shared a Madagascar story in this project. I intentionally searched the websites for the surnames of the House of Burgess members to see if there were any weblogs from African Americans inquiring about Madagascar. I also searched these sites after having been alerted through hearsay that such-and-such family claimed Malagasy descent "from slavery times." As a result of such searches, I was better prepared for encounters with family members of these kinship groups. As an example of how such kin groups may have overlapped, one informant explanation states: I am related to the Ragland, Dickerson, and Carter families.

My father was a Ragland and my mother was from Redland Plantation, a plantation that belonged to the Carters."[15]

I have collected many email testimonies which are actually
fragments of larger family accounts. It is possible to identify them
as fragments by the chronology of events which appear in various
versions, or to surmise that larger sections have been discarded
over time as the message lost some of its importance, or people
simply forgot. Certainly, gaps are present which suggest that the
message has been compressed or otherwise shortened. A few are
presented below.

1) Hi Wendy! My grandfather was born in 1880 his
   father was Malagasy. I do not have much information on him except his name which was Frank
   Kemp and he married Joanna Todd. I do know that
   they lived in Jewel Georgia. I suppose he was a
   slave and based upon the year that my grandfather
   was born my grandfather was around in 1820. I
   hope this helps you.[16]

2) My grandmother is the one from GA and tied in
   with the Malgasy. My grandfather is from D.C.
   They raised me and are very dear to my heart.
   My grandmother's Malagassy line came from
   Oglethorpe and Clarke Counties in Georgia. Their
   surname was Patilla but it was changed to Tiller
   back in 1920. My great grandmother's name was
   Eva Patilla, she married Bennie Simpson and my
   great great grandmother was Lizzie Luvenie Lydosia
   Brown, she married Charlie Paltilla ca. 1895.

In an earlier email, however, the same respondent said:

The line of my ancestors in this area are Charlie Tiller/
Patillo and Lizzie Tiller/Patillo nee Brown. Both were
born ca. 1880. It is family lore at this point that one of
them was Malagassy. They lived in Toccoa, Georgia
in Franklin/Hambersham Counties (depending on the
year)…I don't have any other information and am new
to this line of research. I think that Lizzie was Malagassy though and not Charlie. I have a photograph of

her ca. 1900 and her physical attributes as described
by my grandmother (..long dark hair, very large ears,
...reddish brown skin tone).[17]

Oral Interviews

The people with whom I began personal interviews were also
connected to genealogical studies. Some were members of local
genealogical groups to whom I had presented a lecture about my
research, and who approached me. Others were people who had
been referred to me. Some sought me out to arrange a meeting.
In these personal situations they shared photo albums and other
memorabilia. Most were curious about Madagascar, and had
looked the country up on the internet or in books. As said earlier,
phenotype was often important. Consider the following quote,
shared with me from a third party in the project: "[…] a French-
man gave the family his name, they sailed with the French man off
the Madagascar coast. My great grandfather had long black hair
to his shoulders, with straight bangs: They sailed to America on a
French boat."[18]

The elements of family stories which were about Madagascar
were threads of much bigger family narratives which in each case
went back to at least 1800. In the course of my work, I have found
that the combined use of personal interview and internet interview
greatly improved my chances of getting more textured narratives
and extended the possible time frame for data gathering. The
oral interview was used sometimes as a follow up to an internet
exchange, sometimes as a series of encounters that did not involve
on-line discussion, and sometimes as a series of initial encounters
which were followed up by on-line exchanges and discussion.
Often the stories included residential shifts from Virginia to other
states and descriptions of several branches of the family. In the
first instance, "interview as follow up to an internet exchange,"
my initial contact via on-line discussions had already established
my purpose and my particular interest in any given subject's story.

I would like to think that most exchanges in general were
carried out in the context of inter-subjectivity, wherein both
parties believe that they are in an exchange rather than in a context

of extraction. I define an extraction context as a situation where the interviewer appears as the greatest stakeholder, revealing little about themselves save their professional interest. In such a situation, it is difficult to identify an intersection of shared interest in the narrative in a universe beyond that of the interview environment. In my case interviewees and I shared a sense of purpose, which was to make public stories which had remained either within the family or within fairly limited circles. Lacking a particular forum from which to disseminate such stories, or unwilling to make such a personal commitment for a variety of reasons, my appearance as a willing documenting source was not usually a problematic issue. I believe this was especially true due to the context of the current popularity of genealogical research and increasing interest in African American origins.

In terms of interpretation, my approach was to present myself as one who sought to document each person's representation of his or her family tradition. I explained that I intended to search for contextual historical information, but not to definitively disclaim or uphold any given narrative or testimony. Where appropriate, participants filled out consent forms which assured them of my respect for anonymity. I sought to have interviewees understand that I had no interest in challenging or changing their stories. On the contrary, I struggled to make it clear that my interest was in using their stories to uncover historical facts and documents that might make the narratives more understandable to all concerned.

To begin, I present a short testimony which I recorded by handwritten notes following a telephone conversation with a retiree in Kisimee, Florida:

> A matriarch of a family from North Carolina claimed that her ancestors were slaves of the Duke family there. In the early 1980s she stated in an interview that Malagasy were used as "decorative slaves," often being assigned the work of coachmen, in matching pairs. This woman claimed Malagasy descent through her father. She also stated that her grandmother would tell her the ancestor was known to have said, "We are from Madagascar, they don't beat *we*."[19]

This narrative raises several questions and shows us the transmission of different kinds of messages. To begin with, the interviewee has received information regarding which family in North Carolina owned her ancestors. Secondly, her family narrative has transmitted information about how enslaved family members remembered being used: as "decorative slaves." The message infers that there were other Malagasy slaves that they knew of, or had observed, as the message conveys the hearsay "[…] being assigned the work of coachmen, in matching pairs." Finally, there is a notion of privilege being transmitted, "They don't beat we." This latter sort of message appears in many of the narratives collected – that Malagasy slaves were somehow, sometimes, set apart. Gomez argues in fact that close examination of historical records suggests that particular ethnic groups or persons from particular regions known to planters received particular work.[20]

Perhaps closer examination of Duke family records and of slave trading in North Carolina will tell us something about how Malagasy slaves may have arrived. The case of North Carolina is problematic because not only could such slaves have been brought by families as personal possessions or as commodities by traders, from Virginia; they could also have been brought northward from South Carolina. Gwendolyn Midlo Hall mentions that at least 40 percent of slaves in Barbados were at one time from Madagascar,[21] and Platt also mentions Barbados as an important site for Malagasy slaves.[22] The *Trans-Atlantic Slave Trade Database* also shows that during the same period that the Malagasy slaves arrived in Virginia, almost twice that number arrived in Barbados, along with shipments of slaves from Mozambique.[23] After a few years of correspondence and personal interviews,[24] it was clear that the large majority of the stories I was collecting led back to Virginia, Georgia and North Carolina. Another oral interview excerpt follows below:

> My great-great-grandmother had dark, straight hair and a round, Asian face and Asian eyes. My grandmother would say "Grandpappy was an Australian and Grandmammy was Malagasy." The story is of the Sisco family of North Carolina, Betty Sisco having been sent to Hickman County, Tennessee to the home

of an Iron Master named Montgomery Bell who was Scotch Irish. He founded the Montgomery Bell Academy. Betty Sisco was the daughter of the Malagasy, and she married Columbus Lewis, who was of Australian origin.[25]

A few narratives are characterized by violence. One tells a story of two sisters who were captured in Madagascar and brought through Virginia to Mississippi. In this story, one of the sisters is almost raped by her doctor owner (a Dr. Fine) in Natchez when she stabs him with scissors and runs away. She runs to a nearby plantation where her sister is working. Together they plot their escape and run away to Missouri.[26] Another story, also from Virginia, is marked by chagrin and frustration since little remains of the family's Malagasy story except that one ancestor was from there and should not be forgotten; there is no document trail and no oral references to slave owners of that ancestor.

Written Sources

A classical historical approach works forward from existing archival and other written materials. As an anthropologist, I have sought to use the family narrative as a frame of reference for looking back to the experience of enslavement. Archival materials thus became important references for understanding historical context and establishing chronology. In shifting the historical and social focus, American colonial documents were read and imagined as the records of the "other" from the perspective of the margins. In this reverse focus, the colonial planters and their cohorts inhabit the margins of local African American historical discourse, emerging as sometimes dangerous, capricious, whimsical or generous, but as marginal entities to these "interior" historical texts all the same. While Brian Axel has stated that "one of the important projects of historical anthropology today is to understand not just the status of archival documents but the position of ethnography within the archive...."[27] and this is one of the concerns of the study discussed here, I am more interested in the silences, to use the term in the sense that Trouillot has used it, of the archives of the American colonial past.[28] Archival materials, for instance, have provided insight into the world that Malagasy captives found when they arrived in eighteenth century Virginia, but not the worlds they created.

The account books of John Baylor, trader of Williamsburg, give evidence of the arrival and sale of more than two hundred such slaves.[29] However, it is the voices of living people claiming to be the descendents of slaves from Madagascar that have brought my attention to the vast silences regarding their forebears once they were purchased by individual buyers. That the messages existed at all suggests the other socio-historical processes that existed in tandem with the creation of the colonial and plantation archive. There is an archival silence that follows in the wake of the purchase of the Malagasy slaves. Once purchased, they indeed became American slaves, objects on lists of other commodities.

As mentioned earlier Virginia Platt published an article in the *William and Mary Quarterly* which described the arrival of some 1,200 slaves from Madagascar to ports on the York and Rappahannock Rivers in Virginia between 1719 and 1721.[30] That such a large number of slaves from a place that had never before and never did again contribute appreciable numbers, if any, of slaves to Virginia's work force gives us some idea of the singularity of this intense and short-lived forced migration. Besides the discussion of the political and economic conditions that led to the slaves' arrival, and explanations of why it never happened again, the Platt article does not follow the fate of the slaves once disembarked.[31] The next documents that make part of the patchwork story are the letters of Robert "King" Carter,[32] complimenting the information of Baylor's account books.[33] It is from this moment that written testimony is weak. Although Baylor's books show the sale of "Malagassers" to particular people, and often their gender, the new owners rarely wrote of them as ethnic or cultural entities beyond the reference of "negro," "black slave," or merely "slave." Exceptions are runaway advertisements, and diaries and correspondence, such as that of Robert Carter, who mentions a "Madagascar Jack," in a letter to one of his farm managers.[34]

Neither do the accounts from African American descendents take up where the written trail ends. In most cases they appear to reference back to the late eighteenth century, almost a full one century after the arrival in Virginia. The inter-generational transfer of the captives' cultural identification is not just evidenced in the oral narratives of their descendents. In a few cases families have written down the narratives as they have understood them to be. In some cases, books have been privately published with the family story. Two excerpts from such publications follow.

The book *We Were Always Free* was written by a Madden family member. It includes a photo reproduction of free papers, dated September 18, 1826, for Willis Madden. The Bundy family, who intermarried with the Madden family, are mentioned in the book as relatives. Both families are African American. The text states:

> [...] by the 1810s, perhaps even earlier, they were living east of town (Stevensburg, Virginia, near Culpepper), in an area that had become home to several families of free Negroes, among them the Hackleys, Clarks, Bannisters, and Bundys... Oliver Bannister...had come to the Stevensburg area from Orange County, and also like Sarah, was a mulatto who had formerly been an indentured servant. The Bundys were tall, dark-skinned, and Indian or Asian looking, with slanted eyes and straight hair. They claimed to have come from the island of Madagascar, off Africa (they still looked the same and still claimed to be from Madagascar a century later, when as a child I knew the Bundy family)...It was in this community that Willis Madden reached manhood.[35]

Madden states "They still looked the same and still claimed to be from Madagascar a century later, when as a child I knew the Bundy family." This phrase is fascinating. If we "unpack" this statement, we can learn quite a bit, or at least develop some very good questions. Firstly, the writer does not express surprise that the Bundys were from Madagascar or claimed that they were from Madagascar. Neither does he anticipate shock or surprise from his readers that within an African American community in Culpepper, Virginia, there exists a family who had for almost two centuries, identified themselves as from Madagascar. He includes the information that "with (their) slanted eyes and straight hair...they still looked the same." These factors, such as physical appearance and identification as someone from Madagascar, are not strange to him.

It is also striking that the author states that they "claimed" to be from Madagascar, not that they described themselves as from Madagascar, or were descendents of someone from there. This motif is repeated not only in general references to such narratives within the African American community, but even among those who profess descent from Madagascar. It is seemingly regarded as a story that might be true, but almost unbelievable. Madagascar is, after all, very far away from Virginia and was not the usual source of slaves or black immigrants to the United States of America. Further, nowhere are there public documents which are easily accessible which confirm these claims. Another story from Virginia follows:

> Mrs. Ira Dandridge Bates was born in Hanover County, Virginia. She had eleven brothers and sisters. Her parents, Philip L. and Ida Liggins Dandridge were Hanover residents. Mrs. Bates' father was born on July 18, 1859 in Hanover County and her mother was born March 6, 1871 in Vineland, New Jersey. Her paternal grandmother, Martha J. Gauge Dandridge was a slave in Hanover. However, the other members of her paternal family were all free. Mrs. Bates paternal grandfather was from Madagascar, an island, off the south east coast of Africa. He came to America and lived in Hanover but had to flee often because he was black and the "patty rollers," who were patrollers of slave territory as well as other whites wanted to enslave him. He was a shoemaker and a cabinet maker. According to Mrs. Bates, he had his free papers, a document which the family has preserved.[36]

The free papers are presented in the book and dated 1859. Unfortunately, they are too blurred to discern whether they are manumission papers. If they are not, we must consider whether her grandfather (or great-grandfather?) was not a sailor, or some other sort of emigrant. In the text we see that Mrs. Ira Dandridge Bates describes her grandfather as free. If her father was born in 1859, then her grandfather would have been born perhaps somewhere between 1839 and 1820. However, the way the free papers are described makes it impossible to know whether these are manumission papers or other papers of identification. As mentioned above, in many of the narratives there is confusion regarding generations. People will sometimes refer to great or even great-great grandfathers as their grandfathers. Vansina describes this phenomenon as typical of group oral traditions.[37]

The case of the Bundy and Madden family also illustrates this point. In this text it is not stated whether the Bundy ancestors were slaves or free immigrants. It has also come to my attention that in many cases people refer to someone (and themselves) as "Malagasy," "Molly Glasser," or "Madagasky" when they have actually been born in the U.S. This in itself is interesting in terms of how the tag of Madagascar is used to define and mark a particular, different, history in the community. Vansina states that such repetition must be seen in terms of both its intended and apparent purpose. He states

> The whole corpus of group accounts is constantly and slowly reshaped or streamlined. Some items acquire greater value. As the corpus grows, some items become repetitive or seem to have symmetrically opposed meanings or mnemonic streamlining occurs.... Especially characteristic of this process is the part played by stereotypical elements or clichés.... Once there, clichés may well remain stable over long periods of time or can proliferate further.[38]

The kinship groups which are the families who claim common descent from a Malagasy slave ancestor tend to stress certain phenotypical characteristics in describing themselves, such as straight hair, bronze colored skin, royal origins, and being from Madagascar (instead of a particular place there). This stress on phenotype as a cliché is common to all of the narratives which I have collected to date.

In the context of racialist colonial and pre-Civil War America, the various ethnic distinctions of Madagascar seem to have been shed or discarded in favor of distinguishing "Madagascar" identity from mainland identity. In fact, among all the families which

I have interviewed so far, only two have been able to give some evidence of ethnic origins in Madagascar, and these were families of nineteenth century immigrants.

Re-Visiting Fieldwork Studies
of African Americans

My purpose here is not to present or discuss the past history of ethnographic studies of African Americans, but rather to point out that within this corpus, studies of internal views of past and current relationships to Africa, or various Africas, are rare. With the exception of the field notes of Zora Neal Hurston[39] and the work of Robert Ferris Thompson, inquiries into African American world views expressed by laymen rather than academics have not enjoyed the same growth that related studies have in history and archeology. Ferris Thompson is remembered for his study of elements of Kongo culture in the southeastern United States.[40] In this volume Thompson presents a strong argument that cemetery and funerary decorations in South Carolina show a definite derivative relationship to Kongo art.

In 1980, African American anthropologist John Langston Gwaltney produced the book *Drylongso*, which was an ethnographic journey into the sense of nationhood which he found prevailed in the African American community of that time.[41] This nationhood was based, in Gwaltney's view, on the shared experience of slavery, on subsequent experiences of racism, and family-based ideologies of survival and resistance. The amount of space devoted to the subject of Africa is markedly short. A reading of the book will reveal that Africa is brought up during interviews in its most distant and general form, and the responses show that interviewees responded in kind, remarking on their thoughts of the Africa of the twentieth century or the "Africans who sold them" in the far past.

An interesting characteristic of both Gwaltney's work and the 1930s interviews of the through the Virginia Writers' Project,[42] is that neither focus on the cultural past or present of their subjects. An academic reading of these works, particularly from the anthropological and ethnographic perspective, leads one to question why. I would suggest that certain material at that time was either considered too sensitive, or the study assumed a very shallow past of the subjects, due to their enslavement. More recent publications of the Virginia ex-slave interviews such as *Weevils in the Wheat,* do offer some analysis of social conditions and even African inheritance of the interviewees.[43] However, the analysis of possible cultural patterns, expressions, or memories that are present in the interview texts was not done. The exceptions are notes on "the Negro dialect" which are presented in Appendix 7 of the published interviews, and the accompanying tome to the interviews "The Negro in Virginia."[44]

A review of the questionnaire, thankfully preserved along with the interviews, reveals that there are no questions focusing on particular family practices. One could compare, for example, with similar questionnaires or studies that were being carried out in colonial Africa at that time. These were still early days in American anthropology, for which "Indian" (Native American) culture was the vogue. For the Virginia study there are no ethnographic protocols that cover family networks, rank, or worldview. Most poignantly, there are no questions which are directed towards the origin stories of grandparents, or other family predecessors, although there is one question asking if parents spoke of "Africa."[45]

The treatment of the subject of slavery as a "remembered" experience of African Americans has not been in vogue for a long while. In view of Linda Smith's *Decolonizing Methodologies*[46] one might argue that this in itself is a sign of powerlessness and social insignificance – a so great insignificance that a community is virtually removed from its history as a disembodied object of study. Such a situation perhaps reflects the internalization of a popular folkloric view in America that memories or identification of Africa were quickly wiped out through physical and mental violence.[47] This popular view is held by some African Americans as well as by white, or other Americans. Moreover, the violence of the plantation or other slave experience in the United States and its colonial past has been more researched and more frequently described than the African responses to that violence until recently.

Ira Berlin[48] and other historians have produced significant works which describe African and African American responses up to the late nineteenth century. Historians, psychologists and sociologists have written about African American contemporary life in the last century primarily covering current life and contemporary narratives which speak to the twentieth century. The subject which has received less focus, and which the "Madagascar Narratives" intends to work toward, is the ethnographic view of what slave descendents think about their slave and family pasts now.[49] While there are no longer living witnesses to slavery or to stories about slavery passed directly from a former slave – it remains true that contemporary descendents of slaves have decidedly not been considered a critical source for understanding the nuances of the slave condition that could not have been recorded unless by slaves themselves. Such family narratives can be important sources for contextualizing what the written historical record tells us today.

The sub-field of archeology has by far made the greatest contribution to understanding the history of Africans and their descendents in the U.S. within the discipline of anthropology.[50]In an article about archaeological work in Berkeley County, South Carolina, archeologist Kerri S. Barile found two different versions of the history of one of the buildings on the Middleburg Plantation site.[51] Her experience is instructive in terms of ways that we can look at, listen to, and use family narratives. By piecing together historical land archaeological findings, she ultimately found that the site in question could not have been either of the two buildings described in oral traditions. However, she makes a point worth noting on the issue of oral history:

> ...oral traditions themselves divulge a plethora of information about the 18th-, 19th-, and 20th century relations among white and black populations....This information can be used to decipher meanings among the plantation landscape and the dissemination of power among its' inhabitants. It can also yield possible clues to living conditions, social actions, and the daily lives of both the white elite family and their enslaved African American workforce that are not seen in the written record and cannot be determined archaeologically or architecturally.[52]

Other examples from anthropology are the recently edited volume by Sheila Walker,[53] where a chapter written by her presents an ethnographic view of her childhood in New Jersey, and a volume published by the UCLA project Cultural Studies in the African Diaspora.[54] I suggest that we need to imagine what frameworks can help us to discern the Africa that is entwined in the fabric of America. Family narratives, with their particular references to odd and unusual behaviors, prejudices and customs, are one window. Asking for stories or information about "family customs" is by far a more fruitful field in terms of getting specific localized information about family traditions that may be unique, and that may be signposts to various particular cultural pasts. By contrast, asking whether any given family or persons think they have "African customs" or "African memories" is doomed from the start, since Africa per se was not part of family histories; these would have been regionally and ethnically specific to places in Africa. The use of the term Africa (or Madagascar) is itself an indicator of the chronological context, and perhaps the textural depth, of a narrative. These are compressed terms which accumulated meaning over time for slave descendents. Madagascar became for the Malagasy captive what Africa became for the captives who came from various regions of Africa.

It is possible that there is a prejudice or discomfort in the collection of African American oral narratives that is not evident for such work in similar communities in South America, Africa or the Caribbean. In these environments family narrative becomes a more solid version of "truth" that is used to construct interpretations of African, South American, or Caribbean realities. I can say this because in the course of my research I found myself guilty of this double standard. What I was prepared to believe in Nigerian circumstances was not what I might have believed in Richmond, Virginia. The bar for "truthfulness" shot up in my subconscious when I approached the problem of oral traditions as history in my own country. Such prejudice can be traced back to the generalized assumption that the African American community holds the least promise in terms of oral traditions or contemporary world views as they may relate to Africa. That I was guilty of such double standards did not occur to me until I began hearing narratives that, to coin a phrase of Trouillot, were part of an "unthinkable history."[55]

I had to confront my own prejudice and listen to stories of Virginia and Madagascar as I would have for Cayor and Waalo in Senegal. I learned in this process that even if the cultural present gives evidence and weight to suspicions of historical shallowness, we cannot assume that there is nothing to be learned of the slave experience from native Black communities.[56]

Retrieving Oral Traditions and a Madagascar Past

How then, do we explain repeated instances of these narratives which speak of a slave past and slave progenitors – their plantations, their owners, their appearance, their origins? Of course we can first cite written historical records – the Virginia archives, for example. If documents which support today's claims to Madagascar are not at the center of public records or local written histories does not signify that such stories have no historical grounding. The evidence is in ships' lists, household diaries, farm inventories and the like. The very marginal positioning of the information is evidence of how African American cultural realities of the nineteenth century were ground into humdrum facts or ignored by those who were outside of that cultural reality. Trouillot calls this "banalization," wherein the use of connected tropes help configure a comfortable reality versus an unknowable, or unexpected reality.[57]

In Platt's article the slaves themselves are incidental, and marginal, to the purpose of her discussion which centered on British-American trade policy of the late seventeenth and early eighteenth century. For example, their humanity only comes up when described as a legal topic for judicial rulings of commodities that might be shipped to Virginia, and in a description of one cargo's medical status, which was "distemper of the eyes."[58] The object of this article was not the subject of the slaves per se, but rather the irregularity that the arrival of slaves from that island presents in Virginia history. The primary reason for this irregularity was the problem of taxation of imports arriving directly from another British colonial port. A related reason was the concern the British Foreign Office had regarding pirate activity in the Indian Ocean and private American commercial dealings with pirates in that region.

Since direct trade to Asia was limited the arrival of a large number of slaves from the direction of Madagascar to Virginia was an unusual and probably, singular event. Based on this evidence, one can then surmise that the presence of Malagasy captives in that time and place was itself also unusual, odd, remarkable. It may have been more remarkable for the whites, who had a superior or at least different understanding of Africa's geography and the distance of Madagascar from Virginia, than it was for the West and Central African slaves whom the Malagasy captives, mostly women and children, joined. This may also have been a factor influencing the way that the Malagasy descendents saw themselves and their ancestors.[59]

Assuming that slaves did communicate among themselves, and that tales of origin were shared in the early years, memories of the Malagasy would have traveled kin networks along with other stories of other origins. Recent research suggests that the work of establishing ties was equally intense among individuals from common regional origins (Mandingue, Wolof, and Fula from Senegambia, for instance) as between individuals from geographically and culturally distant origins (Igbo, Mandingo, Kongo).[60] The pressures of daily life under the tobacco plantation regimes assured that English, or a form of it, quickly became a lingua franca. For some reason these narratives were maintained while other narratives were selected out. The value that the social environment, perhaps whites and some blacks, assigned to phenotypes that were more "white" or "mulatto" or "Asian" than black African surely is one reason why. So much has been said on this subject of color prejudice and its origins that I elect not to go further into the topic. However, it is useful to keep it in mind as a factor favoring what in truth was the discarding of some ancestors for the embrace of others. I think, as well, that it cannot be assumed that the identity of "Malagasy" and that of "mulatto" were easily confused among African Americans of the period. People knew "who was who" and their lives often depended on recognizing and assessing their neighbors.[61]

As in the case of the Indian Ocean islands such as Reunion and Mauritius, the blacker the individual or family, and the curlier their hair, the closer they have been associated with savagery and the degradation of the slave state. The difference between Virginia Afro-Malagasy and Afro-Malagasy communities of the Indian Ocean is the placement of such families on the (non-white) social scale. The "Madagascar narratives" seem to reflect a privileged position, or at least a privileged self estimation based on descent from Madagascar. By contrast, the texts which I have read on the Afro-Malagasy in Mauritius and Reunion, for example, do not reflect any superior or special sense of self-worth among Afro-Malagasy in the Indian Ocean diaspora. This may be due to the significant numbers of Asians from the Indian sub-continent in those societies, but only future research can answer this question.

From what we now know of the role of African sailors, freedmen or slave; and of porters and coachmen in circulating information, commentary about the arrival of the Malagasy slaves must have spread quickly to many slave quarters. Were the slaves really Malagasy or from Mozambique? On this subject we have some information, though limited, from Platt's 1969 article. She states that the slaves were picked up between Fort Dauphin in the southeast and the Isle St. Marie in the north-east. Although we cannot know from this what their specific ethnic origins were, we can extrapolate that they may have been from the eastern plains.[62] That they were most probably Malagasy, and not captives from elsewhere, is also indicated in Platt's article. She cites investors' records from the East India Company stating explicitly that Malagasy *natives* should be sought.[63] She also explains that the smuggling of Malagasy slaves was considered difficult because of their different appearance, the British stating that the "Malay" influence in their looks was problematic.[64]

There is some documentation suggesting a sense of difference, of "harboring" an alternative ethnic identity among this community. Platt reports that as early as 1796 a Malagasy woman went to court in St. Mary's County (Maryland) arguing that her enslavement had been a mistake and that "she should not have been made a slave, as she was from Madagascar, which was outside the usual course of the trade" (in slaves).[65] That she would make such a claim reveals an unusual sophistication and familiarity with British law of the colonial period. It hints at the notoriety that the arrival of the Malagasy slaves, and the American ships with their

East Indies cargo, may have had in slave and free communities. Additionally, the woman's claim reflects the tone of the era following the revolutionary war when many slaves hoped that the spirit of independence would affect the way that the white elites and slave holders regarded the status of slaves. This was also a period of numerous manumissions following the Quaker stance on slavery which was announced out of Philadelphia around that time, and the manumission law of Virginia which was passed in 1783. As history has shown, this period of sympathy did not last long and was ended with the slave rebellions of the first decade of the nineteenth century.

Manumission was certainly an element in Virginia which would have favored the retention and elaboration of the slave/captive stories, beyond the obvious one of plantation master family networks and inheritance customs, was early manumission. From the end of the Revolutionary War to the turn of the century, many planter families regularly freed some of their slaves or allowed them to buy their freedom, or buy the freedom of relatives. In Petersburg, for example, nearly half the people in 1790 were slaves, and another 10 per cent were black and free.[66] In 1783 the Virginia legislature passed the bill freeing all slaves "who had contributed toward the establishment of American Liberty and Independence."[67] In talking of the period from 1790 to 1810, Susan Lebsock reports that "The most spectacular growth rate ... was registered by free blacks, who more than tripled their numbers during the two decades ... By 1810, there were more than a thousand free blacks in Petersburg."[68] Lebsock dates the halt of this manumission trend at 1806, when new legislation put an end to slave emancipations in Virginia and installed severely repressive laws for free blacks.[69]

Since many of the slaves were children according to Robert "King" Carter's letters of 1720 and 1721,[70] there is a likelihood that the Madagascar captives in Virginia or their first generation descendents were among those manumitted early by such families as the Carters and the Randolphs. It is likely that Carter bought a good number of the captives as he was an investor in the venture. According to Virginia planter custom, they or their descendents could have ended up in any of the households of Carter's properties as gifts, loans, or inheritance. The eighteenth century Carters' closer "well to do" relatives included the Fitzhugh, Randolph, Lee, Burwell, Wormley, Harrison and Page families.

Carter's correspondence of 1721 also shows discouragement at the large number of women. Although we cannot yet say that there were residential communities which reflected shared Malagasy heritage we can consider kinship networks across various plantations within regions of Virginia as a possibility. Lebsock reports that before 1806, blacks were responsible for one-sixth of Petersburg manumissions, and women accounted for a good part of it.[71] Taking the example of Petersburg, today there are several African American families who cite Petersburg as their family home and who claim descent from Malagasy slaves. These include the Lee, Randolph, Ragland and Ragsdale African American families of that region.[72] The reader may remember the testimony cited above which claimed kinship to African American Lee, Ragland and Randolph lineages.

Free blacks and slaves together outnumbered the whites (of Petersburg) four to three."[73] The Page, Littlepage, and Randolph families all had links to Petersburg and Hanover, Virginia, as well as a presence in and around Williamsburg. For that matter, the Carter family had several Chesapeake properties, and their descendents owned properties near Culpepper as well – all areas that have later turned up family narratives of Madagascar.

The prevalence and tenacity of stories of Madagascar origins in Virginia was no doubt helped along by the arrival of immigrants from Madagascar as free people during the nineteenth century. Oral traditions collected range from stories of religious refugees, to tales of escape with the help of American ship captains and resettlement stories involving partnerships with American commercial agents. The existence of these stories and their historical references suggest a strong tie with maritime trade. The probable presence of Malagasy sailors during the period following the Revolutionary War, whether as slaves or freedmen, is an example. It has been difficult and often impossible to disentangle narratives of slave descendents from narratives of immigrant descendents, which is not surprising.

The story of the arrival and settlement of slaves from Madagascar is a story of an inherited ambiguous identity where one historical thread has been favored over others. Claims to early free status are often vague and not accompanied with clear references to how freedom was obtained or the year. Moreover, some of the descendents of the free arrivals settled in proximity to the sites of earlier slave communities, so that it is likely that in such cases both stories and families overlap. Because of this, it is important to note that oral narratives, like material goods, can themselves be inherited and assumed. Households and individuals may have virtually adopted a common ancestor based on affiliation to a present family network. This also could have affected the rate and expanse of the circulation of family narratives describing a Malagasy ancestor.

The captives' gender structure may have contributed to the longevity and the circulation of the oral texts regarding Madagascar origins. If the majority of the slaves were women, then it was the women who propagated their histories.[74] Women were the primary care givers and probably resided more often with their children than did men, and this may be why the stories prevailed. Lebsock notes that in Petersburg, free African American women were much more likely to remain unmarried than single white women of the working class, and that "the emancipation of a woman in her childbearing years ... struck a blow against the entire slave system, for that single act of emancipation might secure the freedom of generations."[75] It is also not known how many of the women were taken as concubines by the big planters or their overseers.

The Topic of Royalty in the Madagascar Narratives

The topic of royalty runs through many of the narratives. This recurrent theme recalls the Madagascar of the eighteenth and nineteenth centuries, when kings, princes, princesses and queens were the ruling elite around whom courtiers and clients built their social capital. Whether or not any of these stories are actually told by blood descendents of the ruling elites, the emphasis which they assign to the problem of nobility remains as a signature of the societies which they left behind.This emphasis on royalty is proportionately greater in the Madagascar narratives then what one encounters in genealogical discussions about other African heritage among African Americans both on various websites and in personal encounters, in my experience.

Using Vansina's typology, we can isolate various possibilities of why so many of the Malagasy descent narratives emphasize royalty. In this case, "royalty" must be read for its apparent and intended meaning. Intended meaning must be read in this cliché which helps to communicate the singularity and exotic nature of the narrative for the purposes of the performers (those family members who recite the narratives). As a cliché it is a geopolitical reference, emphasizing that these were Malagasy from a kingdom, an organized and centralized polity. Perhaps an earlier narrative had more geographic and political information.

While the apparent reason to claim an inherited genealogically royal past could be for elitist purposes (within the black community), intended meaning may be to signal a former free social status within a hierarchical, stratified society such as that of the Betsimisaraka of the eastern coast, which is where most of the slaves of 1719-1721 probably came from. This infers that the first purpose of the narratives is not dialogue with unrelated families within a generation ("we are better than x"), but a dialogue from generation to generation ("who we are, specifically"). In Malagasy the word for slave, *ondevo*, literally means "reduced to ashes," while the term *olombelo* specifically refers to a living person who is free.[76] In a sense, a slave could not be an ancestor. To become an ancestor one would have had to establish a free status that was "in the blood," inherent to the person and outside of the present condition of captivity. To claim royalty was thus to claim an inherent nobility that referred to a framework outside of the American experience.

Conclusion

As we have seen, all of the stories place particular importance on the physical appearance of their ancestors from Madagascar. Most stories refer to a female grandparent or great-grandparent who insisted on the importance of the story, its claim to Madagascar, and its continuation in succeeding generations. Many place singular importance on early manumission, and consequently, early important social standing in the African American community.

In this research, I have found that many of those claiming Malagasy heritage are of today's middle class in the African American community. I believe that this is both an indication that the people of Malagasy descent married (perhaps with conscious determination) people who looked like them and were upwardly mobile, and the fact that those whose situation in life was a bit better are, in fact, those "who survived to tell the tale." There is reason to believe that both factors are important.

There may be more narratives that are kept within families and which unfortunately are still regarded as silly, manufactured, or strange and yet which have been repeated over generations. There is the possibility that some customs and habits which are derived from a particular place in Africa or Madagascar are remembered as specific family traits rather than ethnic ones. Some continental African identities were forgotten and yet submerged in symbolic and stylized stories which made the information less accessible for the casual observer and therefore less available for ridicule (or punishment). African physical traits became objects of ridicule and African behaviors became less and less the ideal in African American communities of the mid-nineteenth century. When I began interviews in the late 1980s before the internet had become widely popular, the "Madagascar narratives" tended to be shared in closed or close circles where the narrator could not be made fun of for "making up stories," or "attempting to rise above" other African Americans through claims to a known origin.

Earlier I suggest that the family narrative is itself a sort of artifact; as well as it is historical event in its performance and a cumulative site of social process. As I have understood Vansina, narratives often compress or discard historical events because the purpose of the narrative is to *convey a message that is useful and easily retainable* in each generation where it is recited. In the analysis of various testimonies, hearsay, oral traditions and archival data, we begin to discern the purpose of these oral messages. What do they contribute to the kin groups who maintain them?

The Madagascar Narratives have survived because they have responded to a continued need to affirm the humanity and historicity of the kin groups who have maintained them. The common thread for all the narratives is that of attachment to a place of origin of one's ancestors outside of the conceptual and physical space of debasement and captivity. It is also a concern that those ancestors not be forgotten. If there is a cultural retention observable then, among these texts, it is the belief that it is important not to forget one's ancestors from Madagascar. While this belief coincides with the important role the ancestor holds in Malagasy society, the reason this practice of remembrance prevails is that it is needed to enhance one's sense of humanity. While ceremony and ritual have disappeared, the remembrance and sharing of the narrative become the ritual. This ritual functions as an unconscious offering to the ancestor, a responsibility transferred from one generation to the next.

In conclusion, I share the story of the Hope family of Richmond because it clearly demonstrates some of the problems inherent in the collection of these narratives and the tracking of events described in them in the hopes of finding some corroborating evidence. I was contacted by a member of this family early in 2005. This individual had read in a local newspaper about a lecture which I gave in Hanover, Virginia at the invitation of the local community and the Virginia Foundation for the Humanities. She was descended, she said, from a man who was from Madagascar and lived in Richmond around 1790. She explained (via email) that this was part of her family's oral tradition, that a man by the name of Caesar Hope was her direct ancestor, and that he had arrived in the U.S. as a slave from Madagascar. Family history also has it that he worked for Edmund Randolph (son of Sir John), and traveled with him from Williamsburg to Richmond around 1790. She asked me if I might be able to help her with uncovering more information about Caesar Hope. In the interim, the descendant got in touch with a professor of history who often worked in Virginia on the subject of freed slaves. Caesar was among those whom he studied. This was serendipitous, as much more information, in chronological order, became available through his kind assistance.[77] He explained in an email that:

[Caesar] left Williamsburg for Richmond in the late 1780s. He left a remarkable trail through the records which made the essay possible. He died a free man in Richmond ca 1810 or 1811. I do not know how he chose or got the name Hope. Nor do I know where he came from. What I do know is that a slave named Caesar who was emancipated in 1779 under the name John Hope aka Barber Caesar appears in various linked estate accounts all the way back to 1743 when one Benjamin Catton presented a boy before the York County Court to have his age adjudged.... He may have been among 36 slaves transported on two boats the Little Betty sailing from Antigua in late July and the Young David coming from Barbados. It is far more likely that Ceasar disembarked from one of four slave vessels that dropped anchor in the York River between late May and mid-June. Sailing from Bristol England to the west coast of Africa to pick up their human cargoes, the Broomfield, the Henrys Galey, the Goldfinch, and the Williamsburg.

Given the overwhelming numbers of those coming in from Africa – with no more specific location provided – I would argue it is safe to assume that Hope was on one of those ships. There are a couple from the West Indies, but no way of knowing anything more about the origins of individuals on them either. "X" once told me that her family believes that an ancestor was a prince from Madagascar. That might well be, but there is no written historical information that I am aware of that can identify Hope's specific origin or status. I am also not sure of a direct link that can yet be established genealogically between X's family and Ceasar Hope. He disappears from the record ca. 1800. Hope remarried in Richmond a woman named Tenah whom he purchased and freed. In his 1807 will he named Edmund Randolph his executor and instructed him to try and "free two children of his and Tenah's."[78]

I have included this bit of narrative and exchange at the end because it so well demonstrates the problems inherent in working with family oral histories and tracking related events or documented facts in the archives. This story is a good example of the intractable nature of documenting the slave condition, where the individual's past did not matter to the people who were using his labor or even buying his products. There is good reason to believe that a slave arriving from Barbados could very well have been Malagasy. We have seen that more Malagasy arrived in Barbados during the same period than arrived in Virginia. But this detail about Hope was not important to those who presented him to the York County Court. The origin story was expendable and irrelevant to anyone who would have written about Hope, perhaps.

My intention has been to present evidence that there are twenty-first century African American stories, characterized by layers of transitive and evolving identities, which cover several generations. Tracing these dynamic identities gives some insight into the experience not just of enslavement and captivity, but of the creolization process. The embellishments, omissions and emphasis in these oral texts allow a glimpse into what past generations considered important to include, exclude or fabricate in constructing and bequeathing their images of themselves.

Notes

1. For more discussion on this see, for example, Jan Vansina, *Oral Tradition as History* (Madison: University of Wisconsin Press, 1985) 54, 63, 79.

2. Virginia Bever Platt, "The East India Company and the Madagascar Slave Trade," *William and Mary Quarterly* 26 (1969), 548 – 577.

3. Vansina, *Oral Tradition as History*, xi-xii.

4. Vansina, *Oral Tradition as History*, xii.

5. Vansina, *Oral Tradition as History*, 84-88.

6. Vansina, *Oral Tradition as History*, 7, 69.

7. Michel-Rolph Trouillot, *Silencing the Past: Power and the Production of History* (Boston: Beacon Press, 1995), 22.

8. Vansina, *Oral Tradition as History*, 12.

9. In particular, my thanks go to Lorena Walsh, historian at the Colonial Williamsburg Foundation for her assistance and dialogue.

10. Platt, "East India Company," 548-577.

11. Lorena Walsh, *From Calabar to Carter's Grove: The History of a Virginia Slave Community* (Charolottesville: University Press of Virginia, 1997).

12. Some examples are Afrigeneas, www.afrigeneas.com, managed out of the University of Mississipi, and state-focused sites on www.ancestry.com, as well as Genealogy Forum, http://genforum.genealogy.com .

13. I have regularly visited selected family name websites for the last seven years, intentionally on the look-out for queries relevant to my research. In this way, for instance, I followed a thread by several African American Raglands about their family history in Louisa County, Virginia.

14. My thanks to Mary Ann French, historian at the University of Virginia, Charlottesville, for her insight into the problem of surnames. French argues that assuming the slave master's surname was a viable and much used strategy so that slaves could readily identify the communities to which they belonged. Inquiry for understanding how nascent lineages and extended households were viewed and functioned in plantation societies among African descended slaves is a promising topic that deserves further research.

15. Personal interviews in Washington, DC. Conference of the African American Genealogical and Historical Society, 2003.

16. E-mail correspondence, July 20, 2001.

17. E-mail correspondence, October, 2000.

18. Primus family story, Washington, DC, 1989.

19. This was recorded from a conversation with the mother of the late Melvin McCaw, an Africanist and activist who was a former Director of the African American Institute.

20. Michael Gomez, *Black Crescent: The Experience and Legacy of African Muslims in the Americas* (New York: Cambridge University Press, 2005).

21. Gwendolyn Midlo Hall, *Slavery and African Ethnicities in the Americas: Restoring the Links* (Chapel Hill: University of North Carolina Press, 2005), 66-67. Hall states that "A census in Barbados at the end of the seventeenth century counted 32,473 slaves, half of them from Madagascar."

22. Platt, *East India Company*, 557.

23. David Eltis, Stephen Beherendt, David Richardson, and Herbert Klein, *The Trans-Atlantic Slave Trade. A Database on CD-Rom* (Cambridge: Cambridge University Press, 1999).

24. E-mail correspondence from 2001 to 2004, personal interviews in the Washington, DC area during the same period.

25. Interview, 18 March 2001.

26. Gail Melissa Grant, personal interview, Washington DC, 1990.

27. Brian Axel, ed. *From the Margins: Historical Anthropology and its Futures* (Durham: Duke University Press, 2002), 15.

28. Trouillot, *Silencing the Past*, 26-27.

29. John Baylor, *Account Books 1 & 2, 1719-20, 1720-21* (Charlottesville: University of Virginia Special Collections, Manuscript Department).

30. I am grateful to the staff of the Colonial Williamsburg Foundation for the kind assistance they provided in helping me get these texts while I was in Senegal.

31. Except for the case of one woman in Anne County in Maryland, apparently a descendent of these slaves, who protested she should not be enslaved because of the Malagasy origins, cited later in this paper.

32. Louis B. Wright, ed. *The Letters of Robert Carter: The Commercial Interests of a Virginia Gentleman* (San Marino: Huntington Library, 1940).

33. John Baylor, *John Baylor Account Books, I and 2*, 1719-1721.

34. Correspondence of Robert Carter, *Robert Carter Letterbook, 1727-28* (Colonial Williamsburg microfilm number M113, October 10, 1727). In correspondence to Robert Jones, one of Robert Carter's managers in Fairfax County, Carter mentions that he does not want Madagscar Jack to go the New Design Plantation. Whether Jack was himself from Madagascar or reared by Malagasy or had one Malagasy parent, etc. it is evident that the term Malagasy was familiar enough to become part of a slave's name.

35. T.O Madden Jr. and Ann L. Miller, *We Were Always Free: The Maddens of Culpepper County, Virginia, a 200 year family history* (New York: W.W. Norton, 1992), 42-43.

36. Vonita White Foster, "Personal Account of Mrs. Ida Dandridge Bates," in *Black Hanoverians: An Enlightened Past* (Rockville, Virginia: ITS, 1999), 35.

37. Vansina, *Oral Tradition as History*, 20-21.

38. Vansina, *Oral Tradition as History*, 21.

39. Zora Neal Hurston, *Mules and Men* (New York: J.B. Lippincott, 1935). Hurston studied under Franz Boas, and was associated with anthropologist Melville Herskovitz. She undertook field research from 1927-1932 in the southern United States.

40. Robert Ferris Thompson and Joseph Cornet, *The Four Moments of the Sun: Kongo Art in Two Worlds* (Washington, DC: National Gallery of Art, 1981).

41. John Langston Gwaltney, *Drylongso: A Self Portrait of Black America* (New York: Random House, 1980).

42. The Virginia Writers' Project, an activity of the Federal Writers' Project, 1936-1937. See also, Charles L. Perdue, Jr., Tomas Barden and Robert Phillips, ed. *Weevils in the Wheat: Interviews with Virginia Ex-Slaves* (Charlottesville: University Press of Virginia, 1992).

43. Perdue, "Introduction," in *Weevils in the Wheat*.

44. The Work Projects Administration of Virginia Writers' Project, *The Negro in Virginia* (Winston-Salem, North Carolina: John Blair, 1994; New York: Hastings House, 1940).

45. Perdue et al., *Weevils in the Wheat*, Appendix 6, questions #266 "Did you know any slave born in Africa?" and #268 "Did the old folks ever talk about Africa?"

46. Linda Smith, *Decolonizing Methodologies: Research and Indigenous Peoples* (Dunedin: University of Otago Press, 1999).

47. Gwendolyn Midlo Hall also remarks on this tendency of the past to argue that slaves were deliberately and successfully separated in the United States. See Hall, *Slavery and African Ethnicities*, xv.

48. Ira Berlin, *Many Thousands Gone: The First Two Centuries of Slavery in North America* (Cambridge, MA: Belknap Press, 1998).

49. Recent important exceptions include Michael Gomez, *Black Crescent: The Experience and Legacy of African Muslims in the Americas* (New York: Cambridge University Press, 2005); Michael Gomez, *Exchanging Our Country Marks: The Transformation of*

African Identities in the Colonial and Antebellum South (Chapel Hill: University of North Carolina Press, 1998) and Trouillot, *Silencing the Past.*

50. See, for example, the on-line bibliography of the *Newsletter of the African American Archeological Network*, which has several articles which call for interdisciplinary approaches to the study of African American archeological sites, www.clas.ufl.edu/users/davidson. and www.antrho.uiuc.edu/fculty/cfennel/bookmark3htm/ "African Diaspora Archaeology Network"

51. "Testing the Oral History at Middleburg Plantation."

52. "Testing the Oral History at Middleburg Plantation, Berkely County, South Carolina," *Newsletter of the African American Archaeological Network*, no. 26, 1999, electronic version at http://www.diaspora.uiuc.edu/A-AAnewsletter26.html#anchor746411, compiled by T.R. Wheaton, New South Associates.

53. Sheila S. Walker, "Are you hip to the jive? (Re)Writing/Righting the Pan-American Discourse" in *African Roots/American Cultures: Africa in the Creation of the Americas*, ed. Sheila Walker (New York: Rowman & Littlefield, 2001), 1- 45.

54. Dionne Bennet, Valerie Smith, Marcyliena Morgan, ed. *Revolutions of the Mind: Cultural Studies in the African Diaspora Project, 1996-2002* (Los Angeles: CAAS Publications, 2002).

55. Trouillot, *Silencing the Past*, 73-76.

56. I quote this phrase from Joy St. James, Kent State graduate student in Anthropology, 2006.

57. Trouillot, *Silencing the Past*, 96.

58. Virginia Bever Platt, *The East India Company*, 553: "Negroes were construed to be some form of 'Goods Wares Merchandizes and Commoditys,' so they could no longer be brought directly from Madagascar," see 554 n12, for discussion of the East India Act and the description "distemper of the eyes," 568.

59. Gomez, *Exchanging Our Country Marks*, 41.

60. Gomez, *Exchanging Our Country Marks*, 40-41.

61. Ernest J. Wilson, Jr., family discussions, 1970-1981.

62. Scholars of Madagascar, such as Pier Larson, do not think that many, if any, came from the eastern reaches of the Merina plateau (Larsen, personal communication, February 2006).

63. Platt, "*East India Company*," 555-556.

64. Platt, "*East India Company*," 554.

65. Platt, "*East India Company*," 576.

66. Suzanne Lebsock, *The Free Women of Petersburg: Status and Culture in a Southern Town*, 1784-1860 (New York: W.W. Norton & Company, 1984), 6.

67. Writers' Project of the Work Projects Administration, Virginia, *The Negro in Virginia*, 25

68. In that general atmosphere, the Quakers present a particular example. In reading histories of the period it appears that planters, mostly Anglican and Presbyterian, often freed their slaves and transferred responsibility for their upkeep to Quakers, who were known for successfully overseeing such communities or adopting and sponsoring free blacks.

69. Lebsock, *Free Women of Petersburg*, 7.

70. Louis B. Wright, ed. *The Letters of Robert "King" Carter, 1720,* 40- 42.

71. Lebsock, *Free Women of Petersburg*, 91.

72. This information has been collected from personal testimonies regarding family oral traditions. Some informants, such as Lisa. B. Lee, who is related to both Randolph and Lee African American family networks in Virginia, is well known in African American genealogical study circles, and has written her own book on the subject. Ms. Lee's family oral tradition traces Malagasy descent from an emancipated slave in Virginia who traveled to Nova Scotia and returned to Virginia only after several years' residence in Canada. The Ragsdale and Randolph references can be found in blogs on the discussion threads of those surname sites on ancestry.com.

73. Lebsock, *Free Women of Petersburg,* 91.

74. The cargo of the Prince Eugene, 1721 was predominantly women and children. *John Baylor's Account Books, 1721* (May-June).

75. Lesbock, *Free Women of Petersburg,* 102-103, 95.

76. Personal communication, Malagasy researcher Emmanuel Tehindrazanarivelo, September 2, 2001.

77. Dr. Robert Nicholls of Iowa State University has been interested in the contradiction of the two stories and continues to communicate

with the interviewee and myself. The above is an email communication from May 3, 2005.

78.   E-mail correspondence, April 20, 2005.

Chapter 9

Tracing Benguela Identity to the Homeland

Mariana P. Candido

In recent years, studies of the African diaspora have demonstrated that Africans contributed to the formation of societies in the "New World," challenging the idea that the brutality of the slave trade and the "Middle Passage" erased previous identities or made them difficult to remember.[1] Enslaved Africans found strategies to maintain themselves as a group inside colonial societies in the Americas. Classified as "nations," Africans created new social groups shaped by displacement and slavery that connected them to previous shared experiences in the homeland. Scholars have started to focus on the question of what was meant by African ethnicity for the groups of slaves classified into broad categories, such as Yoruba, Mina, Kongo, and others.[2] Some ethnicities or cohorts, such as those identified as "Benguela," have received less attention.[3] Benguela as an ethnonym in the African diaspora was popularized during the late eighteenth and early nineteenth centuries when the coastal town of Benguela in West Central Africa became more prominent as a slave trading port. In the Americas, people who left from this port were given the name of Benguela to indicate their place of provenience. This chapter examines the presence of Benguela slaves in Brazil in the eighteenth and nineteenth centuries, focusing in what Benguela might have meant in West Central Africa.

During the era of the transatlantic slave trade, at least 635,160 slaves left Benguela for the Americas. In a specific and relatively short period between 1790 and 1830, more than 240,000 people embarked upon slave ships at Benguela, representing a major demographic drain.[4] Due to the nature of trade winds and currents in the South Atlantic, as well as the fact that these were all Portuguese colonies, slaves embarked in Benguela mainly landed in Brazil, although in different ports. The average sailing time for ships traveling from Benguela to Rio de Janeiro was 50.8 days opposed to the 49.8 days it took from Luanda. The route from Benguela to Bahia took 41.7 days compared to the 49.8 days necessary to sail from Luanda to Rio de Janeiro.[5] Thus a more favorable Middle Passage travel time could have been one of the motivations for opening the trade route from Benguela. Another reason might have been the price of slaves, which was reported to be lower in Benguela than in Luanda, a factor that certainly increased profits for Atlantic merchants.[6]

Traders from Rio de Janeiro were the most active participants in the transatlantic slave trade from Benguela, which explain the strong Benguela presence in that southeast port town in Brazil.[7] Yet, Benguela slaves were also found in other ports and in the interior of Brazil. This chapter focuses on the African side of the broader diaspora in an attempt to problematize the understanding of African identities in the Americas. This study explores the existence of the ethnic identifier "Benguela" in West Central Africa, where many enslaved people faced displacement and endured the hardships of slavery. Even prior to entering the Middle Passage, frequent migrations and contacts between people of different cultural backgrounds accelerated changes leading to the emergence of new identities on the African continent. Thus, when in the Americas people coming from Benguela and its interior assumed a new identity, they probably were drawing on earlier shifts in how they perceived their ethnicity and community.

The populations in West Central Africa have a long history of migration and cultural change and adaptation,[8] and the transatlantic slave trade accelerated those changes, introducing new elements that forced people to relocate and negotiate their situation as outsiders. This chapter contributes to a better understanding of identity change in Africa, and stresses not only differences but also similarities in human experiences throughout the African diaspora. Scholars have often considered African ethnicities in the Americas as a port designation, rather than an ethnic identifier.[9] In some cases, historians have claimed that African ethnicities were a creation of European colonizers in the late nineteenth and early twentieth centuries.[10] In West Central Africa, as in other places in Africa, ethnicity was constantly being redefined and reshaped, especially since political, social, and cultural boundaries were not always fixed. Ethnicity involved the identification of social relationships through definitions of exclusion and inclusion for a great variety of purposes, and could relate to many other issues, including gender, age, and legal status. Ethnicity was also central to establishing who was inside or outside a given ethnic group, especially in the context of warfare or enslavement. Anyone who did not share the same language, religion, habits, and political affiliation could be considered "an outsider" and potentially a target for enslavement or death.[11] In this sense, ethnicity was shaped by the way people perceived their own identity, and how other people labelled them. Within this flexible characterization, ethnicity was susceptible to change according to the nature of interactions with neighbouring peoples and with variable situations such as warfare or environmental change that could lead to famine and migration.[12]

In this chapter, I argue that Benguela emerged as an ethnic identifier created during the transatlantic slave trade. Not only was it used to designate people exported through the port of Benguela, but it also became a term adopted by people in Benguela. Benguela identity emerged within parts of West Central Africa to specifically refer to the population of enslaved people living in and around Benguela. More research needs to be done to show the similarities and differences in the use of Benguela in West Central Africa and Brazil. Benguela in the African diaspora represented a very heterogeneous group of people from the interior of West Central Africa, which included subjects of the states and chiefdoms of Ndombe, Wambu, Mbailundu, and Nganguela among others. In Benguela, the term appears to be associated with slavery, since in most cases enslaved individuals were called Benguela. This chapter focuses on the presence of Benguelas in

185

Brazil and the emergence of the term in the port town of Benguela. Benguelas formed one of the largest groups of Africans headed to Brazil, and this study offers a rare glimpse into the debate over identities in West Central Africa. Africans brought to the diaspora not only language, religious practices, and cooking habits, but also understandings of how people organized their societies and maintained group cohesion. Certainly informed by previous experiences, Benguelas in Brazil shaped the way identities were transmitted to the New World.

Benguela and its Participation in the Transatlantic Slave Trade

In 1617, the Portuguese explorer Manoel Cerveira Pereira founded the port of Benguela, south of Luanda, which thereafter acquired importance in West Central Africa because of its valuable resources, including copper, ivory, and slaves.[13] The port became fundamental to the exportation of slaves from the heavily populated highlands located in the Benguela hinterland. Benguela was the fourth largest point of departure, after Luanda, Ouidah, and Bonny.[14] The majority of people embarking at Benguela, 67.2 percent, were male. West Central Africa also represented the largest percentage of children among the enslaved population, amounting to 55 percent. The population of children in Benguela itself was approximately 30 percent of the total.[15]

The number of people leaving Benguela was probably higher than has been estimated, considering that many slaves also went from Benguela to other intermediary African ports, such as Luanda. According to Francisco Inocêncio de Sousa Coutinho, governor of Angola (1764-1772), "everything that is good in Angola always comes from Benguela, especially slaves and ivory," a comment that suggests the importance of the trade between the two Portuguese ports in West Central Africa.[16] Until the early decades of the eighteenth century, trade between Benguela and the Americas was not direct, since ships were legally obliged to sail north to Luanda before leaving West Central Africa, in order to register their cargoes and pay duties.[17] Approximately one-third of the slaves shipped from Luanda came from the port town of Benguela, as a result of the lack of custom officials.[18] Consequently, some of the slaves shipped from Benguela across the Atlantic via Luanda might have been identified, when reaching the Americas, as Angola, rather than Benguela. The dispersion of people from Benguela and its interior from different ports makes it more difficult to locate them in the diaspora, since some of them might have stayed in Luanda or assumed new identifying labels in the Americas.

Benguela most likely became an important port due to wind and ocean currents. Ship captains struggled against the currents, pushing ships to sail north along the West Central African coast. Vessels coming from Portugal, Brazil, and Asia often reached Benguela first before sailing north to Luanda, Ambriz, or Loango. At Benguela, crews could re-supply water and food and also repair damaged ships.[19] Despite the difficulties, commerce between Benguela and Luanda was exclusively nautical due to the inability of the Portuguese to use overland routes through Kissama. Luanda-based traders could not travel overland to the highlands in the interior of Benguela because of the resistance of the people of Kissama who blocked the route and opposed Portuguese penetration.[20] Benguela was probably more appealing than other ports because it was far away from European authorities stationed in Luanda, favoring the emergence of a merchant community that was not willing to respect the law and pay taxes.[21]

In 1720s, the Portuguese Crown started authorizing the shipment of slaves from Benguela directly to the Americas, relaxing the requirement for tax collection in Luanda. The change in policy reflected an increase in the Brazilian demand for slaves, especially as a result of the mining boom in Minas Gerais, which required opening more direct routes to Brazil.[22] Decades later, the Portuguese state created the Companhia Geral do Grão Pará e Maranhão and Pernambuco e Paraíba, large trading companies that had a monopoly over the supply of African slaves and the export of minerals and agricultural products to Portugal. Although the Companhias monopolized trade, individuals could request licenses and send their ships to ports controlled by the Portuguese Crown.[23] The shipment of slaves from Benguela to Luanda continued until the late eighteenth and early nineteenth centuries, even though Benguela merchants were also exporting directly to Brazil.

Benguela Ethnicity in Brazil

It is not clear exactly when the first people from Benguela began arriving in Brazil, but by the late eighteenth centurythey were present in Bahia, Rio de Janeiro, Minas Gerais, and, in the far interior of the colony, in Chapada dos Guimarães, in Mato Grosso.[24] In the early eighteenth century an enslaved man in Bahia offered an interesting glimpse into the way Africans employed terms associated with ethnicity. Sometime before 1703, José Benguela was brought to Évora, in Portugal, to face trial. He lived in the parish of Nossa Senhora da Piedade in Bahia and was accused of sodomy in the Inquisition court. In front of the Inquisition judges he identified himself as a "black man, slave of João Carvalho de Barros, single, son of Manoel Luís and Maria; native of Benguela."[25] Thus, in a formal legal venue, José clearly identified himself as originally from Benguela. He, rather than his owner or other officials, claimed Benguela as his place of origin. This case is exceptional in the way that it records how an African man identified himself, as most colonial sources available in Brazil register how slaves were perceived by others.

The discovery of gold mines in Minas Gerais increased the demand for African slave laborand created new trade routes connecting the ports of Salvador and Rio de Janeiro to the interior of Brazil.[26] In Mariana, Minas Gerais, some people were also identified as Benguela by early eighteenth century. In 1723, out of the 1,526 slaves in the parish of Nossa Senhora do Carmo, 106 of them were Benguela.[27] More research is necessary to uncover the routes through which Benguela slaves arrived in the interior. Yet, as the Mariana case shows, the Benguela presence was not limited to the coast of Brazil. The commerce between Benguela and the Brazilian ports increased in the 1720s. By 1722, Rio de Janeiro traders sent a ship to acquire slaves in Benguela. On board, they sent 100 *pipas* (500 litre barrels) of *cachaça,* a distilled alcohol produced from sugar cane in sugar mills in Brazil.[28] A few years later, in 1725, António de Almeida e Souza, captain of the *curveta São Pedro and São Paulo*, asked for royal permission to sail to Benguela.[29] The demand for slave labor in Brazil combined with a growing market in Benguela that was able to provide slaves more cheaply than in the port of Luanda, and resulted in an increase in the number of license requests and slave ships sent to Benguela from Brazilian ports. In 1736, Teodósio da Silva, a trader based in Rio de Janeiro, requested authorization from the king of Portugal, D. João V, to travel to Benguela to buy slaves.[30] The presence of Benguela slaves in Brazil in the first half of the eighteenth century indicates the earlier importance of the Atlantic port, despite the fact that scholars have focused on the late eighteenth century as the period of Benguela's emergence in the Atlantic market.[31]

Parish records have been particularly useful in tracing Benguelas in Brazil and their social networks. In 1719, a woman identified as Benguela had her daughter baptized at Igreja da Sé, in Rio de Janeiro.[32] By baptizing her daughter, this Benguela womanensured that both of them were protected by a network of *irmandades* (brotherhoods) which provided services such as loans, legal counsel, and burial for the dead.[33] A proper burial was important for West Central Africans, Catholics or not, because it ensured that the dead would be remembered and would be able to enter the world of the ancestors.[34] For people from the Benguela highlands, funeral rites guaranteed the proper survival of the *utima*, the spirit, after death.[35] Thus, being a member of a brotherhood in Brazil was a way to participate in a larger community of people who protected each other, including providing funds to a proper Christian burial. Participation in irmandades inevitably meant adopting Catholicism, but the groups became an important form of social interaction among slaves in colonial Brazil. The Catholic Church was one of the few institutions where slaves could participate and be actively involved in a social and religious life. Mariza de Carvalho Soares has identified 397 slave burials in Rio de Janeiro between 1724 and 1736.[36] Out of the total only 20 were identified as Benguela. Eleven Benguelas were buried in the graveyard of the Candelária church, including Maria Benguela (1730), João Benguela (1731), and Pedro Benguela (1733), while 9, including Manoel Benguela (1730), were buried at the *Sé* Church.[37]

It is not clear if the slaves identified as Benguela in Bahia and Rio de Janeiro by the early decades of the eighteenth century had been deported from the port of Benguela or Luanda. It is clear that the identification of the port town as a place of origin was becoming common, as in the case of José Benguela in Bahia. At the same time, the Benguelas in Rio de Janeiro were establishing new social networks through the Catholic Church. Despite being baptized, very few Benguelas (20 out of 397 slave burials) found ways to access a Catholic burial. Few burial registers indicate the difficulties and challenges for social ascension and organization, especially when compared to other African groups, such as Minas.[38] Yet, the continuous arrival of more people identified as Benguela throughout the eighteenth century might have resulted in the increase and re-Africanization of the Benguela population in Rio. The contact of new Benguela arrivals with established slaves of the same origin reinforced links on both sides of the Atlantic. New arrivals would have not only brought over their cultural traditions, and they could have also relayed news from their homelands. Despite the dire circumstances, people could maintain social and cultural links with their communities.[39]

Several scholars have identified Benguelas in Brazil, but what made them different from people classified as Kongo or Angola is not clear. Researchers focusing on slavery in Brazil have emphasized the idea of a culturally homogeneous West Central Africa.[40] Robert Slenes, for example, has advocated for a common cultural heritage whereby members of West Central African groups realized their cultural homogeneity during the Middle Passage and early experiences in Brazil.[41] However, most Africanists tend to emphasize diversity among people from West Central Africa. According to Miller,

> slaves sent to Rio through both Benguela and Luanda in the period after the gold boom thus would have included people from many parts of the forest fringes north of the developing Ruund confederations of warrior chiefs, as well as Kikongo-speakers, Ngangela, and growing numbers of ancestors to the trans-Kwango farmers known a century later as Cokwe, all in significant proportions that diluted the early coherent generations of Umbundu-speakers in southern Brazil.[42]

Although it is evident that the Benguela identity underwent many transformations over time, very little is known about how that identity was created and how it changed. What did Benguela mean to a freed man, such as Francisco Benguela, living in Rio de Janeiro in the 1790s?[43] How was his Benguela identity perceived by other groups, such as someone classified as Mina or Kongo? Did being Benguela mean the same thing to Feliciana Benguela, a slave woman who bought her manumission on June 11, 1817, from her owner Manoel Teixeira de Coelho?[44] Or did it mean something completely different for Bibiana Benguela, a young woman emancipated in Rio de Janeiro in 1834 after the slave schooner *Duquesa de Bragança* was apprehended by the Mixed Commission in Brazilian waters?[45] Certainly neither was enslaved at the same moment in time and probably neither even came from the same location in or around Benguela. Nor were their experiences in Brazil similar. Yet, in the diaspora they were lumped together as members of the same "nation."

The classification into "nations" assumed that African identities were the same just because they embarked at the same port, although is not clear how the Middle Passage brought different groups together, shaping new identities during the crossing. The instability and conflict provoked by the constant search for captives led to rivalries among different groups in the interior of Benguela. Subjects of the states of Mbailundu, Sokoval, and Kakonda raided each other on different occasions, and might have ended up enslaved as captives of war on board of a slave ship.[46] Were the disputes and differences irreconcilable, provoking animosity in Brazil? It is not clear how war and political conflicts affected the way people identified themselves in Africa or in the diaspora. An understanding of African identities in the Americas is only possible if we understand the circumstances in which people were enslaved and how they identified themselves prior to being exported from Africa. Understanding their identity in their place of origin the cultural baggage the so-called Benguelas brought to Rio.

Benguelas in West Central Africa

The historiography of African ethnicities in the Americas has expanded dramatically in recent decades. While some scholars claimed that such identities were New World creations that did not represent previous experience, others explored the connections between places of origins and identities assumed in the diaspora. Carlos Eugênio Soares, for example, claims that African ethnicities in Brazil were "transatlantic slave trade designations, which indicates places and ports of trade rather than people or specific groups."[47] Yet, in Benguela slave owners and Portuguese officials made use of the same terms they used in the Americas to refer to the enslaved population. Slaves were identified by their Catholic name and their place of provenance, which was sometimes in the interior. In the case of locally-born slaves, they were identified as Benguela, exactly like in the Americas. Thus, the transatlantic slave trade and its agents ended up creating new identities in Africa directly associated with the Atlantic world and in some cases, people arrived in Brazil with a Benguela identity constructed in the African coast.

There are few records available that reveal how Africans identified themselves before the twentieth century. The earliest reference that I was able to locate to the term Benguela being used to designate a group of people is from 1718. In that document, Captain Domingos Madeira Velho referred to the "Benguela Blacks and their subjects," when mentioning the people who lived in the coastal town.[48] Several decades later, in 1797, Paulo Pinheiro de Lacerda, a colonial officer, traveled from the port of Benguela to the state of Mbailundu, in the highlands, and wrote a report describing the people he met. He emphasized the multiplicity of people he saw, referring to them by their political affiliation, naming the rulers and the way people called themselves and were called by others ("*como se chamam*").[49] He referred to the people who lived around Benguela as Ndombe (Mundombe in the sources). Ndombe lived in and around the port of Benguela and have been described by the seventeenth-century observer António Cadornega as "the most faithful heathen group in the province [of Benguela]," since they were allies to the Portuguese colonial state from an early date.[50] Besides the Ndombe, Lacerda reported visiting the lands of the rulers of Kilomata, Lombimbe, and Sokoval, and all claimed to be Kilengues (Moquilengues according to Lacerda's account), implying a common identity despite being affiliated with different political unities. Interestingly, he reported that, "Benguelas make use of firearms in their conflicts," noting that some people identified themselves as Benguela by the end of the eighteenth century, although he does not clearly identifying who those people were (See Map 9.1).[51]

MAP 9.1 | BENGUELA'S HINTERLAND

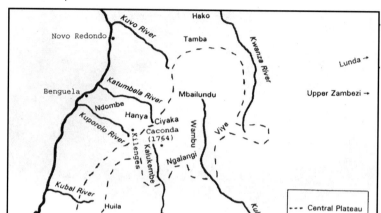

Source: José C. Curto, *Álcool e Escravos. O Comércio Luso-Brasileiro do álcool em Mpinda, Luanda e Benguela durante o Tráfico Atlântico de Escravos (c. 1480-1830) e o seu Impacto nas Sociedades da África Central Ocidental* (Lisbon: Vulgata, 2002), 267.

It is not clear if Lacerda labeled some people as Benguela or if a certain group claimed to be Benguela. In these instances, the term Benguela, usually associated with an African ethnicity created in the Americas, was used to describe people living in West Central Africa.

As in Brazil, official and parish records offer an opportunity to analyze how people were identified by others. In 1790, for example, the Portuguese trader Francisco Dias used the designation Benguela to refer to his slaves. In his will, written a week before his death on August 30, 1790, he identified four of his slaves, Ana, Josefa, Joaquina, and Francisca as Benguela.[52] Dias used a term familiar to specialists of slavery in the Americas.

The use of Benguela as an ethnonym to indicate origin demonstrates the effect of the transatlantic slave trade on the way people organized and identified themselves, leading to a new identity as Benguela, within Africa. In contrast to Africans who lived outside outside Portuguese controlled areas, local slaves were identified by the label Benguela. Like Portuguese and Brazilian residents who had surnames, locally born slaves had a first named followed by Benguela. In 1849, a murder report emphasized the concept of Benguela as an identifier in West Central Africa. João Benguela, a slave, murdered a slave woman, Madalena.[53] As in the Americas, the first name, João, was followed by a place of provenance, Benguela.[54]

Another interesting set of sources that address identification as Benguela, as well as the multiplicity of identifiers in the interior, are slave inventories. Slave inventories started to be compiled in 1845 and 1847 to gather information on the slave population.[55] According to a decree of December 14, 1854, slave owners had to register their slaves within thirty days, and slave owners who did not register their slaves had to free them.[56] One surviving slave register for Benguela in 1859 lists 2,588 slaves.[57] This source is extremely valuable for an understanding of the slave population and identity in Benguela by the 1850s.

The register indicates the heterogeneity of the slave population in Benguela. People were identified by place of origin, usually based on affiliation to a political entity or specific territorial space. Many slaves were from the different polities of the central plateau, which probably indicates the market and region they came from, not necessarily the place they were born or lived before capture. The register carefully recorded the name, age, place of provenance, and physical characteristics that could be used to identify each slave. The document also listed the name of the owner and any special skills slaves had, such as blacksmith, shoemaker, or hairdresser. In 1859, 1,790 slaves, or 69 percent of the slave population of Benguela, were identified as coming from the highlands, from such places as Viye, Kitata, Kiaka, Mbailundu, and Caconda (See Table 9.1).

The presence of slaves from Viye in Benguela was related to the position of that state as one of the main slave markets in the region since the late eighteenth century. In 1800, the market of Viye attracted colonial officials, such as the Portuguese Manoel do Nascimento and the Luso-Africans Manoel Mendes and Caetano Simões, who had deserted the colonial army to act as merchants based in Viye bringing slave coffles to Benguela.[58] The French traveler Jean-Baptiste Douville reported in the late 1820s "the number of captives sold in the market of Viye is around 6,000 yearly; with the proportion of three women to every two men…. the slaves are then sent to Angola and Benguela."[59] The presence of slaves coming from Viye in the 1850s indicates the continuity of this market and the importance and ability of the state and ruling elites to maintain control over slave trade.

TABLE 9.1 | ETHNICITY OF THE SLAVE POPULATION IN BENGUELA, 1859

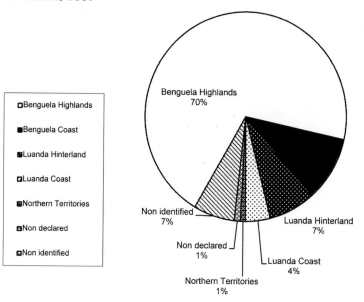

Source: AHNA, Cod 3160, "Benguela, Registro de Escravos, 1859."

Some slaves (10 percent) came from regions near the coast, such as those identified as Egito, Novo Redondo, and Catumbela (See Map 9.1). All coastal-origin slaves accounted for 266 individuals. Curiously, half of the slaves originally from regions close to the coast were identified as Benguela, born in the Portuguese port town. Those people lived in areas under Portuguese control, and probably shared some cultural affinities after years and decades in the same location. This history may have been reflected in their knowledge of some Portuguese, their adherence to Christianity, nominally or not, and their training in specialized skills, such as shoe-making or masonry. Enslaved in a Portuguese colonial town, those slaves probably were integrated in a Lusophone culture and had built a repertoire of knowledge to ensure their survival under slavery. Some slaves constructed social networks in Benguela, perhaps as a way to prevent their sale and deportation to the Americas. In 1797, Floriana Rosa and Vitoriano, both slaves in Benguela, baptized their daughter Lauriana. The family belonged to the highest authority in town, the Governor Alexandre José Botelho de Vasconcelos. To ensure their safety, they named Dona Margarida Botelho de Vasconcelos, wife of the governor, as the godmother of their daughter.[60] Legislation enacted in 1697 stated that local slaves who were sold to transatlantic slave traders and sent to Brazil had to be accompanied by their wives in order to keep families together, even if the wife was a free person.[61] Slaves like Floriana and Vitorino knew Portuguese and probably frequented the local Catholic Church, the *Nossa Senhora do Pópulo*. Living in Benguela they were in close contact with Atlantic traders and were exposed to news coming from Brazil and Portugal. They had knowledge of the colonial language and legislation and recognized the threat that slavery in Brazil represented to them. In the 1830s, several *"crioulos* of Benguela" and *"crioulos"* who were locally-born slaves, arrived in Rio de Janeiro, indicating that these were people born in Portuguese colonial settlements and were to a certain degree acculturated to the Lusophone world.[62]

The slave registers also indicated the presence of slaves from the interior of Luanda, including 196 slaves identified with Ambaca, Golungo, and Cassange, who accounted to 7.5 percent of the slaves. Another 104 individuals, or 4 percent of the slave population, came from the Luanda coast, where they were also exposed to Portuguese culture and language.[63] A small number, 22 individuals or less than 1 percent, came from further north, including those from Ambriz, Kongo, and Cabinda. The places of origin of another 34 people (1 percent) are unknown, and a further 6.5 percent are from places that have not been identified.

The concentration of people from different backgrounds in Benguela unified people from different polities and allowed the amalgamation of identities into something new. The area surrounding Benguela absorbed a large component of this mixed population, who were assimilated into the colonial society, assuming a new name, using a new language, and reconstructing social networks. Or as Pier Larson stresses

> Those who remained behind frequently reconstructed kinship relationships, moved their places of residence, and shifted social organization and cultural practices, creating an internal dispersion comparable in many respects to the experiences of the enslaved in exile from their homes.[64]

Ethnic reconfiguration began in Africa before continuing to do so in the Americas. The Portuguese explorers Hermenegildo Capelo and Roberto Ivens commented on the various groups of people living in Benguela in the 1870s. These included Ndombe, Mbailundu, Viye, and Nganguela, similar to the groups identified in the end of the eighteenth century and into the first half of the nineteenth century, who are also to be identified with people later known as Ovimbundu, although that collective designation was apparently not used at that time.[65]

Moreover, the fact that by the mid-nineteenth century slaves identified themselves or were identified by others as Benguela raises questions of identity and ethnicity in Africa, as well as in the diaspora. It shows ethnic fluidity, stressing how certain ethnicities constructed in the New World could also travel back to Africa.[66] The emergence of a Benguela ethnicity within Africa is clearly associated with the transatlantic slave trade, since by the mid-nineteenth century, only slaves were identified as Benguela. As Terence Ranger commented, "ethnicity was more a matter of role than of origin."[67] And in the cases studied in the diaspora, Benguela identity was associated with bondage. However, it is not clear how this identity developed and changed over time. The existence of a Benguela identity in Africa demonstrates that some of the African "nations" recognized in the Americas were not simply the designation of a port of origin, but perhaps reflected an African creation. Africans, within the continent or in the diaspora, were constantly reshaping their identities to preserve their link with the motherland.[68]

Conclusion

The case of Benguela demonstrates the existence of an identity that did not pre-exist the slave trade, but emerged in Africa. Differentiation among people already existed in Africa, based mainly on linguistic groups and political affiliation. Thus, when people were forcibly sent to the Americas, they already carried with them their identity, that inevitably had to adjust to the realities they faced under enslavement. The displacement, however, was not restricted to the Americas. Africans were also enslaved in Benguela, and as people forcibly displaced, they also adjusted their identity and they way they saw themselves and were seen by others.

The slaves who were settled in Benguela, as well as those who were sent to the Americas, came from a wide range of different places. By the mid-nineteenth century, the slave population in Benguela was ethnically diverse, providing the town with a multiplicity of languages, habits, and behaviors. The fact that large contingents of Benguela slaves came from different regions problematizes questions of identity. Similar to the experience in the Americas, the constant influx of individuals of different ethnicities led to continuous cultural exchanges which shaped the ways in which people identified themselves and others. Slaves transformed their identity prior to their arrival in Benguela into something new, shaping a new identity associated with slavery in a small Atlantic port. In Benguela and its interior, people identified according to the territories of the different states and rulers, but in the context of the slave trade, people who lived in the highlands began to develop some consciousness of a common identity. However, even though people came from different political and territorial units, such as Ngalange, Viye, Mbailundu, and Wambu, they shared cultural affinities. Political fragmentation did not result in isolation. Rather, people who were enslaved had to interact with each other day after day, and through these contacts they came to recognize many common aspects of language and culture. The existence of the term Benguela as ethnic designation in Brazil, and also to a lesser extent in southern Angola, problematizes how African identities evolved and were perceived not only in Africa but also in the Americas. More than a New World creation, these African identities were products of the Atlantic economy that forced internal migration and shifted the ways people recognized each other. Groups of people became Benguela in Brazil through the amalgamation of different people exported through the port of Benguela, which also involved interaction with Luso-Africans. Hence, in Brazil, as Heywood has observed, "enslaved Africans coming from far in the interior would bring not only the culture of their respective African ethnic groups, but also various elements of the Afro-Lusitan culture."[69] People adhered to new identities to escape or survive enslavement in West Central Africa and in the diaspora.

Notes

1. Sidney W. Mintz and Richard Price, *The Birth of African American Culture: An Anthropological Perspective* (Boston: Beacon Press, 1992). The scholarship on the African presence in and contribution to the Americas is vast. See, among others, Pierre Verger, *Fluxo e Refluxo do Tráfico de Escravos entre o Golfo do Benin e a Bahia de Todos os Santos, dos séculos XVII a XIX* (São Paulo: Corrupio, 1987); Colin A. Palmer, "From Africa to the Americas: Ethnicity in the Early Black Communities of the Americas," *Journal of World History* 6, no. 2 (1995), 223-236; Paul E. Lovejoy and David V. Trotman, ed. *Trans-Atlantic Dimensions of Ethnicity in the African Diaspora* (London: Continuum, 2003); Gwendolyn Midlo Hall, *Slavery and African Ethnicities in the Americas* (Chapel Hill: University of North Carolina Press, 2005); Maureen Warner-Lewis, *Central Africa in the Caribbean. Transcending Time, Transforming Culture* (Kingston: University of West Indies Press, 2003); João José Reis, *Slave Rebellion in Brazil: The Muslim Uprising of 1835 in Bahia* (Baltimore: Johns Hopkins University Press, 1993); Mariza de Carvalho Soares, ed. *Rotas Atlânticas da Diáspora Africana: da Baía do Benim ao Rio de Janeiro* (Niterói: Editora da Universidade Federal Fluminense, 2007).

2. See Mariza C. Soares, "A 'Nação' que se tem e a 'Terra' de onde se vem: Categorias de Inserção Social de Africanos no Império Português, século XVIII," *Estudos Afro-Asiáticos* 26, no. 2 (2004), 303-330; Robin Law, "Ethnicity and the Slave Trade: Lucumi and Nago as Ethnonyms in West Africa," *History in Africa* 24 (1997), 205-219; Douglas Chambers, "'My Own Nation': Egbo Exiles in the Diaspora" in *Routes to Slavery: Direction, Ethnicity and Mortality in the Atlantic Slave Trade*, ed. David Eltis and David Richardson (New York: Routledge, 1997); and the chapters in Toyin Falola and Matt D. Childs, ed. *The Yoruba Diaspora in the Atlantic World* (Bloomington: Indiana University Press, 2004). For more on the idea of African nations, see among others, Soares, "A 'Nação' que se tem," 303-330; and John Thornton, *Africa and Africans in the Making of the Atlantic World* (New York: Cambridge University Press, 1992), 195-205.

3. There are very few studies on the Benguelas in Brazil. See Silvia Brugger and Anderson de Oliveira, "Os Benguelas de São João del Rei: Tráfico Atlântico, Religiosidade e Identidades Étnicas (séculos XVIII e XIX)," *Tempo* 13, no. 26 (2009), 177-204. The work of the archeologist Luís Cláudio Pereira Symanski also provides information on the contribution to the material culture of people identified as Benguela in Mato Grosso, Brazil. See his "Slaves and Planters in Western Brazil: Material Culture, Identity and Power" (PhD diss., University of Florida, 2006).

4. *The Transatlantic Slave Trade Database : Voyages*, http://www.slavevoyages.org, shows 354,115 slaves leaving the port of Benguela between 1700 and 1850. Scholars agree that this number is a minimum, restricted to the sources available. Based on calculations of missing voyages and incomplete data, the editors of the *The Transatlantic Slave Trade Database* estimated the number of slaves embarked in Benguela to be around 635,160 people. See David Eltis and David Richardson, "A New Assessment of the Transatlantic Slave Trade," in *Extending the Frontiers: Essays on the New Transatlantic Slave Trade Database,* ed. David Eltis and David Richardson (New Haven: Yale University Press, 2008), 1-60; and Daniel B. Domingues da Silva, "The Coastal Origins of Slaves Leaving Angola, from the 18th to the 19th Century" (Paper presented at the 124th Annual Meeting of the American Historical Association, San Diego, CA, January 2010).

5. *The Transatlantic Slave Trade Database : Voyages*, http://www.slavevoyages.org based on 13 voyages from Benguela and 124

voyages between Luanda and Bahian ports. The length of the Middle Passage between Luanda and Rio de Janeiro is based on 126 voyages and 90 voyages that recorded the number of days it took to sail from Benguela to Rio de Janeiro ports.

6. AHU, Angola, cx. 24, doc. 36, April 17, 1728; and AHU, Angola, cx. 27, doc. 159, December 22, 1734. On better prices for Benguela slaves, see David Birmingham, *Trade and Conflict in Angola* (Oxford: Oxford University Press, 1966), 140-1; and Joseph C. Miller, *Way of Death: Merchant Capitalism and the Angolan Slave Trade, 1730-1830* (Madison: University of Wisconsin Press, 1988), 222–225.

7. Joseph C. Miller, "Legal Portuguese Slaving from Angola. Some Preliminary Indications of Volume and Direction," *Revue Française d'Histoire d'Outre Mer* 62, no. 1-2 (1975), 150-152; Manolo Florentino, *Em Costas Negras. Uma Historia do Trafico de escravos entre a Africa e o Rio de Janeiro* (São Paulo: Companhia das Letras, 1997); José C. Curto, "Movers of Slaves: The Brazilian Community in Benguela (Angola), c. 1722-1832," Unpublished paper presented at the International Symposium "Angola on the Move: Transport Routes, Communications, and History," Berlin, November 2003.

8. Jan Vansina, *How Societies Are Born: Governance in West Central Africa before 1600* (Charlottesville: University of Virginia Press, 2005); Jan Vansina, *Kingdoms of the Savanna* (Madison: University of Wisconsin Press, 1966).

9. Mary Karasch, "Minha Nação': Identidades Escravas no Fim do Brasil Colonial," in *Brasil. Colonização e Escravidão,* ed. Maria Beatriz Nizza da Silva (Rio de Janeiro: Nova Fronteira, 1999), 129; Carlos Eugênio Líbano Soares, *A Capoeira Escrava e Outras Tradições Rebeldes no Rio de Janeiro (1808-1850)* (Campinas: Editora da Unicamp, 2001), 75.

10. Leroy Vail, ed. *The Creation of Tribalism in Southern Africa* (Berkeley: University of California Press, 1989); and Terence Ranger, *The Invention of Tribalism in Zimbabwe* (Gwelo: Mambo Press, 1985).

11. See John Comaroff and Jean Comaroff, *Ethnography and the Historical Imagination* (Boulder: Westview Press, 1992), especially chapter 2; and Frederik Barth, *Los Grupos Étnicos y sus Fronteras* (Mexico: Fondo de Cultura Economica, 1976), 19-22; 36; Mariana P. Candido, *Fronteras de Esclavización: Esclavitud, Comercio*

e Identidad en Benguela, 1780-1850 (Mexico City: Colegio de Mexico Press, 2011), 162-170.

12. Paul E. Lovejoy, "The African Diaspora: Revisionist Interpretations of Ethnicity, Culture and Religion under Slavery," *Studies in the World History of Slavery, Abolition and Emancipation* 2, no.1 (1997), 1-23; and Robin Law, "Etnias dos Africanos na Diáspora: Novas Considerações sobre os Significados do termo 'Mina,'" *Tempo* 10, no. 20 (2006), 109-131.

13. Ralph Delgado, *O Reino de Benguela (do Descobrimento à Criação do Governo Subalterno)* (Lisbon: Imprensa Beleza, 1945), 38-63.

14. David Eltis, Paul E. Lovejoy and David Richardson, "Slave-Trading Ports: Towards an Atlantic-Wide Perspective," in *Ports of the Slave Trade (Bights of Benin and Biafra)*, ed. Robin Law and Silke Strickrodt (Stirling: Centre of Commonwealth Studies, University of Stirling, 1999), 22.

15. David Eltis and Stanley L. Engerman, "Was the Slave Trade Dominated by Men?" *Journal of Interdisciplinary History* 23, no. 2 (1992), 252. See also, Joseph C. Miller, "Central Africans during the Era of the Slave Trade, c. 1490s-1850s," in *Central Africans and Cultural Transformations in the American Diaspora*, ed. Linda Heywood (New York: Cambridge University Press, 2001), 60; and *The Trans-Atlantic Slave Trade Database*, http://www.slavevoyages.org.

16. "Instruções para o Novo Governador de Benguela (1773)," *Textos para a História da África Austral (Século XVIII)* (Lisbon: Publicações Alfa, 1989), 46.

17. AHU (hereinafter AHU), Angola, caixa (cx.) 22, documento (doc.) 58, January 25, 1725; AHU, Angola, cx. 69, doc. 17. July 28, 1784. AHU, Angola, cx. 69, doc. 55, December 16, 1784. AHU, Angola, Cod. 555, fl. 52v-58, January 25, 1758; Roquinaldo Amaral Ferreira, "Transforming Atlantic Slaving: Trade, Warfare and Territorial Control in Angola, 1650-1800" (PhD diss., University of California, Los Angeles, 2003), 79-80; and Miller, "Central Africa during the Era of the Slave Trade," 49.

18. AHU, Angola, cx. 86, doc. 5, July 22, 1797. See also Ferreira, "Transforming Atlantic Slaving," 85.

19. Frédéric Mauro, *Portugal, o Brasil e o Atlântico* (Lisbon: Estampa, 1997), 48-49; and Ferreira, "Transforming Atlantic Slaving," 75-77.

20. Birmingham, *Trade and Conflict in Angola*, 140; Beatrix Heintze, "Historical Notes on the Kisama of Angola," *Journal of African History* 13, no. 3 (1972), 417-18.

21. AHU, Angola Cx. 60, doc. 22. January 26, 1775; AHU, Angola cx. 70, doc. 12. May 4, 1785; AHU, Cod. 542 fl 77v., December 23, 1825; and Ferreira, "Transforming Atlantic Slaving," 70-103. The fifth governor of Benguela, José Botelho de Vasconcelos, finally was provided with a regiment to rule Benguela. AHU, Angola, cx 93-A, doc. 11, November 6, 1799; Carlos Couto, *Os Capitães-Mores em Angola no Século XVIII* (Luanda: Instituto de Investigação Científica Tropical, 1972); Carlos Couto, "Regimento de Governo Subalterno de Benguela," *Studia* 45 (1981), 284-294.

22. AHU, Códice (Cod.) 546, folio (fl.) 2v., December 2, 1725; and fl. 3, January 21, 1726. For more on the Brazilian demand see Charles R. Boxer, *O Império Marítimo Português* (Rio de Janeiro: Nova Fronteira, 2002), 167-173; Laura de Mello e Sousa, *Desclassificados do Ouro. A Pobreza Mineira no Século XVIII* (Rio de Janeiro: Graal, 1985).

23. António Carreira, *As Companhias Pombalinas de Grão Pará e Maranhão e Pernambuco e Paraíba* (Lisbon: Presença, 1983).

24. Lucilene Reginaldo, "Os Rosários dos Angolas: Irmandades Negras, Experiências Escravas e Identidades Africanas na Bahia Setencentista" (PhD diss., Universidade Estadual de Campinas, 2005); Eduardo França Paiva, *Escravidão e Universo Cultural na Colônia, Minas Gerais, 1716–1789* (Belo Horizonte: : Editora da Universidade de Minas Gerais, 2001); Marcos André Torres de Souza Souza and Luís Cláudio Pereira Symanski, "Slave Communities and Pottery Viability in Western Brazil: The Plantatios of Chapada dos Guimarães," *International Journal of Historical Archaeology* 13 (2009), 525-26.

25. Arquivo Nacional da Torre do Tombo (hereafter ANTT), Tribunal do Santo Ofício, Inquisição de Lisboa, Process 6478, December 6, 1703.

26. Stuart B. Schwartz, "The Economy of the Portuguese Empire," in *Portuguese Oceanic Expansion, 1400-1800*, ed. Francisco Bethencourt and Diogo Ramada Curto (New York: Cambridge University Press, 2007), 35. See also Charles Boxer, *A Idade de Ouro do Brasil: Dores de Crescimento de uma Sociedade Colonial* (Rio de Janeiro: Nova Fronteira, 2000), 61; Higgins indicated that 1735-1750 were the years of the gold mining boom in Sabará. Kathleen

J. Higgins, *Licentious Liberty in a Brazilian Gold-Mining Region* (University Park: Pennsylvania State University Press, 1999), 26.

27. Arquivo da Câmara Municipal de Mariana (ACMM), Impostos, Taxas e Multas, Lançamento dos Reais Quintos – 1723, Códice 166. I would like to thank Samila Xavier de Queiroz who has helped me collect the data.

28. José C. Curto, "Luso-Brazilian Alcohol and the Slave Trade at Benguela and its Hinterland, c. 1617-1830," in *Négoce Blanc en Afrique Noire: L'évolution du commerce à longue distance en Afrique noire du 18ᵉ au 20ᵉ siècles,* ed. H. Bonin and M. Cahen (Paris: Publications de la Société française d'histoire d'outre-mer, 2001), 356.

29. AHU, Angola, cx. 22, doc. 58, January 25, 1725.

30. AHU, Conselho Ultramarino, Rio de Janeiro, cx. 32, doc. 106, December 17, 1736.

31. José C. Curto, "Legal Portuguese Slave Trade from Benguela, Angola, 1730-1828: A Quantitative Re-appraisal," *África* 17, no 1 (1993/1994)," 113-115; Birmingham, *Trade and Conflict in Angola,* 154-155; Herbert Klein, "The Portuguese Slave Trade from Angola in the XVIII century," *Journal of Economic History* 32, no. 4 (1972), 894-918; and Miller, "Legal Portuguese Slaving," 152.

32. Arquivo da Cúria Metropolitana do Rio de Janeiro (hereafter ACMRJ), Livro de Batismo da Freguesia da Sé, Assento 44, 1SeBES. I would like to thank Mariza de Carvalho Soares for generously sharing her database of slave baptisms with me.

33. Patricia Mulvey, "Slave Confraternities in Brazil: Their Role in Colonial Society," *The Americas* 39, no. 1 (1982), 39-40.

34. James H. Sweet, *Recreating Africa. Culture, Kinship, and Religion in the African-Portuguese World* (Chapel Hill: University of North Carolina Press, 2003), 176; João José Reis, *Death is a Festival. Funeral Rites and Rebellion in 19ᵗʰ Century Brazil* (Chapel Hill: University of North Carolina Press, 2003), 159-61.

35. Wilfrid Hambly, "The Ovimbundu of Angola." *Field Museum of Natural History, Anthropological Series* 21, no. 2 (1934), 264-68.

36. Mariza de Carvalho Soares, *Devotos da Cor: Identidade Étnica, Religiosidade e Escravidão no Rio de Janeiro, Século XVIII* (Rio de Janeiro: Civilização Brasileira, 2000), 147.

37. ACMRJ, Livro de Óbitos de Escravos. Freguesia da Candelária, 1724-1736.

38. See Mariza de Carvalho Soares, "A Biografia de Ignácio Monte, o Escravo que virou Rei," in *Retratos do Império. Trajetórias Individuais no Mundo Português nos séculos XVI a XIX,* ed. Ronaldo Vainfas (Niterói: Editora da Universidade Federal Fluminense, 2006), 47-68; Mariza de Carvalho Soares, "Can Women Guide and Govern Men? Gendering Politics among African Catholics in Colonial Brazil," *Women and Slavery. Volume II, Americas,* ed. Gwyn Campbell, Suzanne Miers, and Joseph C. Miller (Athens: Ohio University Press, 2007), 79-99; and Manolo Florentino, "Alforrias e Etnicidade no Rio de Janeiro Oitocentista: Notas de Pesquisa," *Topoi* 5 (2002), 9-40.

39. Thornton, *Africa and Africans,* 320.

40. Mary C. Karasch, *Slave Life in Rio de Janeiro, 1808-1850* (Princeton: Princeton University Press, 1987); Michael Gomez, *Reversing Sail. A History of the African Diaspora* (New York: Cambridge University Press, 2005), 65.

41. Robert Slenes, *Malungu, Ngoma vem! Africa encoberta e descoberta no Brasil* (Luanda: Ministerio da Cultura, 1995); and Slenes, *Na Senzala, uma Flor. Esperanças e Recordações na Formação da Família Escrava. Brasil Sudeste, século XIX* (Rio de Janeiro: Nova Fronteira, 1999).

42. Miller, "Central Africa During the era of the Slave Trade," 55.

43. Florentino, "Alforrias e Etnicidades," 9-40.

44. Arquivo Nacional do Rio de Janeiro (hereinafter ANRJ), 1 oficio de notas, Livro (L.) 216, fl 52v-53.

45. ANRJ, Cod. 184 v.3 Escravos Emancipados, Escuna Duquesa de Braganca.

46. For conflicts in the interior of Benguela among different states see Candido, *Fronteras de Esclavización,* 157-205.

47. Soares, *A Capoeira Escrava,* 75. See also Mintz and Price, *Birth of African American Culture.* For a different approach that emphasizes similarities rather than ruptures, see Sweet, *Recreating Africa;* Soares, "A 'Nação' que se Tem," 303-330; and, among others, Linda M. Heywood and John K. Thornton, *Central Africans, Atlantic Creoles, and the Making of the Foundation of the Americas, 1585-1660* (New York: Cambridge University Press, 2007).

48. Ana Paula Tavares and Catarina Madeira Santos, *Africae Monumenta. A Apropriação da Escrita pelos Africanos* (Lisbon: IICT, 2002), 53.

49. Biblioteca Nacional do Rio de Janeiro (hereinafter BNRJ), doc. I-28, 28, 29 "Notícias da Cidade de São Paulo de Benguela e costumes dos gentios habitantes naquele sertão." I am grateful to Roquinaldo Ferreira who shared his transcription of the manuscript with me.

50. António de Oliveira de Cadornega, *História Geral das Guerras Angolanas* (Lisbon: Agência Geral do Ultramar, 1972), vol. 3, 172.

51. BNRJ, I-28, 28, 29,

52. ANTT, FF, JU, Africa, mc 19, n. 13, August 30, 1790.

53. Arquivo Histórico Nacional de Angola (hereafter AHNA), Cod. 461, fl. 91, January 20, 1849.

54. Silvia Hunold Lara, "Linguagem, domínio senhorial e identidade étnica nas Minas Gerais em meados do Século XVIII," in *Trânsitos Coloniais: Diálogos Críticos Luso-Brasileiros*, ed. Cristiana Bastos, Miguel Vale de Almeida e Bela Feldman-Bianco (Lisbon: Imprensa de Ciências Sociais, 2002), 211-12; see also Soares, "A 'Nação' que se Tem," 303-330.

55. See AHNA, Cod, 444, fl., 185v-186, April 5, 1849.

56. Museu Nacional da Escravatura, *A Abolição da Escravatura*, 35-36. AHNA, Cod. 461, fl. 122v., March 19, 1850; and AHNA, Cod. 510, fl. 116v. December 7, 1848.

57. AHNA, Cod. 3160, "Registro de Escravos (Benguela)," 1859.

58. AHNA, Cod. 443, fl. 56, October 18, 1800; AHNA, Cod. 443, fl. 70, March 7, 1801. For the trade route connections, see José Joaquim Lopes de Lima, *Ensaios sobre a statistica d'Angola e Benguella e suas dependencies na costa Occidental d'Africa ao sul do Equador* (Lisbon: Imprensa Nacional, 1844), 17; and Francisco José de Lacerda e Almeida et al., *Lacerda's Journey to Cazembe in 1798* (London: John Murray, 1873), 24. See also Ralph Delgado, *Ao Sul do Cuanza Ocupação e Aproveitamento do Antigo Reino de Benguela* (Lisbon: Beleza, 1944), 1, 339.

59. Jean-Baptiste Douville, *Voyage au Congo et dans l'intérieur de l'Afrique Equinoxiale* (Paris: Chez Jules Renouard, 1832), 2, 145-46.

60. Arquivo do Arçobispado de Luanda (hereinafter AAL), Benguela, Livro de Batismo, 1794-1814, fl. 81-81v, December 30, 1797.

61. In the case of a free wife, according to the legislation, her freedom had to be preserved. See AHU, 101, doc. 38, August 21, 1801.

62. Arquivo Nacional do Rio de Janeiro (hereinafter ANRJ), Cod. 184, volume 3. Escravos Emancipados. See also Luciano Raposo, *Marcas de Escravos. Listas de escravos emancipados vindos a bordo de navios negreiros* (1839-1841) (Rio de Janeiro: Arquivo Nacional, 1990)

63. Beatrix Heintze, "A Lusofonia no Interior da África Central na era pré-Colonial. Um Contributo para a sua História e Compreensão na Actualidade," *Cadernos de Estudos Africanos* 6/7 (2005), 179-207; Jan Vansina, "Ambaca Society and the Slave Trade c. 1760-1845," *Journal of African History* 46, no. 1 (2005), 1-27; Roquinaldo Ferreira, "Ilhas Crioulas: O Significado Plural da Mestiçagem Cultural na África Atlântica," *Revista de História* 155, no. 2 (2006), 17-41.

64. Pier Larson, "Reconsidering Trauma, Identity, and the African Diaspora: Enslavement and Historical Memory in the 19th Century Highland Madagascar," *The William and Mary Quarterly* 56, no. 2 (1999), 356.

65. See Hermegildo Capelo and Roberto Ivens, *De Benguela às terras de Iaca: Descrição de uma viagem à África* (Lisbon: Publicações Europa-América, 1996), 49.

66. Lovejoy, "African Diaspora," 1-21.

67. Terence Ranger, "European Attitudes and African Realities: the Rise and Fall of the Matola Chiefs of South-East Tanzania," *Journal of African History* 20, no. 1 (1979), 64.

68. Paul E. Lovejoy, "Identidade e a Miragem da Etnicidade. A Jornada de Mahommah Gardo Baquaqua para as Américas," *Afro-Ásia* 27 (2002), 34-37; Lovejoy, "African Diaspora," 3; and Larson, "Reconsidering Trauma," 337. See also Kathleen E. Sheldon, *Pounders of Grain. A History of Women, Work, and Politics in Mozambique* (Portsmouth: Heinemann, 2002), 3-15.

69. Linda M. Heywood, "Portuguese into African: The Eighteenth-Century Central African Background to Atlantic Creole Cultures," in *Central Africans and Cultural Transformations in the American Diaspora*, ed. Linda M. Heywood (New York: Cambridge University Press, 2002), 113.

Chapter 10

Art and the History of African Slave Folias in Brazil[1]

Mariza de Carvalho Soares

There are multiple connections between art and history. The objective of this chapter is to discuss two different approaches regarding the uses of images in historical research. In both cases images can be powerful sources for historical research as written documents. During the last decades, images have been receiving a great deal of attention as "sites of memory."[2] However, this perspective avoids considering images as historical sources that can enlarge the comprehension of historical events, in particular when referring to space and sociability of particular groups and places. Images are especially valuable in cases when other historical evidence is rare or incomplete, as is the case of studying slaves in the Americas. The solution is not to choose one approach over another but to develop strategies in differentiating history and memory and new methodological tools that use images, such as paintings, drawings, lithographs, and more recently, photographs. In this study I consider the role of producers of images, the artists, and those who in different ways and times have made use of their production. These topics are often overlooked by scholars. This chapter discusses a collection of primary sources related to congregations within the Catholic brotherhoods of Brazil known as *folia*.

Folia designated a group of people unified by the devotion to a particular saint. As a group they organized celebrations in honor of their patron or patroness, such as the famous *Folia de Reis* and the *folia* of Our Lady of the Rosary. Thus, *folia* both referred to the name of the group and to the celebrations that were mostly parades and processions. Until the nineteenth century, *folias* were organized by Catholic brotherhoods. After reforms in the Catholic Church during the nineteenth century, the Church attempted to distance itself from the festivities and started to prohibit the celebrations. As a result, the *folias* became autonomous. This chapter explores the ways in which descriptions and illustrations of *folias* have shaped a romantic view of slavery in Brazil, without recognizing that early illustrations, particularly those of Carlos Julião, Jean-Baptiste Debret and Johann Moritz Rugendas, provide important information about community formation in Brazil. The paper addresses the ways in which art can inform the history of slavery as revealed through the representations of *folias*.

European Depiction of Slavery in Brazil

For most of the seventeenth and eighteenth centuries, there is very little art related to the slave population. Slaves were rarely depicted, and thus almost never had a "face" in the colonial documents or artistic works. During the seventeenth and eighteenth centuries, foreigners were not welcome in Portuguese overseas colonies. The context of war and international disputes among European states led the Portuguese Crown to prohibit foreigners from traveling in its territories. Only during the Dutch occupation in the seventeenth century foreign artists visited Brazil. The Dutch painters Albert Eckhout and Frans Post were the most important European artists who traveled to Pernambuco during the period and made portraits of landscape and people.[3]

In the nineteenth century visitors from Europe came to Brazil regularly.[4] The focus of this chapter is on the early period of foreign visitation between 1780 and 1830, and specifically on the images and written documents that were produced, with a focus on the representation of slaves in art. The interplay between history and art can be seen with respect to the work of three European artists who visited Rio de Janeiro. Their art can be understood as sites for the representation of slaves and slavery and also as sources for a social history of slavery. In order to explore both dimensions, it is important to consider the context in which these works were produced, including an understanding of who the artists were. The artists, Carlos Julião, Jean-Baptiste Debret and Johann Moritz Rugendas, were in Brazil between 1780 and 1830, and to some extent were contemporaries. While Debret and Rugendas were at the time identified as artists, Julião was a military officer who also painted.[5] They all depicted slavery and slave life in Rio de Janeiro with critical eyes and were able to make important social observations.

Born in Piedmont, in Italy, Carlos Julião (c.1740-1811) moved to Portugal, where he began a career as a military engineer, devoting himself to technical design. He supposedly traveled on expeditions to America, Asia, and Africa, although there are some doubts about part of his travels. Sometime between 1770 and 1800, Julião arrived in Rio de Janeiro. Of his trip to Brazil, he left behind an album composed of a collection of plates of Rio de Janeiro and Minas Gerais. Unfortunately, he left no written comments or descriptions about his work, which remained unpublished until 1960, when the *Biblioteca Nacional*, in Rio de Janeiro, published his plates. The album has an introductory text by the librarian and expert in iconography, Lygia da Fonseca Fernandes Cunha.[6]

As a young French painter, Jean-Baptiste Debret (1768-1848) took sketching courses at the Academy of Fine Arts (Académie des Beaux-Arts) and at the Technical College (École Polytechnique) in Paris, and worked with Jacques-Louis David (1748-1825).[7] After the collapse of Napoleon's regime, with no prospect of jobs in France, Debret went to Brazil, where he remained from 1816 to 1831. In Rio de Janeiro, he taught historical painting at the Imperial Academy of Fine Arts (Academia Imperial de Belas Artes), where he was one of the founding artists.[8] Based on his experiences in Rio, Debret arranged for the publication of his prints in two volumes, *Voyage Pittoresque et Historique au Brésil*, which appeared in Paris in 1834 and 1839. Each plate is accompanied by a long descriptive text, wherein there is important additional information about the depicted scenes.[9]

Johann Moritz Rugendas (1802-1858) was born in Augsburg, Germany. Well trained in painting and drawing, he took courses at the Academy of Fine Arts at Munich (Münchener Kunstakademie). After reading the reports of the naturalists Johann Baptiste von Spix and Karl Friedrich Philipp von Martius, and observing the landscapes of Thomas Ender (1793-1875), he decided to travel to Brazil. He arrived in Rio de Janeiro in 1821 as a member of the scientific expedition of the Prussian naturalist, Baron Georg Heinrich von Langsdorff. After a quarrel with von Langsdorff, Rugendas quit the expedition and remained in Brazil on his own until 1825. In 1835, after his return to Europe, he published *Malerische Reise in Brasilien*, an album of his travels consisting of a long text and a collection of lithographs. Rugendas did not provide a written description for each plate, even though there is a direct correlation between his text and some plates. The first Brazilian edition (1940) came out with illustrations in black and white that were drawn from the original publication.[10]

Julião, as a military officer, drew military uniforms; Debret was a teacher of historical painting; and Rugendas worked for a scientific expedition of natural history. Each of these assignments required accurate observation. In addition to their artistic skills, these men had qualifications that allowed them to observe and represent the colonial society. These talented men did not just pass through but actually lived in Rio de Janeiro, and they had the opportunity to observe slaves and free people of color on the streets, working inside homes, and at leisure in everyday life. It should be noted that Julião was in Brazil at the end of the eighteenth century, while Debret and Rugendas lived there in the first three decades of the nineteenth century. Hence, despite differences in style, we have continuous observation through art from the end of the eighteenth century and well into the nineteenth. Julião's work is the most important pictorial representation of slaves and manumitted slaves for the late eighteenth century in Rio de Janeiro, and perhaps Brazil. Debret and Rugendas arrived later and therefore attest to the changes the colony went through with the arrival of the Portuguese royal family in Rio de Janeiro in 1808. The point of departure is the assumption that the plates depict urban slave *folias* at the time the art was produced.

When Julião did his work, there was no Fine Arts Academy in Brazil. It was only after the arrival of Debret and other French artists that a Fine Arts Academy was inaugurated in 1816. Besides

Debret and Rugendas, the Vienna born Thomas Ender visited Brazil.[11] All of them attempted to represent Brazil and its society through their art and by giving a "face" to slaves. Their work crystallized the images of slavery in Brazil in the nineteenth century. They represented slavery, but also an aristocratic society and its lifestyle, which should be understood as part of the same historical context. Slavery in their works is never portrayed as violent, but as part of the rich and aristocratic style of life of the Brazilian elite. As a consequence, the representation of slavery is clean, textured, and, in a way, beautiful. The violence and the ugliness of the system are excluded from their work as published in their "picturesque" albums. These images have shaped the memory of slavery in Brazil, in many ways until the present. Inexpensive editions of Rugendas and Debret's plates have made their work well known through school textbooks, television programs, movies, Web sites and even in many restaurants and urban murals. Thus, foreign artists and their work has provided the foundation for a "folk" representation of slavery that persists into the twenty-first century.

To demonstrate the importance of these artists and their influence on the construction of the visual representation of slaves and later of a memory of slavery itself, I begin by discussing the importance of their art in illustrating contemporary Brazilian perceptions of slavery. A school textbook provides a case in point. The collection *História* by Roberto Martins is used in high schools. Volume 6 of the collection has two chapters about slavery. The first one contains nine illustrations: among them two by Debret and two by Rugendas. There are four illustrations in the second chapter on slavery. Among them one is by Debret and two by Rugendas.[12] It is the art of Debret and Rugendas that is used to depict Brazil. They painted landscapes, different local populations, plants and animals. And their work is available and accessible to Brazilian high school students, portraying a glamorized version of colonial life and slavery in Brazil. These images have been used exhaustively as the "official" visual description of slave life in Brazilian society. More than half of what these artists painted involved slaves, in part because of the centrality of the institution to Brazilian society. Although their illustrations represent the nineteenth century, their work has even been applied anachronistically to the sixteenth, seventeenth, and eighteenth centuries. The work of these artists has become a powerful and timeless representation of slavery in Brazil.

Debret and Rugendas' plates can be purchased almost anywhere in Rio de Janeiro, including in the streets or newsstands. In *O Brasil de Rugendas*, from Rugendas, there are 100 plates. Half of them contain slaves or former slaves, not considering plates where slaves are depicted as part of the landscape. *O Brasil de Debret* presents 104 plates, of which 51 portray slaves or former slaves. In Julião's album, *Riscos Iluminados,* slaves or former slaves are the main characters in 21 of 43 plates. Debret is the artist who depicted the largest number of plates involving slaves. He is also the most well-known in contemporary Brazil. Debret's *Viagem Pitoresca* contains 139 plates, of which 67 depict slaves or former slaves. Since many of his plates contain two or three pictures in the same plate, there are actually 79 images of slaves. An Internet search, May 14, 2010, revealed 30,700 entries for "Jean-Baptiste Debret." Apart from urban scenes full of slaves, Debret also painted the royal family and official ceremonies. Debret also drafted a flag for the young prince D. Pedro, later the first Emperor of Brazil. After the independence of Brazil in 1822, this flag became official, although later substituted with the Republican flag in 1889. Yet, the Republican flag maintained the same colors and the shape of flag designed by Debret, with a yellow rhombus on a green rectangle.

The Brazilian magazine *Casa Vogue* is one of many examples in which these artists are used today. For example, Debret's plates are presented as part of a "New Look" for local styling for houses and apartments (Figure 10.1). The magazine, targeting mainly the elite of Brazil, brings to the foreground Debret's slave selling baskets; on the back wall there is an aristocratic man walking on the street. On the table, there is a sculpture of a slave man. *Casa Vogue* promotes the decoration of houses in a "colonial style." Tapestries and plates are used to represent the colonial and imperial times, supposedly bringing back an early Brazilian aristocratic way of life, without discussing or problematizing the historical period. Exhibiting art that celebrates slavery inevitably reinforces a nostalgic vision of the past and reinforces a hierarchical vision of Brazilian society.

FIGURE 10.1 - *CASA VOGUE*

Source: No. 238, March 2009, p. 35. Decor by Fabrizio Rollo, and Photograph by Romulo Fialdini. Courtesy of *Casa Vogue.*

The representation of slaves and of slavery in Brazil was a result of the art of foreign artists. Visiting Brazil, they followed the rising of the Brazilian nation and gave a face for slaves and for slavery that continues to shape how Brazilians view the past. Foreign artists distanced themselves from what they saw and painted something that would attract the attention of the public. They were very cautious about "cleaning" any signs of violence in their work. The dirty and grotesque side of slavery is absent in the scenes they show; what they sell is "picturesque." Later, their work was appropriated as a neat, clean and beautiful representation of a period when slaves performed most work. European art became the means of conveying slavery in a form that now indicates high status. Debret, in particular, has been used to demonstrate the beauty of the slave past. Art made by foreign artists contributed to the memory of slavery in Brazil and, eventually, became the "face" of slaves. This sanitized vision is present in all modern visual supports, such as television, magazines, and cinema, in particular. Thus, Debret's *Voyage pittoresque* has become a site of memory.

Julião, Debret and Rugendas are important not only because of the repercussion of their work in modern Brazil, but also because of the richness of the social events they painted. The three of them depicted festivals and celebrations organized by slaves and former slaves, many of them transplanted Africans converted to the Catholic Church. Among these festivals are the *folias,* the celebrations of congregations within Catholic brotherhoods. *Folias* were common in Rio de Janeiro by the late eighteenth century. The *folias* involved street processions composed of black royal "courts" identified with the *reinados* (reigns) of the kings (*reis*), queens (*rainhas*), emperors (*imperadores*), and empresses (*imperatrizes*). The royal courts marched in the parades dancing and singing, and their supporters and viewers made financial contributions. During the *folias* parades, the brotherhoods collected alms to support the festivals in honor of their patron saints. Some of these *folias* elected Africans to the courts. Among them the "kings of Kongo" were the most famous,[13] but there were also African kings of different provenances, including Mina kings.[14] African reinados existed under colonialism and lasted into the nineteenth century and were found almost all over Brazil.

During the first half of the twentieth century Brazilian folk studies and cultural anthropologists considered that the *folias* represented "Afro-Brazilian culture" and "Brazilian folklore."[15] Some *folias* still exist in different parts of Brazil. Based on the studies of anthropologists, scholars claim the *folias* honor the slavery memory, frequently illustrating their books with beautiful plates of the artists or later works.[16] At the same time, as a counterpart, others criticize the use of art as a source for historical information, even frequently repeating each other, reinforcing general patterns that actually create difficulties in historical analysis instead of resolving the methodology of the use of art.[17]

Fundamentally, the Catholic background is essential to the *folias*, because slaves and manumitted slaves were able to gather together within lay brotherhoods.[18] The religious background of the *folias* is clear in the art of Debret and Rugendas, but is not obvious in Julião's plates. The *folias* caught the attention of travelers for their "picturesque" performance, as well as for the commotion they caused in the streets and the social relevance of the events. Members of the *folias* attracted viewers but they also interacted with the public, dancing, singing and playing musical instruments. Yet, most historians have ignored the social importance of the *folias*. Julião, Rugendas and Debret convey different information about Brazil and the Portuguese colonial state and the Catholic background. If their work reinforced the idea of the *folias* as royal processions, they also bring out some interesting information that helps to understand how the *folias* of African people operated as organizational groups for slaves and manumitted Africans who came from different places.[19]

Black Catholic Brotherhoods as Organizational Groups

In Brazil during the second half of the eighteenth century the reproduction of the slave population relied on the arrival of African slaves through the Atlantic trade. In 1763, the city of Rio de Janeiro became the capital of the colony of Brazil and its population increased quickly, including the slave population. The biggest transatlantic slave route going toward Rio left from Angola. The route from Mozambique only increased along the nineteenth century. The route from Bight of Benin, that the Portuguese called Mina Coast (Costa da Mina), to Rio de Janeiro was always a minor route when compared with Angola. Although Mina people represented a relatively small number of transplanted Africans in Rio, they were strongly organized in Catholic brotherhoods. Mina people usually worked in the docks, at the markets, and around the city as petty traders, what made them very visible for all travelers and residents. Called as "Mina," people from the Mina Coast were easily identifiable by observers, repeatedly described by most of the written and visual documents during the nineteenth century.[20]

Upon arriving to the city, as in all other places, enslaved Africans had to re-build their lives as slaves, outside of their native land and far from their relatives and folks. African-born slaves were baptized after a quick introduction to the Catholic doctrine; among them a minority had the chance to enroll in a Catholic brotherhood where Africans could gather. Africans affiliated to brotherhoods constituted the elite among the slave population. In Rio de Janeiro, most Africans from Angola joined the brotherhood of Our Lady of Rosary (Irmandade de Nossa Senhora do Rosário). Slaves from the Mina Coast were separated into a large number of smaller brotherhoods, one of them the Brotherhood of *Santo Elesbão*, founded in 1740. Brotherhoods organized by Africans always involved some kind of ethnic background and were strongly referenced to their African past. Inside a highly hierarchic society regimented by social privileges, Africans also established a new hierarchy for themselves. To become affiliated to a brotherhood was a demonstration of Catholic fervor and high social status. It was not only a matter of being inside or outside the colonial sphere, but an indication of knowing the position of each person and group in the colonial world. Usually, slaves could become members but not be in charge of brotherhoods, which were always controlled by free blacks or manumitted African, depending on the regulation of each brotherhood.[21]

For a long time historians considered brotherhoods as a place of accommodation and retention opposed to groups of maroons (*quilombos*) who would be the symbol of the resistance against slavery in the Americas. Maroons always existed, but they were not necessarily the only option or the most important one for those seeking freedom. Abolition of slavery only came in 1888 and for most of the eighteenth and nineteenth centuries individual manumission was one of the most frequent ways to reach freedom.[22] In Rio de Janeiro, a large proportion of Mina slaves had to pay for their manumission to achieve freedom.[23] For them, the so called "letter of manumission" (*carta de alforria*), and later "letter of freedom" (*carta de liberdade*), was an expensive passport for freedom. Many times manumission letters were bought collectively by the members of the brotherhoods.

If brotherhoods were part of the Catholic Church agenda to bring recently arrived African, seen as heathens, to Christianity, they also became space for African interaction. Africans could organize themselves and elaborate explanations for their displacement, submission, and humiliation within Brazilian colonial society. Beyond conversion and instruction of the Catholic doctrine, brotherhoods were responsible for the health of their members, as well as burials, and for the care of widows and children of the deceased members. Once introduced to baroque Catholicism, converted African slaves believed that the more alms they paid, the faster their soul would be redeemed. Brotherhoods, with their celebrations, processions, and pompous funerals, were place of socialization away from the native land, called simply "my land" (*minha terra*).[24] To belong to a brotherhood was also a strategy for transplanted Africans who had to survive in such a hierarchic and slave based society.[25] Even if this social hierarchy put slaves below all the other members of the Catholic Church, as is the case of converted Africans, they were still considered members of the Church, and where not apart anymore. Through conversion they could change their social status and their identity. The baptism "rescued" them from a heathen environment and displayed them among Christians. Even if an African remained enslaved to the end of his or her life, he or she could convert and acquire the identity of a "Son of God," sharing the eternal afterlife with those called "whites" and other "people of color" who were already Christian.

Despite their importance, brotherhoods were not very visible. The members congregated within poor churches built in the

FIGURE 10.2 – CARLOS JULIÃO, "STREET PROCESSION OF A BLACK BROTHERHOOD"

Source: Carlos Julião, *Riscos iluminados de Figurinhos de Brancos e Negros dos Uzos do Rio de Janeiro e Serro do Frio* (Rio de Janeiro: Biblioteca Nacional, 1960), Plate XXXVIII. Courtesy of Biblioteca Nacional, Rio de Janeiro.

outskirts of the city, in regions where the white colonial elite did not visit. The only time the brotherhoods attracted attention was during the *folias*. The parades went to the main square in front of the palace in order to honor the viceroy (*vice-rei*).[26] The members of the brotherhoods in their unusual costumes attracted attention, although observers probably did not fully associate the *folias* with the brotherhoods to which the participants belonged. Foreign artists observed *folia* in different occasions. Julião drew kings and queens followed by small groups in procession (Figure 10.2), probably as he saw *folia* in Rio de Janeiro. Debret depicted a royal court in the Church of Rosary, in Rio Grande do Sul (Figure 10.3), while Rugendas portrayed the royal couple in the middle of a crowd in an unknown place (Figure 10.4). The illustrations demonstrate the importance of the *folias* in different

FIGURE 10.3 – JEAN-BAPTISTE DEBRET, *QUÊTE POUR L'ENTRETIEN DE L'ÉGLISE DU ROSAIRE* ("COLLECTING DONATIONS AT THE CHURCH OF THE ROSARY")

Source: Jean-Baptiste Debret, *Voyage Pittoresque et Historique au Brésil* (Paris: Firmin-Didot Frères, 1834-1839), vol. 3, plate 30. Also see Jean-Baptiste Debret, *O Brasil de Debret* (Belo Horizonte, Editora Villa Rica, 1993), Plate 90, courtesy of Biblioteca Nacional, Rio de Janeiro.

regions of Brazil. They are general representations, not necessarily portraying a single event. The plates show the role of *folias* as African organizations. Debret mentioned that street processions of kings and queens were prohibited in the city of Rio de Janeiro after 1808. According to him, the authorities believed they might be thought to mock the Portuguese royal court recently installed in Rio de Janeiro. Debret's illustration shows the Brotherhood of the Rosary in Rio Grande do Sul (Irmandade do Rosário do Rio Grande). He probably went to Rio Grande do Sul, and witnessed the religious celebrations prohibited in Rio. Despite the official prohibition, Debret depicted a funeral cortege in Rio de Janeiro and called it "the funeral of a black king's son." Clearly a procession of kings and queens, Debret never associated the funeral he witnessed in Rio with *folia,* regardless of the similarity in both events.[27] Through an observation of the plates, it becomes clear that religious processions and funeral corteges were both practices of brotherhoods, and their *folias*.[28]

Figure 10.4 – Johann Moritz Rugendas,
Fête de Ste Rosalie, Patrone des Nègres

FÊTE DE STᵉ ROSALIE, PATRONE DES NÈGRES.

Source: Johann Moritz Rugendas, *Voyage Pittoresque dans le Brésil, Malerische Reise in Brasilien* (Paris: Firmin-Didot Frères, 1834-1839). Also see João Mauricio Rugendas, *O Brasil de Rugendas* (Belo Horizonte, Itatiaia, 1998), Plate 99, courtesy of Biblioteca Nacional, Rio de Janeiro.

Besides the images of the king and queen, the texts of Debret and Rugendas indicate the presence of a third character. Julião's illustration shows a procession of a king and a queen. Close to them, a man carries an umbrella (*parasol*). Julião also portrays other characters who could be children or people of a lesser social status than the royal couple. Because he did not leave a written description or even a title for the plate, it is difficult, if not impossible, to know which folia he depicted, since in the 1780s there were many folias in the city.[29] Debret's illustration of the collection of alms by the Brotherhood of the Rosary introduces a third character near the queen and king, called in his description, "captain of the black guard." Rugendas' plate also contains a man near the queen and king. The description in Rugendas' chapter entitled "Portraits and Customs" describes this third person as a "minister of the state."[30] Thus, using different scenes and descriptions, the three artists establish the presence of a third person in addition to the royal couple. The work of art makes sense when it is recognized that in the Mina brotherhoods this third element is the *agau*, a Gbe military title from West Africa, which in Brazil, assumed the role of protector of the royal couple, as described by the members of the Mahi *folia* at the brotherhood of Saint Elesbão.

Catholic street processions were accompanied by a particular flag (*bandeira*) that identified the patron saint of each brotherhood. The *folias* also had their own flags. Julião shows a plain flag, with no saints; Rugendas displays flags of different colors and a banner (*estandarte*) with no recognized insignia or patron saint; while Debret does not portray any flag, maybe because the procession is portrayed inside the church and not on the street. None of them had the insignia of Our Lady of the Rosary or any other patron saint. This lack of detail might be an omission. This absence is hardly consistent with the attention to detail in other features of *folias*. Perhaps the artists were more interested in demonstrating common elements, the procession itself, the special costumes, the musical instruments, as well as the principal characters, the king, the queen, and the captain of the guard. While kings and queens wore crowns, the third character had his hat adorned with feathers, a well-known sign of distinction. One can assume that Julião and Rugendas witnessed many processions and hence provided a generalized illustration of what they perceived as a "custom."[31] However the artists attempted to synthesize their observations, the "custom" was a feature of the social practices, and the members of the *folias* recognized that three main characters had to perform. The existence of this trio – king, queen and captain/minister – suggests an analysis of the meanings of politics and power within the brotherhoods as displayed in their *folias*. The statutes of the brotherhoods (*compromissos*) regulated the election of kings and queens but do not usually mention this third position. The art establishes the role this man had in the *folias* and by extension in the brotherhoods. The plates, taken as visual sources and their corresponding written sources, reveal the distribution of prestige and power within the *folias*.

Contemporary documents on the *folia* of the Mina-Mahi organized within the Catholic Brotherhood of Santo Elesbão confirm
the political role of the third character portrayed by Julião, Debret
and Rugendas. In 1786, the recently elected Mahi king wrote a
report narrating the history of the Mina-Mahi *folia,* also called
Mina-Mahi Congregation (Congregação Mahi). The Mahi people
came from north of the kingdom of Dahomey. They had been
enslaved and sent to Brazil beginning in the first decades of the
eighteenth century and continuing until the end of the Atlantic
slave trade to Brazil in 1850.[32] In 1786 the Mahi elected kings
and queens, and also dukes, counts, marquis and generals.[33] The
position of general appears to correspond to the captain/minis-
ter depicted in the illustrations. In the Mina-Mahi Congregation
the general was called *agau*, the title of the army commanders in
Dahomey and perhaps in neighboring areas from where the Mahi
and most of the members of the brotherhood of Santo Elesbão
came.[34] Additional information about the Mahi *folia* demonstrates
the position of the agau was of great importance, and not only
honorific. He was in charge of many activities, including accompanying, serving and protecting the royal couple, and the *folia*
itself, as shown in the plates.[35] The *folias* depicted by Julião,
Debret and Rugendas can be much better understood through an
analysis of written documents that describe the members of *folias*
in their everyday life.

The Organization of the *Folias*

In order to appreciate who the kings of the *folias* were, I have
chosen to focus on Ignácio Monte. Monte was elected the first
Mahi king in Rio de Janeiro in 1762, alongside his wife, Victória,
who became queen. The Mahi assembled at the Church of the
Brotherhood of Santo Elesbão, from where, their *folia* started its
processions. As king and queen, Monte and Victória probably led
the processions through the streets much as depicted by Julião,
Debret and Rugendas. The Mahi *folia* proceeded to the Church
of the Rosary and also to the palace of the viceroy, which would
make them visible to any available artist passing by.

Ignácio Monte left the Bight of Benin before the middle of the
eighteenth century. The man who came to be a king arrived Brazil

as a slave in 1741. In 1742, he was baptized as Ignácio Mina and later was known as Ignácio Gonçalves do Monte, a name he acquired from his master Domingos Gonçalves do Monte. He was manumitted in 1757, after paying 350,000 *réis* for his freedom. In 1759, he married Victória, a Mina-Coura who also had been manumitted. He became a successful leader of his people and a captain of the Black militia. He also had a barbershop where he practiced his skills as a successful barber and bleeder (*barbeiro-sangrador*).[36] In Rio he identified with other Mina as Mina-Mahi, who considered themselves a distinct group within the Brazilian categorization that recognized people speaking one of the Gbe languages as "Mina." In 1762, Monte organized the first Mahi *folia,* occupying the position of king of the Mahi people in Rio de Janeiro. The Black Brotherhoods were not specifically ethnic organizations, although people of the same ethnic backgrounds could gain ascendancy in a particular brotherhood. The Mahi in Rio did exactly that, using a strong sense of a common background to launch a Mahi *folia*. As recorded in documents that served as the basis for this analysis, he was king of the Mahi until he passed away in 1783.[37]

The barbershop probably explains Monte's social position and his network among the Mahi and other Africans in Rio. In Brazil, barbers required a special license to work. They could bleed (by cupping or using leaches), and treat external diseases and bruises; some of them had a special license to be dentists. In English the usual word for barbers who performed those activities is barber-surgeon but in Brazil the word "surgeon" does not apply since a slave could not be a surgeon. In addition to this, a surgeon could treat internal diseases, which barbers could not. In the Portuguese empire, the most elevated level in the medical career was the physician, limited to free people. Each of these positions required a special license issued by the Portuguese royal medical institution (*Fisicatura Mor do Reino*). Barbeiro-sangrador were much respected among the slave population and beyond.[38] As a barber, Ignácio Monte accumulated money and met people who certainly recognized his prestige and supported him as the king of the *folia*. In 1786, Francisco Alves de Souza replaced Monte as the Mahi king. His wife, Rita Sebastiana was the new queen, and Luiz Roiz da Silva was elected the agau.[39]

Folias and brotherhoods were spaces where African slaves and former slaves could express themselves and build social networks, as the case of Ignácio Monte demonstrates. Barbershops, as the one owned by Monte, were places of work but also of socialization.[40] As shown in Debret's illustration of a barber shop (Figure 10.4), free and enslaved Africans met people at barber shops, searched for cures for their ills, found dentists and even had socks mended. The barber, Luiz Francisco do Couto, belonged to the Mahi Congregation and sewed stockings for a living, for example.[41] Barbers like Monte and Couto were part of the elite among slaves and freed slaves who had skills that separated them from the rest of the black population. Many Mina people in Rio de Janeiro were professionals who performed important roles within their brotherhoods, where they were able to build different networks. The sign hanging over the door in Debret's illustration announces: "*barbeiro, cabellereiro, sangrador, dentista e deitão bichas*" ("barber, hairdresser, bleeder, dentist and work with leaches"). There is no mention of other activities, but we can see men sewing socks and sharpening a knife.[42] Of course barbers also shaved beards and cut hair. Thus, barbers were used to dealing with knives and needles and scissors. These items of iron were associated with blacksmiths and hence belonged to the confraternities of the blacksmiths, devoted to Saint George (*São Jorge*), both in Portugal, and in Rio de Janeiro.[43]

Other sources support the association of barbers with needlework. A vocabulary written in Minas Gerais in 1741 to teach slave masters some Gbe terms contains words related to barbers and their skills.[44] Slave owners identified terms such as "barber" (*atamchólátô*), "head" (*ta*), "hair" (*dábâ*), "louse" (*jô*), and "louse egg" (*józim*) with Africans transplanted from the Bight of Benin. The sentences masters were supposed be able to say included, for example: "I shave the beard" (*máhi chuléatam*). Debret's written description and plate, together with the *Vocabulário*, reveal the everyday life of barbers and their barbershops, including the fact that cutting someone's hair involved the hard task of fighting lice. The *Vocabulário* also include sentences apparently not related to barber activities, as *áhigam guhi* ("I will sharpen a knife"), and *máhitoavó* ("I will sew"). However, Debret's plate illustrates that sharpening knives and sewing stockings were barbershop activities. Debret's illustration depicts the tasks performed within barber shops, information that is "silenced" in written accounts.

FIGURE 10.5 – JEAN-BAPTISTE DEBRET, "BOUTIQUE DE BARBIERS"

Source: Jean-Baptiste Debret, *Voyage Pittoresque et Historique au Brésil* (Paris: Firmin-Didot Frères, 1834-1839), vol. 2, plate 12. Also see Jean-Baptiste Debret, *O Brasil de Debret* (Belo Horizonte. Editora Villa Rica, 1993), Plate 36, courtesy of Biblioteca Nacional, Rio de Janeiro.

Images can illustrate the past, not only as sites of memory, but also as historical sources. Historians can benefit from visual images left by travelers who visited Brazil to reconstruct the history of slavery. Images unveil the role of Africans and their descendents in the city life of Rio, not only in cultural and religion expressions, such as the *folias,* but also in daily activities, such as the case of the Debret's plate on the barbershop. Again, by drawing on various types of sources historians can magnify their view of the whole picture of slavery in Rio de Janeiro and the skills performed by Africans. Images by themselves do not tell the history of slavery. Like other sources, such as written documents or oral reports, images have to be understood in context and in comparison with other evidence. Debret did not link the Rosário brotherhood with the barbershop, for example. A close look by a historian, however, reveals the interconnection of three of his plates (the donations at the Church of the Rosário; the funeral of the son of the "black" king, not analyzed here, and the barbershop).

The artists who visited Brazil provide new knowledge about slavery. Through their paintings that emphasize the bright and colorful *folias*, historians can view the diverse cultural and religious practices performed by Africans and their descendents. Alongside written accounts, images reveal the organization of networks linked to ethnic groups. Analyzed in conjunction with accounts, works of art reveal that *folias* reunited transplanted Africans who made use of the Catholic practice of devotion to create congregations based on ethnic ancestry. The brotherhoods operated as networks, while the barbershop served as a meeting place. The Mahi king Ignácio Gonçalves do Monte was a barber who engaged with other barbers around his barbershop, at least some of whom were also members of his royal court. He used to dance in the streets with his queen Victória to collect alms, and accompanied by his *agau*, covered by a parasol. Although Mahi documents do not mention the role of the agau, the artwork of Julião, Debret and Rugendas stress how agau accompanied the king and the queen in *folias*. The sources demonstrate the importance of the *folias* as an occasion for transplanted Africans to maintain strong ethnic networks. By crossing visual and written sources, it is possible to uncover the social relevance of the *folias* at the end of theeighteenth and beginning of the nineteenth centuries in Rio de Janeiro, and by extension to other parts of Brazil. In this chapter, I have called attention to the importance of art as visual documents for the historical reconstruction that challenges the "memory of slavery" as currently romanticized through the popularization of the art of Julião, Debret and Rugendas.

Notes

1.   In 2005, I presented a preliminary version of this text at the Harriet Tubman Institute (York University), and at Centre Interuniversitaire d'Études sur les Lettres, les Arts et les Traditions (Université

Laval). I want to thank Paul Lovejoy, Bogumil Jewsiewicki, and Ana Lucia Araujo for their comments during both occasions. I also want to thank Leia Pereira da Cruz, technician at the Sessão de Iconografia, Biblioteca Nacional, Rio de Janeiro, for information about the different editions of Debret and Rugendas, works referenced in this paper. I am indebted to Henry Lovejoy, who translated the first version of this paper. *Casa Vogue* gave me permission to reproduce the cover of the special issue. I also want to thank the Bibioteca Nacional for permission to use the plates of Carlos Julião, Jean-Baptiste Debret and Johannes Rugendas.

2. For a bibliography on history and memory, see Pierre Nora, "Entre mémoire et histoire. La problématique des lieux," in *Les lieux de mémoire, La République,* ed. Pierre Nora (Paris: Gallimard, 1984), vol. 1. His study does not specifically address slavery but is relevant in thinking about sites of memory for slave societies in the Americas. See Mariza de Carvalho Soares, "Nos Atalhos da Memória: Monumento a Zumbi," in *Cidade Vaidosa. Imagens Urbanas do Rio de Janeiro,* ed. Paulo Knauss (Rio de Janeiro: Sette Letras, 1999), 117-35.

3. For Frans Post and his art depicting slaves in Brazil, see Mariza de Carvalho Soares, "Engenho sim, de açúcar não: o engenho de farinha de Frans Post," *Varia Historia* 25, no. 41 (2009), 61-83.

4. By this time their paintings and lithographs were being sold in Europe. Thus from the beginning of the nineteenth century the representation of Brazil in European art always included African slaves, and slave sociability.

5. It was only around the middle of the nineteenth century that artistic representations of the city of Rio de Janeiro in general and slaves in particular came to be more abundant, particularly after the arrival of the daguerreotype and photograph. On photographs of slaves in nineteenth-century in Brazil, see Boris Kosoy and Maria Luiza Tucci Carneiro, *O Olhar Europeu. O Negro na Iconografia Brasileira do século XIX* (São Paulo: Editora da Universidade de São Paulo, 1994).

6. See Carlos Julião, *Riscos Iluminados de Figurinhos de Brancos e Negros dos uzos do Rio de Janeiro e Serro do Frio,* Introdução histórica e catálogo descritivo por Lygia da Fonseca Fernandes Cunha. (Rio de Janeiro: Biblioteca Nacional, 1960). The original album is held in the collection of the Biblioteca Nacional in Rio de Janeiro. Regarding Carlos Julião, see Silvia Hunold Lara, "Customs and

Costumes: Carlos Julião and the Image of Black Slaves in Late Eighteenth-century Brazil," *Slavery and Abolition* 23, no. 2 (2002), 123-46. Julião's plates XL, XLI, XLII came out in C. R. Boxer, *The Golden Age of Brazil, 1695/1750. Growing Pains of a Colonial Society* (Berkeley and Los Angeles: University of California Press, 1962), based on the original plates at Biblioteca Nacional, Rio de Janeiro. As far as I know, Boxer was the first historian to use these illustrations about slavery in Brazil.

7. Jacques-Louis David managed an important studio in France portraying members of the French nobility, and is usually described as the painter of Napoleon. His most famous works are *Le Premier Consul franchissant les Alpes au col du Grand-Saint-Bernard* (Vienna: Kunsthistorisches Museum, 1800) and *Madame Récamier* (Paris: Louvre, 1800). Gérard Gros and Ingres were also his students.

8. For a biography of Debret, see J. F. de Almeida Prado, *O Artista Debret e o Brasil* (São Paulo: Companhia Editora Nacional, 1989); Júlio Bandeira, "Debret e a Corte no Brasil," in *O Brasil Redescoberto*, ed. Carlos Martins (Rio de Janeiro: BNDES, 1999); and Rodrigo Naves, *A Forma Difícil: ensaios sobre arte brasileira* (São Paulo: Ática, 1996).

9. Jean-Baptiste Debret, *Voyage pittoresque et historique au Brésil, ou séjour d'un artiste française au Brésil, depuis 1816 jusqu'en en 1831 inclusivement, époque de l'avénement et de l'abdication de S. M. D. Pedro 1er, fondateur de l'Empire brésilien. Dedié à l'Academie des Beaux-Arts de l'Institut de France par J. B. Debret, premier peintre et professeur de l'Académie Impériale Brésilienne des Beaux-Arts de Rio de Janeiro, peintre particulier de la Maison Impériale, membre correspondant de la classe des Beaux-Arts de l'Institut de France, et Chevalier de l'Ordre du Christe* (Paris: Firmin Didot et Frères, 1834-39). The first Brazilian edition came out in 1940 as Jean-Baptiste Debret, *Viagem Pitoresca e Histórica ao Brasil* (São Paulo: Livraria Martins Fontes, 1940). This edition includes the full text and the plates in black and white. For a later edition with plates in color, but with no text, see *O Brasil de Debret* (Belo Horizonte: Itatiaia, 1998).

10. Johann Moritz Rugendas, *Malerische Reise in Brasilien* (Paris and Mülhausen: Engelmann et Cie, 1835). French edition: Maurice Rugendas, *Voyage pittoresque dans le Brésil* (Paris: Engelmann & Cie., 1835); João Mauricio Rugendas, *Viagem pitoresca através*

do Brasil (São Paulo: Livraria Martins, 1940); and João Mauricio Rugendas, *O Brasil de Rugendas* (Belo Horizonte: Itatiaia, 1998).

11. Ender was from Vienna and went to Brazil in 1817 with the archduchess Maria Leopoldine von Österreich, the bride of the Prince D. Pedro, who became Emperor of Brazil in 1822.

12. José Roberto Ferreira Martins, *História: 6a. série* (São Paulo: FTD, 1997), vol 6, 136-45. For further information about the press, see www.ftd.com.br. FTD is one of the largest Brazilian publisher for high schools.

13. For Kongo kings, see Marina de Mello e Souza, *Reis negros no Brasil escravista. História da Festa de coroação de rei Congo* (Belo Horizonte: Editora da Universidade Federal de Minas Gerais, 2002).

14. For Mina kings, see Mariza de Carvalho Soares, *Devotos da Cor. Identidade étnica, Religiosidade e Escravidão no Rio de Janeiro, século XVIII* (Rio de Janeiro: Civilização Brasileira, 2000).

15. For a general description of the *folias* see Luiz da Câmara Cascudo, *Dicionário do Folclore Brasileiro*. 1st edition 1954 (Rio de Janeiro: Edições de Ouro, n/d), 402-403. Brazilian anthropologists were strongly influenced by Melville Herskovits, in particular, with respect to acculturation, cultural dynamics and cultural transmission. His book *Man and his Works* was translated into Portuguese in 1964 after being well known since it came out in English. See Melville J. Herskovits, *Man and his Works* (New York: Alfred A. Knopf, 1948).

16. For a new interpretation of the cultural approach of the *folias* see Martha Abreu, *O Império do Divino. Festas religiosas e cultura popular no Rio de Janeiro, 1830-1900* (Rio de Janeiro: Nova Fronteira, 1999).

17. For the debate, see Lara, "Customs and Costumes," 125-46; and Robert Slenes, "African Abrahams, Lucretias and Men of Sorrows: Allegory and Allusion in the Brazilian Anti-slavery Lithographs (1827-1835) of Johann Moritz Rugendas," *Slavery and Abolition* 23, no. 2 (2002), 147-68.

18. See Mariza de Carvalho Soares, "O Império de Santo Elesbão na cidade do Rio de Janeiro, no século XVIII," *Topoi* 4 (2002), 59-83.

19. For the detailed argument on the provenances of groups, a concept I developed building from Fredrik Barth's concept of organizational groups, see Soares, *Devotos da Cor*, chapter 3.

20. For a description of African born slaves, in particular Mina people in Rio de Janeiro, see Mariza de Carvalho Soares, "From Gbe to Yoruba: Ethnic Changes within the Mina Nation in Rio de Janeiro," in *The Yoruba Diaspora in the Atlantic World,* ed. Toyin Falola and Matt Childs (Bloomington: Indiana University Press, 2004), 231-47.

21. These brotherhoods worshiped such "black" Catholic saints as Santo Elesbão, Santa Efigênia, Santo Antônio da Mouraria, Santo Antônio do Categeró, and São Domingos. Two of them were "white," Nossa Senhora do Rosário and Senhor do Bonfim, the later portrayed as Jesus dead on the cross. Regarding brotherhoods in Rio de Janeiro in the eighteenth century, see Soares, *Devotos da Cor,* chapter 4.

22. During the eighteenth century freedom was a personal privilege of the free and manumitted black elite. In the nineteenth century, when abolitionism became an important political force in Brazil, "black" intellectuals bravely fought for the general abolition of slavery.

23. Manolo Florentino, "Alforrias e Etnicidade no Rio de Janeiro Oito-centista: notas de Pesquisa," *Topoi* 5 (2002), 9-40.

24. For the idea of "nations" (*nações*) and "lands" (*terras*), see Mariza de Carvalho Soares, "A 'nação' que se tem e a 'terra' de onde se vem: categorias de inserção social de africanos no Império portu-guês século XVIII," *Estudos Afro-Asiáticos* 26 (2004), 303-30.

25. For the importance of "black brotherhoods" in colonial Brazil, see A. J. R. Russell-Wood, *The Black Man in Slavery and Freedom in Colonial Brazil* (New York: St. Martin's Press, 1982).

26. Biblioteca Nacional do Rio de Janeiro (hereafter BN-RJ), Rio de Janeiro, Regra ou estatuto por modo de um diálogo onde, se dá notícia das Caridades e Sufragações das Almas que usam os pretos Minas, com seus Nacionais no Estado do Brasil, especialmente no Rio de Janeiro, por onde se hão de regerem e governarem fora de todo o abuso gentílico e supersticioso; composto por Francisco Alves de Souza preto e natural do Reino de Makim, um dos mais excelentes e potentados daquela oriunda Costa da Mina. BN-RJ (MA) 9,3,11 (ant. 5,3,12) [24].

27. See Debret, *Viagem pitoresca,* plate 16 [Tomo II, 185-186].

28. Julião, *Riscos Iluminados*, Plate XXXVIII; *O Brasil de Rugendas* (Belo Horizonte: Itatiaia, 1998), plate 99 (first edition, 4ª. Div p Pl

19); *O Brasil de Debret* (Belo Horizonte: Itatiaia, 1993), Plate 90 (first edition, vol. I, plate 30).

29. See Soares, *Devotos da Cor*, chapter 4.

30. Debret, *Viagem pitoresca*, 187; Rugendas, *Viagem pitoresca*, 26-27. Rugendas' description is based on Henry Koster's description of the election and coronation of a Kongo king in Pernambuco. Koster (ca.1793-1820) was the administrator of a sugar plantation and lived in Pernambuco for some years. He was a Portuguese entrepreneur of British parents and wrote a book narrating his travels; see *Travels in Brazil* (London: Longman, Hust, Rees & Brown, 1816), 273-75.

31. According to Silvia Lara "Julião's drawings also represent a larger unit: the dominions of the Portuguese in the lands of America. Thus, in a synecdoche play, Bahia or Rio, territories in the Portuguese empire, stood emblematically for the whole, that is, the entire universe of the Conquistas, the lands conquered by the Crown and subject to its domination." The flags represented all the black brotherhoods of which there were many during the time the artists would have walked and observed the streets of Rio de Janeiro. Lara, "Customs and Costumes," 131.

32. For further information about the Mahi and other Mina peoples in Brazil see Soares, "A 'nação' que se tem e a 'terra' de onde se ve," 303-30. For Mahi in Africa, see Robert Cornevin, *Histoire du Dahomey* (Paris: Éditions Berger-Levrault, 1962); and Robin Law, *The Slave Coast of West Africa 1550-1750. The Impact of the Atlantic Slave Trade on an African Society* (Oxford: Clarendon Press, 1991).

33. The *estatutes* of the *folia* organized by the Mahi congregation were copied as part of a long report about the Mina-Mahi in Rio de Janeiro written in 1786. See Soares, *Devotos da Cor,* chapter 6. The manuscript is presently part of the collection of the Biblioteca Nacional do Rio de Janeiro (hereafter cited as BN-RJ, Regra ou Estatutos).

34. For the *agau,* see Law, *Slave Coast of West Africa*, 271, 325, 328.

35. BN-RJ, Regra ou Estatutos.

36. For Brazil see in particular *Tratados I, III* and *XI* by Luís Gomes Ferreira, *Erário Mineral*, ed. Júnia Ferreira Furtado (Belo Horizonte, Fundação João Pinheiro; Rio de Janeiro, Fundação Oswaldo Cruz, 2002). For more details about African barbers and bleeders

in Rio and on board slave ships, see Mariza de Carvalho Soares, "African Barber-Surgeons in Brazilian Slave Ports: A Case Study from Rio de Janeiro," paper presented at the *Black Urban Atlantic Conference*, University of Texas at Austin, April 1-3, 2009, and forthcoming in *The Urban Black Atlantic during the Era of the Slave Trade*, ed. James Sidbury and Jorge Canizares-Esguerra.

37. Arquivo da Cúria Metropolitana do Rio de Janeiro (hereafter ACMRJ), Habilitações Matrimoniais, Ignacio Gonçalves do Monte, cx. 1648, doc 22.119; ACMRJ, Livro de Testamentos e Óbitos da Freguesia da Sé, 1776–1784, Will of Ignacio Gonçalves do Monte, fls. 442v-444; BN-RJ, Regra ou Estatutos. See also Soares, *Devotos da Cor,* chapter 6.

38. For barbers and bleeders in Portugal, see Joaquim Barradas, *A Arte de Sangrar de Cirurgiões e Barbeiros* (Lisbon: Livros Horizonte, 1999). For Brazil see in particular *Tratados I, III* and *XI* by Luís Gomes Ferreira, *Erário Mineral*.

39. BN-RJ, Regra ou Estatuto, fl. 24.

40. See Max Gluckman, *Custom and Conflict in Africa* (Oxford: Basil Blackwell, 1955).

41. ACMRJ, Livro de Testamentos e Óbitos da Sé, 1776–1784. Testamento de Luiz Francisco do Couto, fl. 42v. For an online collection of ecclesiastical records, see www.historia.uff.br/curias.

42. *O Brasil de Debret*, plate 36 [first edition, plate vol II, 12].

43. For further information about bleeders (*sangradores*) in Portugal, see Barradas, *A Arte de Sangrar.* For the devotion of barbers to Saint George, see Georgina Silva dos Santos, *Oficio de Sangue. A Irmandade de São Jorge e a Inquisição na Lisboa Moderna* (Lisbon: Edições Colibri, 2005). The main regulation for barbers (*Regimento do Barbeiro*) dated to 1620 and can be found in Barradas, *A Arte de Sangrar,* Apêndice 2-5, 237-47.

44. See António da Costa Peixoto. *Obra Nova de Língua Geral da Mina.* Manuscrito da Biblioteca Pública de Évora e da Biblioteca Nacional de Lisboa publicado e apresentado por Luis Silveira e acompanhado de comentário filológico de Edmundo Correia Lopes (Lisbon: Agência Geral das Colônias, 1945), 205-225; or the new edition by Yeda Pessoa de Castro, *A língua Mina-Jeje no Brasil. Um falar Africano em Ouro Preto do século XVIII* (Belo Horizonte: Fundação João Pinheiro, 2002). See also Olabiyi Yai, "Texts of Enslavement: Fon and Yoruba Vocabularies from Eighteenth-and-

Nineteenth-century Brazil," in *Identity in the Shadow of Slavery,* ed. Paul E. Lovejoy (London: Continuum, 2000), 102-112; and Silvia Hunold Lara, "Linguagem, domínio senhorial e identidade étnica nas Minas Gerais de meados do século XVIII," *Trânsitos Coloniais: Diálogos Críticos Luso-Brasileiros* (Lisbon: Imprensa de Ciências Sociaisa, 2002), 205-225.

Chapter 11

"So That God Frees the Former Masters from Hell Fire:" Salvation Through Manumission in Nineteenth Century Ottoman Algeria

Yacine Daddi Addoun

Why is it so difficult to examine slavery in the Muslim world? The overwhelming silence on the subject raises questions about how slavery has been perceived in the past and why silence seems to be necessary in the present.[1] By analyzing manumission records that have survived from the eighteenth and nineteenth centuries, this study demonstrates that the manumission of slaves was closely associated with efforts at personal salvation.[2] The question of who benefited, therefore, resurfaces as a leitmotif when talking about slavery in Muslim societies in relation to the descendants of both masters and slaves. In Algeria, the memory of slavery is suppressed, in part because remembering slavery implies acknowledging that slavery existed and that masters and their descendants profited from it, and still are profiting from it, even after its abolition. The descendants of former masters avoid stirring up memories of the distant past and knowledge that their forefathers were involved in slavery because of shame. The story of slavery is considered to be something of the past that is indeed over, and should remain as part of the past, but the very silence that pervades the issue demonstrates a continued importance.

Even for descendants of slaves, it is unwise to acknowledge the heritage to slavery, which implies that their forefathers were heathens, non-believers, who as foreigners in Algeria were subjected to exploitation in servitude. The disparaging association of skin color with slavery has been a constant reminder among descendants of slaves who thereby still experience discrimination. As proof we only need mention that nowadays in some places in North Africa and the Arab world, people who are black are called "slaves" (*'abd/'abīd*), as if the terms for slaves and blacks are synonymous.This kind of racialized association reveals that slavery was a central institution in North Africa and cannot easily be ignored, despite efforts to do so. Employing the terms slave and black as equivalent shows that slavery is not erased from collective memory. Though the subject is publicly avoided, it has not been forgotten. The silence continues to comfort or impose a sense of avoidance of difficult issues and uncertainties on all sides. This silence is only broken publically in situations of conflict or in more or less controlled ritual contexts.[3]

Masters and slaves represent opposite poles in the history of slavery. The current reactions of the descendents of both masters and slaves reflect the past, nonetheless. On the one hand, some attempt to apologize for slavery (especially in the southern parts of Algeria), while on the other hand, the descendents of slaves take pride in the sub-Saharan warrior tradition of the Bambara. Researchers are caught between the suspicion of the former and the reserve of the latter, and are never seen as a neutral part in the research equation, especially in situations of interview and field study. Researchers are objectively situated in a specific social space, and this position is never ignored by their interlocutors, who present conflicting memories of the past or attempt to suppress the past.

We should be critical of both points of view because the descendants of masters and the descendants of slaves are located in their respective social spaces with biased positions about slavery and its aftermath. Their current social positions, places of habition, their political orientation, and economic niches evoke the past associated with slavery. However, there is a self-imposed curtain of censorship regarding slavery which was lowered at the time of independence in 1962. With the end of the bloody war of independence and the death of colonialism, there was no place for exploitation. Thus, all citizens of Algeria were to be considered equal before the law. Issues of slavery, servitude, and discrimination were part and parcel of colonialism, and as such they were to be bundled and shelved in the past. However, by promoting this policy, Algerian authorities contributed to silencing the past and effectively maintained the *status quo*. Officials and intellectuals knowingly or not tended to support the descendants of slave masters and reinforced racial prejudices against the descendants of slaves by avoiding public debate. Current attitudes suggest that efforts to recognize that slavery has a persistent legacy beyond colonialism will take a long time.

This chapter seeks to address the following questions: "Who benefits from the study of slavery in the Muslim World?" "Who benefits from its oblivion?" A just society requires that everyone acknowledges where they came from and the role of their ancestors in the past. A clear understanding of the past and strategies to empower those who were alienated from spaces of power can bring a better future. In the case of the historical denial of slavery in Algeria, the silences, different viewpoints, allusions and unspoken misunderstandings have been devastating. The weight of a loaded past rests on the shoulders of the descendants of slaves. They continue to be excluded and suffer discrimination. Because of ignorance of Islamic law, the descendants of slaves have often been denied their socio-cultural heritage. The history of slavery and the slave trade in North Africa must, therefore, be critically examined.

Documents relating to the manumission of slaves are an important historical source for the study of slavery in the Islamic world, and in this case, Algeria.[4] Manumission records reveal the intricacies of slavery and allow scholars to glance into the domestic sphere, almost inaccessible in other sources. The challenge is to analyze individual manumission cases to understand different social contexts and spaces. For the most part, manumission records tend to over-represent the dominating ideologies of slave masters and do not adequately convey the perspectives of former slaves who came from diverse ethnic groups. Despite the fact that the documents were produced by slave masters and clerics, the voice of the enslaved can be found in a close reading. An analysis of documentation relating to the manumission of slaves offers an opportunity to consider the nature of master-slave relations in the past at the crucial moment when the relationship shifted to clientship.

The manumission documents used in this study are held in the Archives Nationales d'Algérie (ANA) classified under the records of the Muslim courts (*al-maḥākim al-shar'iyya*). Documents after the 1850s are housed at the Archives du Ministère de la Justice (AMJ). However, this collection can only be accessed with permission of the administrative authorities. It is difficult to view these documents unless one is a relative or family member of the people directly involved with the past, which makes this collection inaccessible. Archival restrictions demonstrate policies related to the censorship of the past and control of knowledge. By denying access to historical evidence, archives and their bureaucrats reinforce the *status quo* and prevent questions from being asked about the past. As a result, researchers can only speculate on the sort of information obtainable in the *al-maḥākim al-sharᶜiyya* collection of manumission records after 1850.

This chapter is an examination of the different types of manumissions in Algeria between the 1730s and the 1850s. I argue that manumission documents comprised three different tpes of contract. The first, and most obvious, was the contract of manumission itself, between master and slave, through which the slave status was eliminated. The second contract, which was implicit, and a consequence of the first one, was made between the patron (ex-master) and client (ex-slave). The status of the manumitted slave changed but this did not make him free as a freeborn; he and his descendents would still be linked to the master's family, as clients. It is worth noting that the Islamic term for patron and clientin Arabic was the same: *mawlā*. And, the last contract was between the ex-master and God through which the master could guarantee his or her eternal salvation. In short, a major factor in the manumission of many slaves had to do with a contract with God that would compensate the master with heavenly reward.

In arguing so, I am not dismissing the idea that emancipation – in this case manumission – is a social necessity for the host society, as Farid Khiari demonstrates for the case of white slaves in the Regency of Algiers.[5] Rather, I examine the issue form the point of view of the motives of the masters, or from the stand point of methodological individualism and not from perspective of some holistic structuralism.

In the archives of the Muslim courts of the Regeny of Algiers, the *al-maḥākim al-sharʿiyya* contains a collection of manumission cases. These documents are accessible on microfiche but some of the duplication is of poor quality. The original *maḥākim al-sharʿiyya* collection at the ANA was cataloged by Chihab Eddin Yelles. He was responsible for labeling and numbering each box, volume and individual documents. He also provided brief summaries of each document highlighting the key information available in each on of them, such as the date of each document in the *hijrī* and Gregorian calendars. The Yelles catalog has obviously become a useful tool for any researcher interested in working with this collection. Table 11.1 presents the distribution of manumission records according to the volumes cataloged by Yelles.

TABLE 11.1: DISTRIBUTION OF THE MANUMISSION RECORDS IN THE YELLES CATALOG

VOLUME #	# OF DOCUMENTS
1	50
2	8
3	10
4	143
5	20
6	91
7	35
8	2
Total	359

Yelles did not summarize the documents of Volume 4, box 59, number 1. He only mentions that this box contained manumission records numbered 1 to 93.[6] The documents number 52 to 56 are missing from this box.[7] Also, I could not locate ten other documents, nor was I able to locate volume 6, which is believed to be missing. Yet, Fatiha Loualiche was able to use this volume, which she reproduced as an appendix and includes 91 records.[8] Despite its importance, the Yelles catalog is only accessible at the ANA. I therefore worked on a set of 243 documents, which with the apparent missing volume 6, make a total of 359 documents as recorded in table 11.1. The number of records is actually more than this total because in certain circumstances there were two different records written on one page relative to one case and one person.[9]

The *maḥākim al-sharʿiyya* collection can only be considered a sample of manumissions in Ottoman Algeria. It is not suggested here that the documents are representative of slavery throughout the entire Regency of Algiers. For example, there is not one manumission record whose beneficiary was white, Christian or European. Even though it is known that "white" slaves existed in Algeria as late as 1816, these documents do not support this fact. There is evidence in Portuguese sources of Algerian masters issuing contractual manumissions (*mukātaba*) to 14 slaves from Portugal as late as 1813.[10] These 14 enslaved Portuguese had clearly arranged legal manumission with their masters in the presence of a *qāḍī*. However, what happened to such manumission cases in Algerian sources is not known. It is possible that the records were lost when the Ottoman Archives were destroyed during the invasion of the French Army. Moreover, Abdeljelil Temimi has compiled a partial catalog of the archives, in which he mentions several examples whereby the archivists, who were supposed to be taking care of the collections, destroyed records or sold documents.[11] Nonetheless, the documents provide a window into the history of slavery.

The Manumission Records

Manumission records provide information on daily life under slavery and thereby reveal the Algerian social structure from the mid-eighteenth to the mid-nineteenth century. Although there were at least ten different modalities of manumission, most can be divided into two categories. First are those that took place during the lifetime of the master, which included simple manumissions, conditional manumissions, if the conditions was set before the death of the master, and manumissions one day before the death of the master. The second category consists of manumissions that occurred after the death of the master, including manumissions by probate, *post mortem* manumission, and testimonial manumission (see Table 11.2).

TABLE 11.2: TYPES OF MANUMISSION IN THE ANA 1730s-1850s

TYPES OF MANUMISSION	NUMBER OF DOCUMENTS	PERCENTAGE
Simple	193	75.1%
Unspecified	15	5.8%
Probates	11	4.3%
Post Mortem	8	3.1%
Execution of a Will	6	2.4%
Manumission one day/death	6	2.3%
Testimonial	5	1.9%
Formalizing	5	1.9%
Predetermined	3	1.2%
Lost Copies	3	1.2%
Conditional	2	0.8%
Total	257	100%

As can be seen in Table 11.2, virtually all manumissions, including simple manumissions accounting for 77 percent of all cases, had as their purpose personal and spiritual reward either for the master or for someone else specifically named.These different manumission modalities will be discussed in detail below.

Although written records were extremely important in Muslim societies, especially contracts,[12] sometimes there were reasons that prevented agents from obtaining official manumission certificates in the presence of a judge (*qāḍī*) and witnesses (*'udūl*). This is the reason for probate certificates and testimonies of manumission, whereby slaves were manumitted after the death of their masters without proof. In cases like this, slaves or the heirs of the deceased master gathered witnesses in order to show that the master had the intention of freeing his or her slave. Witnesses could also report that the deceased master had already manumitted the slave previously, although no written proof was available. In either case, free and freed witnesses testified to confirm the slave's claims. According to the records available, 6.5 percent of all cases were manumissions by probate (*iktifā'*) or by such testimony. The difference between the two was the type of document produced. The *qāḍī* was assigned to undertake the probate, which had to be signed by two witnesses, *ʿudūl*. The second situation only presented the facts and the testimony of the person who witnessed the manumission pronounced by the deceased master. In these cases, too, it can be seen that a principal if not the only reason for manumission was for the spiritual benefit of the master.

In certain circumstances, slaves could go to the *qāḍī* with witnesses to establish their manumission in the absence of written documentation. Of the total number of documents consulted, cases such as these represented 2 percent. The small number might be related to the fact that months or even years could pass between the act of manumission and the formal recognition. In one example, the sisters Khaddāwaj and Mūnī manumitted their house slave Faṭīma, without providing her with a certificate. After Mūnī passed away, her inheritance went to her nephews Muḥammad and Aḥmad. What happen to Fatima after Mūnī's death is not clear, but seven months later toward the end of March in 1838 Fatima received a certificate.[13] In many cases, several years could pass before manumissions were recognized on paper. In another example, a slave named Mbārka was manumitted years before he received the paperwork to prove it.[14] The demand for copies of manumission papers demonstrated how important these documents were as a guarantee of freedom. Moreover, these cases show that it was not enough to be simply known as a freed slave to be really manumitted. Individuals needed documents to prove their freedom.

Among the different types of manumission, the most common was simple manumission, whereby the master granted a slave his/her freedom in belief that God would recognize the "good deed." Of the total number of manumission records, more than 75 percent were of this category. Among these cases, reasons were never given as to why the master decided to set the slave free, although there were three cases in which slaves were bought specifically to be manumitted.[15] In those cases, the motivation can be explained by the fact that the individuals wanted to expiate their sins through manumission but did not own a slave and hence had to buy someone. For example, a native of Miliana in north-western Algeria, Ḥājj Muḥammad b. ʿAbd al-Qādir, known by the nickname La ʿraj (the lame person), bought the slave, Fātiḥ, from Qaddūr al-Ḥanafī b. Muṣṭafā, also known as Bin al-Khaznājī, for his niece, Roza b. Muḥammad Khaznājī. Fatiḥ was bought for 45 riyāl dūrū. Upon completion of the transaction, Fātiḥ was freed by Qāʾid Mubārak, a former slave of Roza, who was sent by her with power of attorney expressly to execute Fātiḥ's manumission. It is clear from the context that Qaddūr al-Ḥanafī would not have sold this slave, who was born in his house (shūshān), if he was not certain that Fātiḥ would be manumitted by the buyer.[16]

Post Mortem manumission (*tadbīr*) refers to cases whereby after a master died the slave was manumitted. The difference between *post mortem* manumission and mention in a will (*waṣiyya*) is that in the former cases the outcome could not be changed or cancelled. Wheras, wishes expressed in a will can be altered during the life of the master. Moreover, after the pronouncement of the *tadbīr* the slave could no longer be bought or sold.[17] Maybe to protect slaves and guarantee that the wish of masters would be carried out whatever the circumstances, in certain wills it was stipulated, "the slave will become free one day before the sickness takes the life of his master."[18] That way, the slave freed by will, will have his manumission guaranteed. Because while *post mortem* manumissions were executed from the capital of the deceased, the manumission by a will is carried out from the third of the capital. As the diseased has the right only to the third of his possessions, the rest belongs to the heirs by law, and hence could not be part of the will. Therefore, a slave had a greater chance of being freed from *post mortem* manumission than a slave only being mentioned in a will. If in the eventuality that both types of manumissions were mentioned in the inheritance, i.e. *post mortem* manumission and a slave only being mentioned in a will, the former (*mudabbar)* was given the priority.

It was also possible for masters to put certain conditions on slaves in order for the manumission to be carried out (ʿitq muqa-

yyad). In these cases, there was only a sample of three documents to choose from, whereby two of which appeared in *post mortem* manumissions. In those two cases, the conditions were that the slave had to serve their master well and that they did not try to flee or run away. In the third case, the will of the mistress Nafūsa bt. ʿAbd al-Raḥmān stipulated the conditions on her slave Saʿāda must serve her mistress well and that Nafūsa "could sell her slave without anyone having the right to dispute or challenge this decision"[19] These examples illustrate the power of the master over his or her slaves, who were subject to the whims of their owners, who could set conditions that had to be met in order to achieve freedom. The evidence suggests the negotiation over space that was fundamental to the achievement of freedom.

It was equally possible for a master to declare his/her slave free at a predetermined date, in a sort of formal promise written into a contract. There were only three cases of this type of manumissions. Toward the end of April 1834, the mistress al-Zahrāʾ bt. Aḥmad b. ʿAbd Allāh granted her slave Faṭīma a *post mortem* manumission as well as a gift of a third of all her inheritance. Then, al-Zahrāʾ wanted to make a pilgrimage to Mecca and wanted her slave to accompany her. On the Sept. 27, 1841, al-Zahrāʾ drew up a contract whereby there was a clause in which her slave would be manumitted one year after the date of the contract. She renegotiated her manumission to occur earlier, and go on a trip to Mecca with her mistress. By virtue of this contract, Faṭīma would have been freed in September of 1842. It was stipulated moreover that when they reached Mecca, Faṭīma would have the choice of staying or returning back to Algeria with her mistress.[20] Thus, predetermined manumission was similar to conditional manumission but the conditions potentially involved restrictions on the date of manumission.

Umm Walad manumissions involved female slaves who were to be freed because they gave birth to offspring by their masters. The majority of legal schools declared that these women would be free, by their right, at the death of the master, unless they were manumitted beforehand.[21] Their legal statute was called *umm walad* and it granted the automatic manumission of slave women who had had children. For example, ʿĀʾisha was the slave of

Maḥmūd b. Ḥusayn b. Būṣālī, a hairdresser in Algiers. In 1840, he acknowledged that ʿĀʾisha was the mother of their child ʿAbd al-Raḥmān. He put into motion the umm walad statute in his will.[22] Thus, concubinage with offspring offered a chance for a female slave to become a free person.[23] In the documents housed at the ANA, there were only two other cases, much like this example, whereby manumissions were granted through umm walad status.[24]

The Structure Of Manumission Documents

The texts of manumission documents are standardized and structured. Some sections were mandatory, whereas other parts were advised, and some were optional. In the most common types of manumission, or those labeled "simple," the structure typically included the seal of the qāḍī or his signature at the top of the page followed by the names of two witnesses, and the name of the manumitted slave and the motive for the manumission. The document concluded with the signature of the ʿadl and the date of the contract. Sometimes, the date only indicated the year.[25] Simple manumissions always started with the expression "Praise be to God." All these elements in the manumission document were mandatory and if they were not included, the contracts would be deemed incomplete, and without legal value.

Beside these mandatory sections, most manumission documents included short physical descriptions of the person being manumitted. The descriptions were probably optional, and most describe adult slaves. Details on children never mentioned physical appearance.[26] Physical descriptions facilitated recognition of the manumitted slave without the possibility of much confusion. In essence, these descriptions could be considered a type of identity card before photographs.[27] Descriptions usually started by conveying the physical build in sketchy terms, such as short (qaṣīr), average height (rubʿī), tall (ṭawīl) and sometimes strong arms and legs (ghaliḍal-aṭrāf), or with long or short limbs.

Skin color was another way to describe someone, which was very often included in the manumission reports. Table 11.3 shows the skin color of 257 manumitted slaves.

TABLE 11.3: SKIN COLOR OF MANUMITTED SLAVES

COLOR	TOTAL	PERCENTAGE
Liver color (*kabdi (at) al-lawn*)	123	48%
Black (*aswad/sawdā'*)	62	24%
Not mentioned	61	24%
Red (*aḥmar/ḥamrā'*)	11	4%
Total	257	100%

The three main color categories in the documentation included liver color (*kabdī 'l-lawn*), black (*aswad*) and red (*aḥmar*). The most common color was liver color (*kabdī 'l-lawn*) at 48 percent, although it is not known exactly what that color is, what it referred to or why that term was used, although it obviously referred to a dark brown color. There were 62 cases where the person was described as black or blackish and 11 cases where the person was described as red. In 61 cases, no skin color was provided, although it can be assumed that the people were black. Most, if not all, of the manumission cases, then, refer to black slaves, and most probably coming from sub-Saharan Africa rather than being born into slavery.

Information about language helps us to identify the origins of slaves in the Regency of Algiers. The languages spoken by the manumitted slaves were sometimes included in the description section. Table 11.4 presents the languages spoken by manumitted slaves.

TABLE 11.4: LANGUAGES OF MANUMITTED SLAVES

LANGUAGE	TOTAL	PERCENTAGE
Arabic	145	56.4%
Not mentioned	91	35.4%
Language of Jenne or from Jenne	16	6.2%
ʿAjamī	3	1.2%
A little bit of Arabic	2	0.8%
Total	257	100%

As indicated in table 11.4, Arabic was the main language spoken by manumitted slaves, or almost 57 percent of all 257 cases. These people probably acquired Arabic on their own initiative as a second language when they were inserted (not to say integrated) into Algerian society and culture. It seems clear that fluency in Arabic increased the chances of being freed. Approximately 35 percent of the 257 cases (91 cases) make no mention of which language the person spoke. Only ten cases mention that the manumitted slave spoke the Jenne language (Janāwaiyya or Ganāwiyya), while there were six other cases where the manumitted slaves came from this region. The term Jenne specifically referred to the city on the Niger River that was connected to the trans-Saharan slave trade. During this period Jenne was an important hub that attracted merchants. Slaves sold in Jenne came from different parts of West Africa, but the language of the town was Bambara, and people over much of the region spoke Bambara, Malinke, Dioula or a related Manding language. It is therefore difficult to speculate on where people identified as coming from Jenne actually came, other than in the interior of the western Sudan. On the one hand, this shows the presence of a multicultural slave population in the north of Algeria, and on the other hand, it is clear that the Algerian population largely ignored more specific sub-Saharan Africa identities and labeled everybody as coming from Jenne or Guinea, understood as people from western Africa south of the Sahara in general.

Loualiche misunderstood the term Janāwiyya. She thought the manumissions referred to women from Genoa. In fact, the slave girls identified by Loualiche were enslaved girls who came from Jenne or Guinea. Loualiche misinterpreted the Arabic root JNWY in Jinwiyya to mean Genoese, which is a possible reading but clearly mistaken.[28] The reason for this confusion can be explained by the lack of an *alif* in a number of instances. Loualiche did not read this as *janāwiyya* because of confusion over the ancient spelling in Arabic with occurrences of *isqāṭ*, whereby the *alif* is commonly left out, as in the example of ʿAbd al-Raḥmān, which can be written ʿAbd al-Raḥman, or *samāwāt* which can be written *samawāt*. Therefore, it is possible to interpret the word *janāwiyya* (or in Algerian Arabic *Jnāwiyya*), pronounced *Ganāwiyya* (*Gnāwiyya*), to mean someone from Genoa,[29] rather than a person coming from Jenne in the Bilād al-Sūdān.[30] However, the meaning is clear, since in some manumission records, the physical description refers to black skin and "Sūdānic" facial markings, which establishes that these slaves were indeed sub-Saharan Africans.

In all cases, the sex of the manumitted slaves and masters were included. Table 11.5 presents the total numbers of males and females manumitted, showing whether their owner was male or females. According to table 11.5, many more females were manumitted, amounting to 71.1 percent.

TABLE 11.5: MANUMITTED SLAVES BY SEX

MASTERS	SLAVE NUMBERS		TOTAL
	FEMALE	*MALE*	
Female	81	26	
Male	116	49	
Total	197	75	272
Percentage	72.4%	27.6%	100%

TABLE 11.6: NUMBER OF MASTERS AND MISTRESSES WHO MANUMITTED SLAVES BY SEX

SLAVE	MASTER NUMBERS		TOTAL
	FEMALE	*MALE*	
Female	82	101	
Male	25	48	
Total	107	149	256
Percentage	41.8%	58.2%	100%

This probably reflects the fact there were more female slaves in Algeria in the eighteenth and nineteenth centuries than males, as well as opportunities of manumission which were available to women during this period.[31] In comparison, as shown in table 11.6, there were many women who freed their slaves, accounting to 41.8 percent of the owners whose gender can be identified. Of the 258 cases in this sample, males represented 58.2 percent of the total. The combination of tables 11.5 and 11.6 allows us to correlate ownership based on sex with the gender of the enslaved. While mistresses tended to free male slaves and female slaves at almost the same ratio, masters tended to free more female slave than males. Although male owners manumitted more slaves than women, the difference was relatively minor, considering that men probably owned many more slaves than women.

Contracts Between Patron and Client

Manumission did not mean the end of subordination. Even after a slave was manumitted, he or she was still subject to exploitation since freedom could only be considered partial. Manumission contracts stipulated the nature of the freedom to be enjoyed. For example, one manumission contract stated the terms of this freedom as follows: "He is manumitted by lawful and effective liberation; the freed-man is no longer connected to slavery or servitude, and joins the free Muslims in their rights and duties." The document states that "he shall go forth where he appears to be in the land of God." However, while freedom was defined as to deny the right of the former master "to exercise any control upon him," it also stated clearly, "except the relationship between patron and client (walā'), to whom by right, conforms to _sharī'a_."[32] In such terms, manumitted freedom, whether acquired, contracted or bought, was restricted within the terms of the patron-client relationship.

The manumitted slave was legally connected to his or her former master, even if both parties wished to terminate that relationship. Islam did not recognize the manumitted slave without formal links to the slavery days (sā'iba), which seems to be have common in the pre-Islamic period. _Shī'ī-imāmī_ legislation has retained this kind of manumission, although restricted to cases of mandatory manumission, such as in cases of manumission for expiation of sins (kaffāra).[33] In _shī'ī_ law, manumission was analogous to divorce, which entailed the serious intention to sever the relation between the couple and required sobriety, among other conditions, in order for the act to be valid.[34] This was not the case in _sunnī_ and _ibāḍī_ law, whereby manumission was valid even if the master was drunk, angry, or when manumission was invoked in the name of the devil.[35]

Some jurists argued that the act of manumission was comparable to giving birth, in that the master who granted manumission would benefit in power (ahliyya), possession (milkiyya) and protection (walāya).[36] Contemporary scholars maintained that after manumission the relationship between master and ex-slave were characterized by equality. The term *walā'* is ambiguous because it can mean either patron or client. According to this interpretation, a former slave master could not be differentiated from his or her slaves socially or legally. For those who defended this interpretation, the use of the same term *walā'* to designate patron or client is proof that slavery was forgotten.[37] Indeed, in manumission records, the use of such a vague term to describe both patron and client suggests that a sense of equality was theoretically established.[38] However, that sense of equality was only partially true. To distinguish the manumitted slave and the master, the specialized literature always used terms such as *al-mawlā 'l-a'lā* (the top client) and *al-mawlā 'l-asfal* (the bottom client) to convey the relationship of dependency and its link with former bondage.[39]

Higher social position did not require clear statement. Ambiguous language also reinforced social differentiation and hierarchical social organization. An Algerian proverb exemplifies how language could be used to play upon social position, "I call you 'my master' but you must know your own position."[40] No one is fooled when it is about status. By the use of term *walā'*, social distinctions were not so obvious, yet those involved knew who was subordinated or who had the upper hand. For example, in a marriage contract, it was clearly stated that Sālim was manumitted by Muṣṭafā Pāshā, probably the Dey of the Regency of Algiers (1797-1805). The wife, of Sālim, Mubāraka, was also manumitted, although the name of her patron was not recorded.[41] In another example of a marriage contract, the groom Mas'ūd was identified as a manumitted slave and client of Muḥammad al-Būrāsī.[42] Indeed, despite the equality of position suggested by the term *walā'*, in reality, nobody confused the positions of patron and client. The patron was the one who "gave life" to the slave through manumission. As such, the relationship between the two was comparable to the relationship of parent and child, as clearly stated in a tradition of the Prophet that "clientship is like the relationship between parents and child and cannot be transferred by sale or gift."[43] The logical consequence of this homology is a mutual heritage between master and slave in the case where one of the two would neither be the inheritor nor the agnate. The asymmetry of the relationship however made it so that the legal authorities agreed unanimously that the patron could inherit from his or her client but not vice versa.[44] Only the Ibāḍī tradition did not recognize inheritance between client and patron. According to Ibāḍī interpretation, when a former slave dies without a parent, his inheritance is divided among Muslims of the same nation (jins) of the manumitted slave. In the absence of this identity, the inheritance was divided among people who had the same color of skin, even if they were of different ethnic groups. If this identification could not be established, then the inheritance went to the poor Muslims in the region where he lived. Finally, a deceased manumitted slave, contrary to other categories of Muslims, could bequeath his entire possessions to whomever he wished by will.[45] In exchange for the right to inherit, the patron was required to protect his former slave. This protection was specifically relevant to cases of homicide. Essentially, the patron was considered as an agnate and was required to pay for spilt blood ('āqila).[46]

Despite the interpretation that manumission brought equality between master and former slaves, the newly manumitted individuals had to find strategies to overcome the lack of kin and build new relationships through marriage or incorporation into an extended family. In order to create these new social links, former masters and slaves maintained their relationships as patrons and clients.

A patron was obliged to provide for the needs of his or her manumitted slaves when they were sick. Invalids had to be looked after until they completely recuperated. Male children had to be cared for until they reached puberty, while females until they were married.[47] The master, at least theoretically, could not renounce his clients even they were causing problems. Clients were required to treat their patrons with respect, pay visits during religious festivals, and show them all kinds of expressions of deference.

Contract of Eternal Salvation

The manumission documents demonstrate the intentions behind freeing slaves. In fact, in the majority of records consulted, masters expressed their motivation for freeing slaves was "for the love of the God supreme, and to hope for his pardon." Expressions from the Qur'ān, echoed in the documents, emphasize the hope of spiritual compensation for good deeds. In some manumission documents we indeed read that "God compensates charitable souls"[48] and "does not deny retribution for well-doers."[49] In the quest for eternal salvation, manumission documents contain verses from the Qur'ān and traditions from the *sunna,* such as "In order for God to free the master from hell, he releases a slave from slavery limb by limb."[50]

In the sample of manumission cases, there were forty-five examples where masters freed their slaves not for their own benefit but in request for a third party, who could be a deceased relative. The names of such relatives are mentioned in the records. For example, in the first week of June 1823, al-'Arbī, a silk vendor, and his brother, Ḥasan, sons of Ḥājj 'Alī, manumitted their slave Sa'āda. They declared that the reward for this act should go to their deceased father.[51] In another example, Ḥusayn Pāshā, the last Dey of the Regency of Algiers (1818-1830), manumitted his slave Mbirīka and her little daughter Yāsmīna on July 10, 1827. He mentioned that he wanted this act of piety to be credited to his manumitted slave Mbārka.[52] Requests for divine acceptance and reward could vary, but they were always included in the same order in the manumission cases. Even if the request was not written directly into the text, as was the case of Ṭaḥāwī et de Ṭulayṭilī's books, that ideology was implied. Expressions of divine retribution were in the spirit of every Muslim who manumitted a slave. Indeed, the hope of divine reward was the motivation for most cases of manumission. In some cases, Muslims bought slaves only to free them and display their good will in the eyes of God and society. Generosity and piety were valuable attributes for the faithful. In this way, manumissions can be seen as contracts for eternal salvation through which Muslims sought a place in Paradise. As profane as this transaction must seem, it remains never the less one of the most important motivations why Muslims manumitted their slaves.

Conclusion

Despite the fact that slavery is a taboo subject is contemporary Algeria, documents available in the national archives reveal the role of slavery in the Regency of Algiers during Ottoman occupation. Based on manumission records, I have explored the ways manumission was perceived by slave masters. Different kinds of manumission stress the variety of ways through which slaves could achieve their freedom. While slave women who had given birth to a child by her master were freed, male slaves and other women who were not sexually involved with their owners could employ strategies to achieve freedom that involved the pious hopes of their masters. In some cases, a loyal slave was rewarded with freedom. In others, freedom was tied to specific conditions. Despite the differences, manumission indicates room for negotiation within a society where slavery was a key institution.

Slaves by definition were outsiders. In Muslim societies this pattern was evident because slavery was associated with a past of Unbelief as a non-Muslim. Thus the memory of being an outsider was never erased. Former slaves had to find strategies to overcome their identity as aliens. As a result, clientship and dependency maintained the links associated with bondage. Although legally freedom brought masters and their former slaves close, the reality of patron-client relationships stressed hierarchy and domination.

Manumission records indicate that rather than constituting a selfless act, masters freed their slaves as an expression of faith and submission to God. Masters even offered freedom in the name of deceased relatives to make sure God would reward the act. The way manumission operated in the Regency of Algiers left a strong legacy in twentieth-century Algerian society. The emphasis on generosity and piety has led Algerians to believe that slavery was mild and masters had good intentions. Moreover, this belief had consequences on the nature of slavery at the time, and its effect on history in the Islamic world is widespread. Nonetheless, the space for emancipation in Muslim jurisprudence and religious belief influenced perceptions of slavery, but did not lead to a movement for the abolition slavery.[53] On the contrary, the emphasis on divine retribution led to the continuation of mechanisms of social differentiation and subordination rather than a rupture with the practice of slavery. Comparatively, the perverse effect of the frequency of manumissions was the persistence of slave demand in Algeria.[54] Freedom was not followed by fully social, political and economic integration of former slaves into Algerian society.

Notes

1. Chouki El Hamel calls it in the context of North Africa a culture of silence: "one Islam, one nation, (al-maghrib al-'arabi), one culture, one language, and a silence." See "'Race', Slavery and Islam in Maghribi Mediterranean Thought: The Question of the *Haratin* of Morocco." *Journal of North African Studies* 7, no. 3 (2002), 29.

2. I use the concept of manumission rather than enfranchisement or emancipation to highlight the fact that these slaves were never considered free as freeborn, in the sense that Claude Meillassoux gives to this term. See *The Anthropology of Slavery: The Womb of Iron and Gold* (Chicago: University of Chicago Press, 1991), 118-121.

3. In reference to different *dīwān* de Sīdī- Bilāl and such other community organizations located throughout Algeria. See Émile Dermenghem, *Le culte des saints and l'islam maghrébin* (Paris: Gallimard, 1954), 255-297.

4. Historians call for the exploitation and study of these sources for a period of time. See J. O. Hunwick, "Black Slaves in the Mediterranean World: Introduction to a Neglected Aspect of the African Diaspora," in *The Human Commodity: Perspectives on the Trans-Saharan Slave Trade*, ed. Elizabeth Savage (London: Routledge, 1992), 30; J. O. Hunwick, "African Slaves in the Mediterranean World: A Neglected Aspect of the African Diaspora." *Global Dimensions of the African Diaspora*, ed. Joseph E. Harris (Washington, DC: Howard University Press, 1993), 315.

5. Farid Khiari, *Vivre et mourir en Alger: l'Algérie ottomane aux XVIe-XVIIe siècles: un destin confisqué* (Paris: L'Harmattan, 2002), 71-73.

6. Documents n 61 and n 84 relate to manumissions, but are not manumission records.

7. Including vol. 2, box, 282, new n 115, document n 73 ف; vol. 5, box 64, new n 6, document n 147 ف, vol. 7, box 109-110, new n 97, 99, 109, 112, 113, 114, 35, documents n°s 38 ف, 40 ف, 89 ف, 45 ف, 15 ف, 14 ف, 2 ف respectively.

8. For the documents reported by Loualiche, and which are not included in my calculations because volume 6 of the Yelles Catalogue was missing, see Fatiha Loualiche, *Fi'at al-mu'taqīn*, 192-195.

9. See box 109-110, new n 72, document n 7 ف. The documented cases include a *post mortem* manumission dated *muharram* at the beginning of 1190 h., i.e., the last third of February 1776. After sixteen years and before the death of the mistress, her slave was manumitted by a simple manumission statement dated by *dhu 'l-hijja* in the year 1206 h., corresponding to the last third of July 1792. This case appears on the same page in the right margin of the preceding document. Document n 25, box 59, is the case of a testimonial manumission dated to middle of the month of *muharram* 1246 h., corresponding to the end of May 1831. In the same document, the same person was freed by simple manumission dated 11 years after the first act, on *jumādā 'l-thāniya* 1258, corresponding to 12 July 1842.

10. Arquivo Histórico Ultramarino (AHU), Norte de África, box 409: 1813 (Cativos em Argel).

11. Abdeljelil Temimi, *Sommaire des registres arabes et turcs d'Alger* (Tunis: [s.n.], 1979), 9-14.

12. In relation to the forms and contracts, see Shams al-Dīn Muhammad b. Ahmad al-Manhājī al-Asyūtī, *Jawāhir al-'uqūd wa mu'īn al-qudāt wa 'l-muwaqqi'īn wa 'l-shuhūd*, Hamīd al-Faqī (ed.), [s.l.], [s.d.], 2ᵉ éd., 2 vols; Ahmad b. al-Mughīth al-Tulaytilī, *al-Muqni' fī 'ilm al-shurūt*, Duhā 'l-Khatīb, ed., (Beirut: Dār al-Kutub al-'Ilmiyya, 1420 h / 2000). In relation to the importance of written culture in Islam, see Émile Tyan, *Le notariat et le régime de la preuve par écrit dans la pratique du droit musulman*, [s.l.], [s.d.], 2ⁿᵈ ed.; Tyan, *Histoire de l'organisation judiciaire en pays d'islam* (Leiden: Brill, 1960).

13. Box 109-110, new n. 82, document n. 16 ف.

14. Box 3, new n. 85, document n. 08/38 ف.

15. Documents: Box 46/1, new n. 65, document n. 244 ف; box 109-110, new n. 86, document n. 37 ف; box 65-66-67 new n. 31, document n. 61 ف.

16. Documents: box 65-66-67 new n. 31, document n. 61 ف.

17. See Abū Bakr b. Mas'ūd al-Kāsānī *Badāi' al-sanā'i' fī tartīb al-sharā'i'* (Cairo: Matba'at al-Imām, 1971) vol. IV, 180.

18. See the first category in table 11.2.

19. Box 59, new n 44.

20. Box 58, new n 87, document n 9 ف.

21. See Kāsānī, *Badā'i' al-ṣanā'i'*, IV, 182-196.

22. Box 58 new n 182 document n 108 ف.

23. For further analysis of concubinage and freedom see Paul E. Lovejoy, "Concubinage and the Status of Women Slaves in Early Colonial Northern Nigeria," *Journal of African History*, 29, no. 2 (1988), 245-266.

24. See box 65-66-67, new n 59, document n 8 ف and box 58, new n 22, document n 191 ف.

25. Box 59, new n 76, manumission of Mubārak by her master *qā'id* Muṣṭafā.

26. Note that in this category manumitted children were called <u>shūshān</u> or *jūjān*, terms also used in Tunisia, and therefore terms probably originating from Hausa. The terms *bačučan* (pl. *čučanawa*) were slaves born in the house whereby it was taboo to sell them. See Marc Henri Piault, "Captifs du pouvoir et pouvoir des captifs," Claude Meillassoux, ed. *L'esclavage en Afrique précoloniale* (Paris: F. Maspero, 1975), 344-346.

27. The description of al-Asyūṭī was the most detailed. See *Jawāhir al-'uqūd*, ii, 57-81.

28. Fatiha Loualich, "Fi'at al-mu'taqīn," 185-186.

29. This is the feminine form of the word. The masculine form is *jan-awiyya* is *janawi,* but Arabic speakers in the northwest of Africa pronounce it *Jnāwiyya* and *Jnāwawi* (more commonly pronounced *gnāwiyya gnāwi*). For Arabic pronunciation of Jenné, see, Al-Sa'dī, *Tārīkh Es-Soudan*, trad., O. Houdas (Paris: E. Leroux, 1900), 22, n1. See also Marcelin Beaussier and Mohamed Ben Cheneb, *Dictionnaire pratique Arabe-Français* (Algiers: La Typo-Litho, J. Carbonel et La Maison des Livres, [1887], 1958).

30. This misreading is widespread. See Farid Khiari, *Vivre et mourir en Alger: l'Algérie ottomane aux XVIe-XVIIe siècles: un destin confisqué* (Paris: L'Harmattan, 2002), 155.

31. Lovejoy also makes this point for the Sokoto Caliphate, see "Concubinage in the Sokoto Caliphate," *Slavery and Abolition* 21, no.2 (1990), 159-189. José C. Curto makes the same argument for the case of Luanda in Angola, see Curto "'As If From a Free Womb:' Baptismal Manumissions in the Conceição Parish, Luanda, 1778-1808," *Portuguese Studies Review* 10, no. 1 (2002), 26-57.

32. These manumission forms appeared in almost all the documents and reference books. See Abū Jaʿfar Aḥmad b. Muḥammad, al-Ṭaḥāwī, *Al-shurūṭ al-ṣaghīr mudhyyalan bimā ʿuthira ʿalayhi mina 'l-shurūṭ al-kabīr*, Baghdād: Maṭbaʿat al-ʿAynī, vol. 2, 1974, 704-25; al-Ṭulayṭilī, *al-Muqniʿ*, 223-225.

33. See the compilation of ʿAlī Aṣghar Marawārīd, *Silsilat al-yanābīʿ al-fiqhiyya*, X, *Al-ʿitq wa 'l-tadbīr*, Bayrūt, Dāt al-Turāth al-Dār al-Islāmiyya, 1410 h / 1990, especially the opinion of Abū al-Qāsim ʿAlī b. al-Ḥusayn al-Ūsī, 283-284.

34. Marawārīd, *Silsilat al-yanābīʿ*, X, 283-304, among others.

35. Kāsānī, *Badāʾiʿ al-ṣanāʾiʿ*, IV, 236.

36. Kāsānī, *Badāʾiʿ al-ṣanāʾiʿ*, IV, 236.

37. See for example, Maḥmūd ʿAbd al-Wahāb Fāʾid, *Al-riqq fī 'l-Islām* (Cairo: Dār al-Iʿtiṣām, 1989), 92-99.

38. Note that in Arabic, there are many terms with more than one meaning beyond the terms stated here.

39. Kāsānī, IV, 236 and 248.

40. "*Ana ngul-'lak sīdī wa-'nta 'aʿraf qadrak.*"

41. Some documents do not mention the heir for one reason or another. In such cases, it is apparent that the spouse, suitor, *qāḍī* and the *ʿudūl* were known to the former master of the spouse. This probably meant that these people were present during the hearing.

42. See box 108-109, new n 96, document n 48 ف.

43. "Al-walāʾu luḥmat^un ka-luḥmati 'l-nasab." See, Shihāb al-Dīn Abī 'l-Faḍl Aḥmad b. ʿAlī b. Muḥammad Ibn al-Ḥajar al-ʿAsqalānī al-Shāfiʿī. *Talkhiṣ al-ḥabi-r fī takhrīj aḥādīth al-Rāfiʿī al-kabīr* (Beyruth: Dār al-Kutub al-ʿIlmiyya, 1419 h – 1998 AD), vol. 4, 510-512.

44. See Kāsānī, *Badāʾiʿ al-ṣanāʾiʿ*, IV, 236 et 239-242; Qayrawānī, *al-nawādir wa-'l-ziyādāt*, XIII, 250-251; As for the shīʿī law, see the compilation of ʿAlī Aṣghar Marawārīd, *Silsilat al-yanābīʿ* and most notably the opinion of al-Rāwandī in *Fiqh al-Qurʾān*, 262. Shīʿī however do not recognize clientship relationships in cases of mandatory manumission, such as for the expiation of a sin, manumissions in cases where slaves suffered maltreatment, or in the case of slave women who give birth to a master's son (*umm walad*). These manumited slaves were not considered clients (*sāʾiba*) of the former master. In reality they became the clients of the whole

community not only their former master. On this specific point, see *Silsilat al-yanābī'*, X, 261 and *passim*.

45. See Mḥammad b. Yūsuf Aṭfayya<u>sh</u>, <u>Sharḥ</u> *kitāb al-nīl wa* <u>shifā'</u> *'l-'alīl*, XV, 516-529. There is an opinion according to which the patron inherits from his or her client and *vice versa*, but this is exceptional; see Aṭfayya<u>sh</u>, <u>Sharḥ</u> *kitāb al-nīl*, XIV, 22.

46. See Kāsānī, *Badā'i' al-ṣanā'i'*, IV, 238. In <u>Shī</u>'ī literature, the price of blood is called *jarīra*.

47. For more details, see Aṭfayya<u>sh</u>, <u>Sharḥ</u> *kitāb al-nīl*, XIV, 20-25.

48. *Qur'ān*, XII, 88.

49. *Qur'ān*, XII, 90. These two expressions appear in most of the records.

50. This ḥadī<u>th</u> is mentioned in all authentic collections of prophetic traditions (*Ṣaḥīḥ*) with some differences in details. Cf. Bu<u>kh</u>ārī, *Ṣaḥīḥ*, al-Riyāḍ, Bayt al-Afkār al-Dawliyya, 1419 h/1998, 477; Muslim b. al-Ḥajjāj al-Qu<u>sh</u>ayrī al-Nīsābūrī, *Ṣaḥīḥ Muslim*, Bayrūt, Dār Ibn Ḥazm, 1995, II, 926-927.

51. Box 58, new n 69, document n 214 ف.

52. Box 59, new n 66. When the case involved an important person, somebody was sent to execute the manumission. The name of this person is always mentioned. In this case, it was the son-in-law of the Pā<u>sh</u>ā, Maḥmūd. This proceedure is also used in cases involving women emancipating their slaves. Women did not usually go to see the *qāḍī*. Instead, they sent a kin (*maḥram*) who would be their representative.

53. This argument is examined in detail in my analysis of the Arabic literature pertaining to slavery; see Yacine Daddi Addoun, "Abolition de l'esclavage en Algérie, 1816-1871" (PhD diss. York University, 2010).

54. See Hunwick, "African Slaves in the Mediterranean World," 315.

Bibliography

A Abolição do Tráfico e da Escravatura em Angola. Documentos. Luanda: Ministério da Cultura, 1997.

Adediran, Biodun. "Islam and Political Crises in Kétu: A Case-Study of the Role of Muslims in a Nineteenth Century Yoruba Polity." *Ife Journal of Religion* 3 (1982-1989), 3-18.

Aiton, Arthur Scott. "The Asiento Treaty as Reflected in the Papers of Lord Shelburne." *Hispanic American Historical Review* 8, no. 2 (1928), 167-177.

Ajayi, J.F.A. "Samuel Ajayi Crowther of Oyo." In *Africa Remembered: Narratives by West Africans from the Era of the Slave Trade,* edited by Philip Curtin, 289-316. Madison: University of Wisconsin, 1967.

Ajayi, J.F.A and Robert Smith. *Yoruba Warfare in the Nineteenth Century.* Cambridge: Cambridge University Press, 1964.

Alber, Jean-Luc. "Les ressorts d'une africanité réinventée à Maurice." In *Fabrication des traditions, Inventions de la modernité,* edited by Dejan Dimitrijevic, 99-118. Paris: Éditions de la Maison des sciences de l'Homme, 2004.

Alencastro, Luiz Felipe de. "Le versant brésilien de l'Atlantique-Sud: 1550-1850." *Annales: Histoire, Sciences Sociales* 61, no. 2 (2006), 339-382.

Anonymous. "Les Sites Touristiques - Village Ofia (Sous-Préfecture De Kétou)." Ofia, Bénin, n.d.

Anonymous. "The Story and the Biography of Abidogun Adebi Osundade Adebeji Family." 1-8. Ofia, Benin, n.d.

Anonymous, "Testing the Oral History at Middleburg Plantation, Berkeley County, South Carolina," *Newsletter of the African American*

Archaeological Network 26 (1999) http://www.diaspora.uiuc. edu/A-AAnewsletter26.html#anchor746411.

Apter, Andrew. "Herskovits's Heritage: Rethinking Syncretism in the African Diaspora." *Diaspora* 1, no. 3 (1991), 235-259.

Araujo, Ana Lucia. "Mémoires de l'esclavage et de la traite des esclaves dans l'Atlantique Sud: enjeux de la patrimonialisation au Brésil et au Bénin." PhD diss., Université Laval, École des Hautes Études en Sciences Sociales, 2007.

Araujo, Ana Lucia. "Renouer avec le passé brésilien: la reconstruction du patrimoine post-traumatique chez la famille De Souza au Bénin." In *Traumatisme collectif pour patrimoine: Regards croisés sur un mouvement transnational,* edited by Bogumil Jewsiewicki and Vincent Auzas, 305-330. Québec: Presses de l'Université Laval, 2008.

Araujo, Ana Lucia "Enjeux politiques de la mémoire de l'esclavage dans l'Atlantique Sud: La reconstruction de la biographie de Francisco Félix de Souza." *Lusotopie* XVI, no. 2 (2009), 107-131.

Araujo, Ana Lucia. *Public Memory of Slavery: Victims and Perpetrators in the South Atlantic.* Amherst, NY: Cambria Press, 2010.

Asiwaju, A. I. "The Alaketu of Ketu and the Onimeko of Meko." In *West African Chiefs: Their Changing Status under Colonial Rule in Africa,* edited by Michael Crowder and Obaro Ikime, 134-160. York: Africana Publishing, 1970.

Asiwaju, A. I. *Western Yorubaland under European Rule 1889-1945: A Comparative Analysis of French and British Colonialism.* Atlantic Highlands, NJ: Humanities Press, 1976.

'Asqalānī, Shihāb al-Dīn Abī 'l-Faḍl Aḥmad b. 'Alī b. Muḥammad Ibn al-Ḥajar al-Shāfi'ī (al-). *Talkhiṣ al-ḥabi-r fī takhrīj aḥādīth al-Rāfi'ī al-kabīr.* 5 vols. Beirut: Dār al-Kutub al-'Ilmiyya, 1419 h – 1998 AD.

Assmann, Jan. *Religion and Cultural Memory.* Stanford: Stanford University Press, 2006.

Assone, Sedley Richard. *Le Morne, territoire marron!* Port-Louis: Éditions de la Tour, 2002.

Axel, Brian, ed. *From the Margins: Historical Anthropology and its Futures.* Durham, NC: Duke University Press, 2002.

Babatunde, Emmanuel D. "The Gelede Masked Dance and Ketu Society: The Role of the Transvestite Masquerade in Placating Powerful Women While Maintaining the Patrilineal Ideology." In *West African Masks and Cultural Systems*, edited by Sidney L. Kasfir, 45-64. Tervuren, Belgium: Musée Royal d'Afrique Centrale, 1988.

Bako-Arifari, Nassirou. "La mémoire de la traite négrière dans le débat politique au Bénin dans les années 1990." *Journal des Africanistes* 70, no. 1-2 (2000), 221-231.

Bandeira, Júlio. "Debret e a Corte no Brasil." In *O Brasil redescoberto*, edited by Carlos Martins, 55-72. Rio de Janeiro: BNDES, 1999.

Barber, James. "Journey to Ketu." In *Church Missionary Society Archives*. Birmingham, Great Britain, 1853.

Barnes, Sandra, ed. *Africa's Ogun: Old World and New*. 2d ed. Bloomington: Indiana University Press, 1997.

Barradas, Joaquim. *A arte de sangrar de cirurgiões e barbeiros*. Lisbon: Livros Horizonte, 1999.

Barth, Frederik. *Los grupos étnicos y sus fronteras*. Mexico City: Fondo de Cultura Economica, 1976.

Barth, Heinreich. *Travels and Discoveries in North and Central Africa Being a Journal of an Expedition Undertaken Under the Auspices of H. B. M'S Government in the Years 1849-1855*. Vol. 1. London: Frank Cass, 1965.

Bastide, Roger. "Mémoire collective et sociologie du bricolage." *L'Année sociologique* 3, no. 21 (1970), 65-108.

Battell, Andrew. *The Strange Adventures of Andrew Battell of Leigh, in Angola and the Adjoining Regions*. London: The Hakluyt Society, 1901.

Baussant, Michèle. "Penser les mémoires." *Ethnologie Française* 37, no. 3 (2007), 389-394.

Baussant, Michèle. *Du vrai au juste*. Québec: Presses de l'Université Laval, 2005.

Baum, Robert Martin. *Shrines of the Slave Trade: Diola Religion and Society in Precolonial Senegambia*. New York: Oxford, 1999.

Bay, Edna G. "Protection, Political Exile and the Atlantic Slave-Trade: History and Collective Memory in Dahomey." In *Rethinking the African Diaspora: The Making of a Black Atlantic World in the Bight of Benin and Brazil,* edited by Kristin Mann and Edna G. Bay, 42-60. London: Frank Cass, 2001.

Bay, Edna G. "Protection, Political Exile, and the Atlantic Slave Trade: History and Collective Memory in Dahomey." *Slavery and Abolition* 22, no. 1 (2001), 22-41.

Bay, Edna G. *Wives of the Leopard: Gender, Politics and Culture in the Kingdom of Dahomey.* Charlottesville: Virginia University Press, 1998.

Beltrán, Gonzalo Aguirre. *Obra antropológica II: la población negra de México estudio etnohistórico.* Mexico City: Fondo de Cultura Económica, 1989 [1946].

Benezet, Anthony. *Some Historical Account of Guinea, Its Situation, Produce and the General Disposition of its Inhabitants with an Inquiry into the Rise and Progress of the Slave Trade, Its Nature and Lamentable Effects.* London: Frank Cass, 1968 [1771].

Bennet, Bennett, Valerie Smith and Marcyliena Morgan, ed. *Revolutions of the Mind: Cultural Studies in the African Diaspora Project, 1996-2002.* Los Angeles: CAAS Publications/ UCLA, 2002.

Berlin, Ira. *Generations of Captivity:A History of African-American Slaves.* Cambridge, MA: Belknap Press of Harvard University Press, 2003.

Berlin, Ira. *Many Thousands Gone: The First Two Centuries of Slavery in North America.* Cambridge, MA: Belknap Press, 1998.

Berlin, Ira. "From Creoles to African: Atlantic Creoles and the Origins of African-American Society in Mainland North America." *William and Mary Quarterly* 53, no. 2 (1996): 251-288.

Berlin, Ira. "Time, Space, and the Evolution of Afro-American Society on British Mainland North America." *American Historical Review* 85 (1980), 44-78.

Birmingham, David. *Trade and Conflict in Angola: the Mbundu and Their Neighbours under the Influence of the Portuguese 1483-1790.* Oxford: Clarendon Press, 1966.

Blier, Suzanne Preston. *African Vodun: Art, Psychology, and Power.* Chicago: University of Chicago Press, 1995.

Bowen, Thomas J. *Adventures and Missionary Labours in Several Countries in the Interior of Africa from 1849 to 1856.* 2nd ed. London: Frank Cass, 1968 [1857].

Bowser, Frederick P. *The African in Colonial Peru, 1524-1650.* Stanford: Stanford University Press, 1974.

Boxer, Charles R. *O Império Marítimo Português*. São Paulo: Companhia das Letras, 2002 [1969].

Braga, Júlio Santana. "Notas sobre o 'Quartier Brésil' no Daomé." *Afro-Ásia*, no. 6-7 (1968), 55-62.

Bruce Lockhart, Jamie and Paul E. Lovejoy, ed. *Hugh Clapperton into the Interior of Africa: Records of the Second Expedition 1825-1827.* Leiden: Brill, 2005.

Bukhārī. *Ṣaḥīḥ*. Riyadh: Bayt al-Afkār al-Dawliyya, 1998.

Butler, Kim D. *Freedoms Given, Freedoms Won: Afro-Brazilians in Post-Abolition, São Paulo and Salvador*. New Brunswick, N.J.: Rutgers University Press, 1998.

Byrd, Alexander X. "Eboe, Country, Nation and Gustavus Vassa's *Interesting Narrative*." *William and Mary Quarterly* 63, no. 1 (2006), 123-148.

Camus, Albert. *Le premier homme*. Paris: Gallimard, 1994.

Candido, Mariana. "Enslaving Frontiers: Slavery, Trade and Identity in Benguela, 1780-1850." PhD diss., York University, 2006.

Candido, Mariana. *Fronteras de Esclavización: Esclavitud, Comercio e Identidade en Benguela, 1780-1850*. Mexico City: El Colegio de México Press, 2011.

Capelo, Hermenegildo and Roberto Ivens. *De Benguela às terras de Iaca*. Lisbon: Publicações Europa-América, 1877.

Cadornega, António de Oliveira de. *História Geral das Guerras Angolanas*. Lisbon: Agência Geral do Ultramar, 1972, vol. 3.

Carneiro, Edison. *Candomblés da Bahia*. Salvador: Secretaria de Educação e Saúde, 1948.

Carretta, Vincent. *Equiano the African: Biography of a Self-Made Man.* Athens, GA: University of Georgia Press, 2005.

Carretta, Vincent, ed. *The Interesting Narrative and Other Writings*. New York: Penguin, 2003.

Castillo, M.E. Brenes. "Matina, Bastión del contrabando en Costa Rica." *Anuario de Estudios Centroamericanos* [Costa Rica] 4 (1978), 416-418.

Castro, Yeda Pessoa de. *A língua Mina-Jeje no Brasil. Um falar africano em Ouro Preto do século XVIII*. Belo Horizonte: Fundação João Pinheiro, 2002.

Césaire, Aimé. "Culture et colonisation." In *Œuvres complètes*. Vol. III. Fort de France: Éditions Désormeaux, 1976 [1956].

Chambers, Douglas. "'My Own Nation': Egbo Exiles in the Diaspora." In *Routes to Slavery. Direction, Ethnicity and Mortality in the Atlantic Slave Trade*, edited by David Eltis and David Richardson, 72-97. New York: Routledge, 1997.

Chan Low, Jocelyn. "Les enjeux actuels des débats sur la mémoire et la réparation pour l'esclavage à l'ile Maurice." *Cahiers d'études africaines* 1-2, no. 173-174 (2004), 401-418.

Chan Low, Jocelyn. "De l'Afrique rejetée à l'Afrique retrouvée? Les Créoles de l'Ile Maurice et l'Africanité." *Revi Kiltir Kreol* 3 (2003), 39-50

Chan Low, Jocelyn. "Esclaves, exclus, citoyens?" In *L'esclavage et ses séquelles: mémoire et vécu d'hier et d'aujourd'hui. Actes du Colloque international UOM* (1998), edited by Jean-Clément Jocelyn Chan Low and Mayila Paroomal, 237-272. Port Louis: Presses de l'Université de Maurice, 2002.

Chazan-Gillig, Suzanne. "The Roots of Mauritian Multiculturalism and the Birth of a New Social Contract: Being *Autochtone*, Being Creole." *Journal of Mauritian Studies* 2, no. 1(2003), 64-84.

Cilardo, Agostino. "The Transmission of the Patronate in Islamic Law." In *Miscellanea Arabica et Islamica: Dissertationes in Academia Ultrajectine prolatae anno MCMXC*, 31-52. Leuven: Uitgeverij Peeters en Depatement Oriëntalistiek, 1993.

Clapperton, Hugh. "Hugh Clapperton into the Interior of Africa: Records of the Second Expedition, 1825-1827." In *Hugh Clapperton into de Interior of Africa*, edited by Jamie Bruce-Lockhart and Paul E. Lovejoy, 1-77. Leiden: Brill, 2005.

Clapperton, Hugh. *Journal of a Second Expedition into the Interior of Africa from the Bight of Benin to Socatoo*. London: Cass, 1966.

Comaroff, John and Jean Comaroff. *Ethnography and the Historical Imagination*. Boulder, CO: Westview Press, 1992.

Confino, Alon. "Collective Memory and Cultural History: Problems of Method." *American Historical Review* 105 (1997), 1386-1403.

Cord, Marcelo Mac. *O Rosário de D. Antônio. Irmandades negras, alianças e conflitos na história social do Recife. 1848-1872*. São Paulo and Recife: Fundação de Amparo à Pesquisa do Estado de

São Paulo and Editora Universitária da Universidade Federal de Pernambuco, 2005.

Cornevin, Robert. *Histoire du Dahomey.* Paris: Éditions Berger-Levrault, 1962.

Coquery-Vidrovitch, Catherine. *L'Afrique occidentale au temps des Français: colonisateurs et colonisés (c.1860-1969).* Paris: La Découverte, 1992.

Costa e Silva, Alberto. *Francisco Félix de Souza, mercador de escravos.* Rio de Janeiro: Nova Fronteira, 2004.

Cottias, Myriam. *La question noire. Histoire d'une construction coloniale.* Paris: Bayard, 2007.

Couto, Carlos. "Regimento de Governo Subalterno de Benguela." *Studia* 45 (1981), 285-294

Couto, Carlos. *Os Capitães-Mores em Angola no Século XVIII.* Luanda: Instituto de Investigação Científica Tropical, 1972.

Cunha, Manuela Carneiro da. *Negros, estrangeiros: os escravos libertos e sua volta à África.* São Paulo: Brasiliense, 1985.

Curtin, Philip D. *The Atlantic Slave Trade: A Census.* Madison: University of Wisconsin Press, 1969.

Curto, José C. *Enslaving Spirits, The Portuguese-Brazilian Alcohol Trade at Luanda and Its Hinterland, C. 1550-1830.* Leiden: Brill, 2004.

Curto, José C. "The Legal Portuguese Slave Trade from Benguela, Angola, 1730-1828: a Quantative Re-appraisal." *África* 17, no. 1 (1993/1994), 101-116.

Curto, José C. "'As If From a Free Womb:' Baptismal Manumissions in the Conceição Parish, Luanda, 1778-1808," *Portuguese Studies Review*, 10, 1 (2002), 26-57.

Curto, José C. "Movers of Slaves: The Brazilian Community in Benguela (Angola), c. 1722-1832." Paper presented at the International Symposium "Angola on the Move: Transport Routes, Communications, and History," Berlin, November 2003.

Curto, José C. "Luso-Brazilian Alcohol and the Legal Slave Trade at Benguela and its Hinterland, c. 1617-1830." In *Négoce Blanc en Afrique Noire: L'évolution du commerce à longue distance en Afrique noire du 18e au 20e siècles,* edited by H. Bonin and M.

Cahen, 351-69. Paris: Publications de la Société française d'histoire d'outre-mer, 2001.

Daddi Addoun, Yacine. "L'Abolition de l'esclavage em Algérie: 1816-1871," PhD diss., York University, 2010.

Dalzel, Archibald. *The History of Dahomy, an Inland Kingdom of Africa.* 2nd ed. London: Frank Cass, 1967 [1793].

Daniel, Levy and Nathan Sznaider. "Memory Unbound: The Holocaust and the Formation of Cosmopolitan Memory." *European Journal of Social Theory* 5, no. 1 (2002), 87-106.

Debret, Jean-Baptiste. *Voyage pittoresque et historique au Brésil.* Paris: Firmin Didot et Frères, 1834-1839.

Defoe, Daniel. *A Plan of the English Commerce: Being a Compleat Prospect of the Trade of this Nation, as well the Home Trade as the Foreign in Three Parts.* Oxford: Basil Blackwell, 1928 [1728 and 1730].

Delgado, Ralph. *O Reino de Benguela (do Descobrimento à Criação do Governo Subalterno).* Lisbon: Imprensa Beleza, 1945.

Denis, Dohou Codjo. "Influences brésiliennes à Ouidah." *Afro-Ásia* 12 (1976), 193-209.

Dermenghem, Émile. *Le culte des saints and l'islam maghrébin.* Paris: Gallimard, 1954.

Dias, Jill. "Novas Identidades Africanas em Angola no Contexto do Comércio Atlântico." In *Trânsitos Coloniais: Diálogos Críticos Luso-Brasileiros*, edited by Cristiana Bastos, Miguel Vale de Almeida and Bela Feldman-Bianco, 293-320. Lisbon: Imprensa de Ciências Sociais, 2002.

Donnan, Elizabeth. "The Early Days of the South Sea Company, 1711-1718." *Economic and Business History* 2 (1929), 419-450.

Donnan, Elizabeth, ed. *Documents Illustrative of the History of the Slave Trade to America. The Eighteenth Century.* Vol. 2. New York: Octagon Books, 1965 [1931].

Douville, Jean-Baptiste. *Voyage au Congo et dans l'intérieur de l'Afrique Equinoxiale.* Vol. 2. Paris: Chez Jules Renouard, 1832,

Drewal, Henry John, and Margaret Thompson Drewal. *Gelede: Art and Female Power among the Yoruba, Traditional Arts of Africa.* Bloomington: Indiana University Press, 1983.

Duncan, John. *Travels in Western Africa in 1845 & 1846: Comprising a Journey from Whydah, through the Kingdom of Dahomey, to Adofoodia in the Interior.* Vol. 1. London: Cass, 1968 [1847].

Dunglas, Edouard. "Contribution ál'histoire Du Moyen-Dahomey (Royaume d'Abomey, de Kétou et de Ouidah)." *Études Dahoméennes* I-III, no. 20, 21 (1957-1958).

Dyson, Freeman. "Our Biotech Future." *New York Review of Books*, July 17, 2007.

Edwards, Paul and James Walvin. *Black Personalities in the Era of the Slave Trade.* London: Macmillan, 1983.

Edwards, Paul and Rosalind Shaw. "The Invisible *Chi* in Equiano's *Interesting Narrative.*" *Journal of Religion in Africa* 19 (1989), 146-156.

El Hamel, Chouki. "'Race', Slavery and Islam in Maghribi Mediterranean Thought: The Question of the *Haratin* of Morocco." *Journal of North African Studies* 7, no. 3 (2002), 29-52.

Eltis, David. "The Transatlantic Slave Trade: A Reassessment Based on the Second Edition of the Transatlantic Slave Trade Database." Paper presented at the 120th American Historical Association Annual Meeting, Philadelphia, January 4, 2006.

Eltis, David et al. *The Trans-Atlantic Slave Trade Database*: http://www.slavevoyages.org.

Eltis, David, Stephen Beherendt, David Richardson, and Herbert Klein. *The Trans-Atlantic Slave Trade. A Database on CD-Rom.* Cambridge: Cambridge University Press, 1999.

Eltis, David and Stanley L. Engerman. "Was the Slave Trade Dominated by Men?" *Economic History Review* 46, no. 2 (1993), 308-323.

Eltis, David, Paul E. Lovejoy and David Richardson. "Slave-Trading Ports: Towards an Atlantic-Wide Perspective." In *Ports of the Slave Trade (Bights of Benin and Biafra)*, edited by Robin Law and Silke Strickrodt, 12-34. Stirling: Centre of Commonwealth Studies, University of Stirling, 1999.

Eltis, David and David Richardson. *Extending the Frontiers: Essays on the New Transatlantic Slave Trade Database.* New Haven, CT: Yale University Press, 2008.

Equiano, Olaudah. *The Interesting Narrative and Other Writings.* Edited by Vincent Carretta. New York: Penguin Books, 2003.

Eriksen, Thomas Hylland. *Common Denominators. Ethnicity, Nation-building and Compromise in Mauritius.* Oxford: Berg, 1998.

Fadipe, N. A. *The Sociology of the Yoruba.* Edited by Francis Okedeji and Oladejo Okedeji. Ibadan, Nigeria: University of Ibadan Press, 1970.

Fāʾid, Maḥmūd ʿAbd al-Wahāb.*Al-riqq fī ʾl-Islām.* Cairo: Dār al-Iʿtiṣām, 1989.

Falola, Toyin and Matt D. Childs, ed. *The Yoruba Diaspora in the Atlantic World.* Bloomington: Indiana University Press, 2004.

Faulkner, Valentine. "Journal of Itinerary from Ebute Meta to the Kétu Territory via Oyo, Badagry, Ado, Okeodan, and Ilaro, July-August, 1875." In *Church Missionary Society Archives.* Birmingham, Great Britain, 1875.

Ferreira, Luís Gomes. *Erário Mineral,* edited by Júnia Furtado. Belo Horizonte/Rio de Janeiro: Fundação João Pinheiro/Fundação Oswaldo Cruz, 2002.

Ferreira, Roquinaldo. "Ilhas Crioulas: O Significado Plural da Mestiçagem Cultural na África Atlântica. *Revista de História* 155, no. 2 (2006), 17-41.

Ferreira, Roquinaldo Amaral. "Transforming Atlantic Slaving: Trade, Warfare and Territorial Control in Angola, 1650-1800." PhD diss., University of California, Los Angeles, 2003.

Fika, Adamu Mohammed. *The Kano Civil War and British Overrule 1882-1940.* Ibadan: Oxford University Press, 1978.

Florentino, Manolo. "Alforrias e etnicidades no Rio de Janeiro oitocentista: notas de pesquisa." *Topoi* 5 (2002), 9-40.

Florentino, Manolo. *Em Costas Negras. Uma Historia do Tráfico de escravos entre a África e o Rio de Janeiro.* São Paulo: Companhia das Letras, 1997.

Forbes, Frederick E. *Dahomey and the Dahomans. Being the Journals of Two Missions to the King of Dahomey and Residence at His Capital in the Years 1849 and 1850.* Vol. 1. London: Frank Cass, 1966 [1851].

Foster, Gwendolyn Audrey. *Class Passing. Social Mobility in Film and Popular Culture.* Chicago: Southern Illinois Press, 2005.

Foster, Vonita White. *Black Hanoverians: An Enlightened Past.* Rockville, Virginia: ITS, 1999.

Freyre, Gilberto. *Casa-Grande & Senzala*. São Paulo: Global Editora, 2003 [1933].

Gilroy, Paul. *The Black Atlantic. Modernity and Double Consciousness*. Cambridge, MA: Harvard University Press, 1993.

Ginsberg, Elaine K. and Donald E. Pease, ed. *Passing and the Fictions of Identity*. Durham, NC: Duke University Press, 1996.

Gleason, Judith. *Agotime: Her Legend*. New York: Grossman, 1970.

Goddard, S. "Town-Farm Relationship in Yorubaland: A Case Study from Oyo." *Africa* 35, no. 1 (1965), 21-29.

Gollmer, Charles Andrew. "Journal Extracts for the Half Year Ending September 25, 1859." In *Church Missionary Society Archives*. Birmingham, Great Britain, 1859.

Gomez, Michael. *Black Crescent: The Experience and Legacy of African Muslims in the Americas*. New York: Cambridge University Press, 2005.

Gomez, Michael. *Reversing Sail. A History of the African Diaspora*. New York: Cambridge University Press, 2005.

Gomez, Michael. *Exchanging Our Country Marks: The Transformation of African Identities in the Colonial and Antebellum South*. Chapel Hill: University of North Carolina Press, 1998.

Goslinga, Cornelius Ch. "Curaçao as a Slave-trading Center During the War of the Spanish Succession (1702-1714)." *Nieuwe West-Indishe Gids* (*New West Indian Guide*) 52 (1977), 1-50.

Goslinga, Cornelius Ch. *The Dutch in the Caribbean and the Guianas, 1680-1791*, ed. Maria J.L. van Yperen. Assen: Van Gorcum & Company, 1985.

Gunning, Sandra, Tera W. Hunter, and Michele Mitchell. "Gender, Sexuality, and African Diasporas." *Gender and History* 15, no. 3 (2003), 397-408.

Guran, Milton. *Agudás: Os "Brasileiros" do Benim*. Rio de Janeiro: Editora Nova Fronteira, 1999.

Gwaltney, John Langston. *Drylongso: A Self Portrait of Black America*. New York: Random House, 1980.

Hacking, Ian. *Historical Ontology*. Cambridge, MA: Harvard University Press, 2004.

Halbwachs, Maurice. *On Collective Memory*. Chicago: Chicago University Press, 1992 [1926].

Halbwachs, Maurice. *Les cadres sociaux de la mémoire.* Paris: Presses Universitaires de France, 1952 [1925].

Hall, Gwendolyn Midlo. *Slavery and African Ethnicities in the Americas: Restoring the Links.* Chapel Hill: University of North Carolina Press, 2005.

Hambly, Wilfrid. "The Ovimbundu of Angola." *Field Museum of Natural History, Anthropological Series* 21, no. 2 (1934), 89-361.

Hamza, Ibrahim. "Slavery and Plantation Society at Dorayi in Kano Emirate." In *Slavery on the Frontiers of Islam*, edited by Paul E. Lovejoy, 125-148. Princeton, NJ: Markus Wiener, 2004.

Harding, Rachel E. *A Refuge in Thunder: Candomblé and Alternative Spaces of Blackness, Blacks in the Diaspora.* Bloomington: Indiana University Press, 2000.

Hartog, François. *Régimes d'historicité. Présentisme et expérience du temps.* Paris: Seuil, 2003.

Hazoumé, Paul. *Le Pacte de Sang au Dahomey.* Paris: Institut d'Ethnologie, 1956.

Heijer, Henk den. "The Dutch West India Company, 1621-1791." In *Riches from Atlantic Commerce,* edited by Johannes M. Potsma and Victor Enthoven, 77-114. Leiden: Brill, 2003.

Heintze, Beatrix. "Historical Notes on the Kisama of Angola." *Journal of African History* 13, no. 3 (1972), 417-418.

Heintze, Beatrix. "A Lusofonia no Interior da África Central na era pré-colonial: Um Contributo para a sua História e Compreensão na Actualidade." *Cadernos de Estudos Africanos* 6/7 (2004/2005), 179-207.

Herissé, A. Le. *L'Ancien Royaume de Dahomey.* Paris: La Rose, 1911.

Herskovits, Melville. *Les bases de l'anthropologie culturelle.* Paris: Payot, 1952.

Heywood, Linda M., ed. *Central Africans and Cultural Transformations in the American Diaspora.* New York: Cambridge University Press, 2002.

Higgins, Kathleen. *Licentious Liberty in a Brazilian Gold-Mining Region.* University Park: Pennsylvania State University Press, 1999.

Hill, Polly. *Population, Prosperity and Poverty: Rural Kano, 1900 and 1970.* New York: Cambridge University Press, 1977.

Hill, Polly. "From Slavery to Freedom: The Case of Farm Slavery in Nigerian Hausaland." *Comparative Studies in Society and History* 18, no. 3 (1976), 395-426.

Hirsch, Marianne. *Family Frames, Photography Narrative and Post-memory.* Cambridge, MA: Harvard University Press, 1997.

Hogendorn, Jan S. "The Economics of Slave Use on Two 'Plantations' in the Zaria Emirate of the Sokoto Caliphate." *International Journal of African Historical Studies* 10 (1977), 369-383.

Hunwick, J. O. "Black Slaves in the Mediterranean World: Introduction to a Neglected Aspect of the African Diaspora." In *The Human Commodity: Perspectives on the Trans-Saharan Slave Trade,* edited by Elizabeth Savage, 5-38. London: Routledge, 1992.

Hunwick, J. O. "African Slaves in the Mediterranean World: A Neglected Aspect of the African Diaspora." In *Global Dimensions of the African Diaspora,* edited by Joseph E. Harris, 289-323, Washington, DC: Howard University Press, 1993.

Hurston, Zora Neal. *Mules and Men.* New York: J.B. Lippincott, 1935.

Ibitokun, Benedict M. *Dance as Ritual Drama and Entertainment in the Gèlèdè of the Kétu-Yorùbá Subgroup in West Africa.* Ilé-Ife, Nigeria: Obàfemi Awólowo University Press, 1993.

Jackson, Maurice. *Let This Voice Be Heard: Anthony Benezet, Father of Atlantic Abolitionism* Philadelphia: University of Pennsylvania Press, 2009.

Jewsiewicki, Bogumil. "Patrimonialiser les mémoires pour accorder à la souffrance la reconnaissance qu'elle mérite." In *Traumatisme collectif pour patrimoine: Regards croisés sur un mouvement transnational,* edited by Bogumil Jewsiewicki and Vincent Auzas, 3-12. Quebec: Presses de l'Université Laval, 2008.

Jewsiewicki, Bogumil. *Mami wata. La peinture urbaine au Congo.* Paris: Gallimard, 2003.

Jewsiewicki, Bogumil and Jocelyn Létourneau, ed. *L'histoire en partage, usages et mises en discours du passé.* Paris: L'Harmattan, 1996.

Johnson, James W. *The Autobiography of an Ex-Coloured Man.* New York: Dover, 1995 [1921].

Jordaan, Han. "The Curaçao Slave Market: From *Asiento* Trade to Free Trade, 1700-1730." In *Riches from Atlantic Commerce,* edited by Johannes M. Potsma and Victor Enthoven, 219-257. Leiden: Brill, 2003

Julião, Carlos, *Riscos iluminados de figurinhos de brancos e negros dos uzos do Rio de Janeiro e Serro do Frio* (Introdução histórica e catálogo descritivo por Lygia da Fonseca Fernandes Cunha), edição fac-simile comemorativa do quinto centenário do Infante D. Henrique. Rio de Janeiro: Biblioteca Nacional, Ministério da Educação e Cultura, 1960.

Karasch, Mary. *A Vida dos Escravos no Rio de Janeiro, 1808-1850*. São Paulo: Companhia das Letras, 2000.

Karasch, Mary. "Minha Nação': Identidades Escravas no Fim do Brasil Colonial." In *Brasil: Colonização e Escravidão*, ed. Maria Beatriz Nizza da Silva, 127-141. Rio de Janeiro: Nova Fronteira, 1999.

Kāsānī, Abū Bakr b. Mas'ūd (al-). *Badāi' al-ṣanā'i'fī tartīb al-sharā'i'*, 7 vols. Beirut: Dār al-Kutub al-'Ilmiyya, 1986.

Kiddy, Elizabeth W. *Blacks of the Rosary. Memory and History in Minas Gerais, Brazil.* Pennsylvania: Pennsylvania State University Press, 2005.

Klein, Herbert. "Tráfico de escravos." In *Estatísticas Históricas do Brasil, Séries econômicas, demográficas e sociais de 1500 a 1985.* Rio de Janeiro: IBGE, 1987.

Klein, Herbert. "The Portuguese Slave Trade from Angola in the XVIII Century." *Journal of Economic History* 32, no. 4 (1972), 894-918.

Klein, Martin A. "Studying the History of Those Who Would Rather Forget: Oral History and the Experience of Slavery." *History in Africa* 16 (1989), 209-217.

Klooster, Wim. "Curaçao and the Caribbean Transit Trade." In *Riches from Atlantic Commerce: Dutch Transatlantic Trade and Shipping, 1585-1817*, edited by Johannes Postma and Victor Enthoven, 203-218. Leiden: Brill, 2003.

Kritzman, Lawrence D., ed. *Realms of Memory: Rethinking the French Past*, trans. Arthur Goldhammer. New York: Columbia University Press, 1998.

Lapierre, Nicole. "Le cadre référentiel de la Shoah." *Ethnologie Française* 37, no. 3 (2007), 475-482.

Lara, Silvia Hunold. "Customs and Costumes: Carlos Julião and the Images of Black Slaves in Late Eighteenth-Century Brazil." *Slavery and Abolition* 23, no. 2 (2002), 125-146.

Lara, Silvia Hunold. "Linguagem, domínio senhorial e identidade étnica nas Minas Gerais em meados do Século XVIII." In *Trânsitos*

Coloniais: Diálogos Críticos Luso-Brasileiros, edited by Cristiana Bastos, Miguel Vale de Almeida e Bela Feldman-Bianco, 205-225. Lisbon: Imprensa de Ciências Sociais, 2002.

Larsen, Nella. *Passing*. New York: Penguin Classics, 1999.

Larson, Pier. "Reconsidering Trauma, Identity, and the African Diaspora: Enslavement and Historical Memory in 19th Century Highland Madagascar." *The William and Mary Quarterly* 56, no. 2 (1999), 335-362.

Lavabre, Marie-Claire. "Roger Bastide, lecteur de Maurice Halbwachs." In *Maurice Halbwachs: espace, mémoires et psychologie collective*, edited by Yves Deloye et Claudine Haroche, 161-171. Paris: Publications de la Sorbonne, 2004.

Laville, Rosabelle. "Prospects for Creole Identity Beyond 2000: An Anthropological Perspective." In *L'esclavage et ses séquelles: mémoire et vécu d'hier et d'aujourd'hui*, Actes du Colloque International organisé par l'UOM (1998), 289-302. Port-Louis: M. des Arts et de la Culture, 2002.

Law, Robin. "The Atlantic Slave Trade in Local History Writing in Ouidah." In *Africa and Trans-Atlantic Memories: Literary and Aesthetic Manifestations of Diaspora and History*, edited by Naana Opoku-Agyemang, Paul E. Lovejoy and David V. Trotman, 257-274. Trenton, NJ: Africa World Press, 2008.

Law, Robin. "Etnias dos Africanos na Diáspora: Novas Considerações sobre os Significados do termo 'Mina.'" *Tempo* 10, no. 20 (2006), 109-131.

Law, Robin. *Ouidah, The Social History of a West African Slaving "Port," 1727-1892*. Athens, OH: Ohio University Press, 2004.

Law, Robin. "A Carreira de Francisco Félix de Souza na África Ocidental (1800-1849)." *Topoi* (2001), 9-39.

Law, Robin. "Ethnicity and the Slave Trade: Lucumi and Nago as Ethnonyms in West Africa." *History in Africa* 24 (1997), 205-219.

Law, Robin. *The Slave Coast of West Africa 1550-1750. The Impact of the Atlantic Slave Trade on an African Society*. Oxford: Clarendon Press, 1991.

Law, Robin. *The Oyo Empire, c.1600-C.1836: A West African Imperialism in the Era of the Atlantic Slave Trade*. Oxford: Clarendon Press, 1977.

Law, Robin, and Paul E. Lovejoy. *The Biography of Mahommah Gardo Baquaqua: His Passage from Slavery to Freedom in Africa and America*. Princeton, NJ: Markus Wiener Publishers, 2001.

Law, Robin, and Kristin Mann. "West Africa in the Atlantic Community: The Case of the Slave Coast." *The William and Mary Quarterly* 56, no. 2 (1999), 307-334.

Lawal, Babatunde. *The Gèlèdè Spectacle: Art, Gender, and Social Harmony in an African Culture*. Seattle: University of Washington Press, 1996.

Lebsock, Suzanne. *The Free Women of Petersburg: Status and Culture in a Southern Town, 1784-1860*. New York: W.W. Norton and Company, 1984.

Lemelle, Sidney, and Robin D. G. Kelley. "Introduction: Imagining Home: Pan-Africanism Revisited." In *Imagining Home: Class, Culture and Nationalism in the African Diaspora*, edited by Sidney Lemelle and Robin D. G. Kelley, 1-16. London and New York: Verso, 1994.

Lemos, Maximiano. *História da Medicina em Portugal: instituições e doutrinas*. Vol. 2. Lisboa : Dom Quixote : 1991 [1899].

Levi-Strauss, Claude. *La pensée sauvage*. Paris: Librairie Plon, 1962.

Levy, Daniel and Nathan Sznaider. "Memory Unbound: The Holocaust and the Formation of Cosmopolitan Memory." *European Journal of Social Theory* 5-1 (2002), 87-106.

Lima, Vivaldo da Costa. "Nações-de-Candomblé." In *Encontro de Nações de Candomblé: Salvador-Bahia*, edited by Vivaldo da Costa Lima, 65-90. Salvador: Universidade Federal da Bahia Centro de Estudos Afro-Orientais, 1984.

Love, Edgar F. "Legal Restrictions on Afro-Indian Relations in Colonial Mexico." *Journal of Negro History* 55, no. 2 (1970), 131-139.

Lovejoy, Paul E. "The Context of Enslavement in West Africa: Ahmad Bābā and the Ethics of Slavery." In *Slaves, Subjects and Subversives: Blacks in Colonial Latin America,* edited by Jane Landers and Barry M. Robinson, 9-38. Albuquerque: University of New Mexico Press, 2007.

Lovejoy, Paul E. "Autobiography and Memory: Gustavus Vassa, alias Olaudah Equiano, the African." *Slavery and Abolition* 27, no. 3 (2006), 317-347.

Lovejoy, Paul E. "Identidade e a Miragem da Etnicidade. A Jornada de Mahommah Gardo Baquaqua para as Américas." *Afro-Ásia* 27 (2002), 34-7.

Lovejoy, Paul E, ed. *Identity in the Shadow of Slavery.* New York: Continuum, 2000.

Lovejoy, Paul E. *Transformations in Slavery: A History of Slavery in Africa.* Cambridge: Cambridge University Press, 2nd ed., 2000.

Lovejoy, Paul E. "The African Diaspora: Revisionists Interpretations of Ethnicity, Culture and Religion under Slavery." *Studies in the World History of Slavery, Abolition and Emancipation* 2, no. 1 (1997): 1-23.

Lovejoy, Paul E. "Concubinage and the Status of Women Slaves in Early Colonial Northern Nigeria." *Journal of African History* 29, no. 2 (1988), 245-266.

Lovejoy, Paul E. "Slavery in the Sokoto Caliphate." In *The Ideology of Slavery in Africa,* edited by Paul E. Lovejoy, 201-243. Beverly Hills: Sage Publications 1981.

Lovejoy, Paul E. *Caravans of Kola: The Hausa Kola Trade (1700-1900).* Zaria: Ahmadu Bello University Press, 1980.

Lovejoy, Paul E. and Jan S. Hogendorn. "Oral Data Collection and the Economic History of the Central Savanna." *Savanna* 7, no. 1 (1978), 71-74.

Lovejoy, Paul E. and David Richardson. "The Internal Crisis of Adaptation: The Impact of British Abolition on the Atlantic Slave Trade in West Africa, 1808-1820." In *From Slave Trade to "Legitimate" Commerce. The Commercial Transition in Nineteenth-Century West Africa,* edited by Robin Law, 32-56. Cambridge: Cambridge University Press, 1995.

Lovejoy, Paul E. and David V. Trotman, ed. *Trans-Atlantic Dimensions of Ethnicity in the African Diaspora.* London: Continuum, 2003.

Lovejoy, Paul E. and David V. Trotman. "Enslaved Africans and their Expectations of Slave Life in the Americas: Toward a Reconsideration of Models of "Creolisation." In *Questioning Creole. Creolisation Discourses in Caribbean Culture,* edited by Verene Shepherd and Glen L. Richards, 67-91. Kingston: Ian Randle Publishers, 2002.

Loualich, Fatiha. "Fi'at alm^cutaqīn bi-madīnat al-Jazā'ir nihāyat al-qarn [al-<u>thā</u>min] ^c<u>ash</u>ar bidāyat al-qarn al-tāsi^cc<u>ash</u>ar min <u>kh</u>ilāl wath̲ā'iq al-maḥākim al-sharᶜiyya: les affranchies [sic] à. Alger fin du XVIIᵉ début du XIXᵉ siècles d'après les actes des Mahâkim Shar'yya,"*Arab Historical Review for Ottoman Studies* 25 (2002), 181-196.

Madden, T.O and Ann L. Miller. *We Were Always Free: The Maddens of Culpepper County, Virginia, a 200 Year Family History.* New York: W.W. Norton and Company, 1992.

Mahadi, Abdullahi. "The State and the Economy: The Sarauta System and its Roles in Shaping the Society and Economy of Kano with Particular Reference to the Eighteenth and Nineteenth Centuries." PhD diss., Ahmadu Bello University, 1982.

Mamigonian, Beatriz Galotti. "To be a Liberated African in Brazil: Labour and Citizenship in the Nineteenth Century." PhD diss., University of Waterloo, 2002.

Mann, Kristin, and Edna G. Bay. "Shifting Paradigms in the Study of the African Diaspora and of Atlantic History and Culture." In *Rethinking the African Diaspora: The Making of a Black Atlantic World in the Bight of Benin and Brazil*, edited by Kristin Mann and Edna G. Bay, 3-21. London: Frank Cass, 2001.

Marawārīd, ᶜAlī Aṣg̲h̲ar. *Silsilat al-yanābīᶜ al-fiqhiyya*, X, *Al-ᶜitq wa 'l-tadbīr*. Beirut: Dāt al-Turāth̲ al-Dār al-Islāmiyya, 1990.

Marquese, Rafael de Bivar. "A dinâmica da escravidão no Brasil: resistência, tráfico negreiro e alforrias, séculos XVII a XIX." *Novos Estudos* 74 (2006), 107-123.

Matory, J. Lorand. "The English Professors of Brazil: On the Diasporic Roots of the Yorùbá Nation." *Comparative Studies in Society and History* 41, no. 1 (1999), 72-103.

Matory, J. Lorand.. *Sex and the Empire That Is No More: Gender and the Politics of Metaphor in Oyo Yoruba Religion.* New York: Berghahn, 1997.

Matory, J. Lorand.. *Black Atlantic Religion: Tradition, Transnationalism, and Matriarchy in the Afro-Brazilian Candomblé.* Princeton, NJ: Princeton University Press, 2005.

Mauro, Frédéric. *Portugal, o Brasil e o Atlântico.* Lisbon: Estampa, 1997.

Mazārī, Ag̲h̲ā bin ᶜUda (al-). *Ṭulūᶜ Saᶜd al-suᶜūd fī ak̲h̲bār Wahrān wa-'l-Jazā'ir wa-Ispāniyā wa-Faransā 'ilā awāk̲h̲ir al-qarn al-tāsiᶜᶜashar*, éd. Yaḥyā Bū ᶜAzīza. Beirut: Dār al-Gharb al-islāmī, 1990.

Meillassoux, Claude. *The Anthropology of Slavery: The Womb of Iron and Gold.* Chicago: University of Chicago Press, 1991.

Melo, D. Miguel Antonio de. "Relatório do Governo de D. Miguel Antonio de Mello." *Boletim da Sociedade de Geografia de Lisboa,* 5th serie, 8 (1885), 548-564.

Mercier, Paul "Notice sur le peuplement Yoruba au Dahomey-Togo," *Études Dahoméennes* 4 (1950), 29-40.

Miller, Joseph C. "Retention, Reinvention, and Remembering: Restoring Identities through Enslavement in Africa and under Slavery in Brazil." In *Enslaving Connections: Changing Cultures of Africa and Brazil during the Era of Slavery,* edited by José C. Curto and Paul E. Lovejoy, 81-121. Amherst, NY: Humanity Books, 2004.

Miller, Joseph C. "Central Africa during the Era of the Slave Trade, c. 1490s-1850s." In *Central Africans and Cultural Transformations in the American Diaspora,* edited by Linda Heywood, 21-69. New York: Cambridge University Press, 2001.

Miller, Joseph C. *Way of Death: Merchant Capitalism and the Angolan Slave Trade, 1730-1830.* Madison: University of Wisconsin Press, 1988.

Miller, Joseph C. "Legal Portuguese Slaving from Angola. Some Preliminary Indications of Volume and Direction." *Revue Française d'Histoire d'Outre Mer* 62, no. 1-2 (226-227) (1975), 135-176.

Mintz, Sidney, and Richard Price. *The Birth of African-American Culture: An Anthropological Perspective.* Boston: Beacon Press, 1992 [1976].

Morgan, Philip D. "The Cultural Implications of the Atlantic Slave Trade: African Regional Origins, American Destinations and New World Developments." In *Routes to Slavery: Direction, Ethnicity, and Mortality in the Transatlantic Slave Trade,* edited by David Eltis and David Richardson, 122-145. London: Frank Cass, 1997.

Moulero, Thomas. "Essai Historique Sur La Ville De Kétou." *La Reconnaissance Africaine.*

Moulero, Thomas. "The Work of Cultural Ethnogenesis." In *History and Ethnicity,* edited by Elizabeth Tonkin, 198-215. London: Routledge, 1989.

Mulvey, Patricia. "Slave Confraternities in Brazil: their Role in Colonial Society." *The Americas* 39, no. 1 (1982), 39-40.

Muniz Sodré, Luís Filipe de Lima. *Um Vento Sagrado: História de Vida de um Adivinho da Tradição Nagô-Kêtu Brasileira.* Rio de Janeiro: Mauad, 1996.

Mwembu, Donatien Dibwe dia and Bogumil Jewsiewicki, ed. *Le travail hier et aujourd'hui. Mémoires de Lubumbashi.* Paris: L'Harmattan, 2004.

Naves, Rodrigo. *A forma difícil: ensaios sobre arte brasileira.* São Paulo: Ática, 1996.

The Negro in Virginia. New York: Writers' Project of the Work Projects Administration, 1940.

Nettels, Curtis. "England and the Spanish American Trade, 1680-1715." *Journal of Modern History* 3, no. 1 (1931), 1-32.

Nietzche, Friedrich. *Considérations inactuelles.* Vol. 2. Paris: Société du Mercure de France, 1899.

Nora, Pierre, ed. *Les Lieux de mémoire.* Paris: Gallimard, 1997, vol. I.

Nora, Pierre. "Between Memory and History: Les Lieux de Mémoire." *Representations* 26 (1989), 7-24.

O'Toole, James M. *Passing for White: Race, Religion, and the Healy Family, 1820-1920.* Boston: University of Massachusetts Press, 2003.

Paiva, Eduardo França. *Escravidão e Universo Cultural na Colônia, Minas Gerais, 1716-1789.* Belo Horizonte: Editora da UFMG, 2001.

Palmer, Colin A. "From Africa to the Americas: Ethnicity in the Early Black Communities of the Americas." *Journal of World History* 6, no. 2 (1995), 223-236.

Palmer, Colin A. "The Company Trade and the Numerical Distribution of Slaves to Spanish America, 1703-1739." In *Africans in Bondage: Studies in Slavery and the Slave Trade,* edited by Paul E. Lovejoy, 27-42. Madison: University of the Wisconsin-Madison Press, 1986.

Palmer, Colin A. *Human Cargoes: The British Slave Trade to Spanish America, 1700-1739.* Chicago: University of Illinois Press, 1981.

Pares, Luis Nicolau. "The Jeje in the Tambor de Mina of Maranhão and in the Candomblé of Bahia." *Slavery and Abolition* 22, no. 1 (2001), 91-115.

Parrinder, George. *The Story of Ketu: An Ancient African Kingdom.* Ibadan: Ibadan University Press, 1967.

Parry, John Horace, Philip Manderson Sherlock and Anthony P. Maingot. *A Short History of the West Indies.* New York: St. Martin's Press, 1987.

Peel, J.D.Y. *Religious Encounter and the Making of the Yoruba.* Bloomington: Indiana University Press, 2000.

Peel, J.D.Y. "The Work of Cultural Ethnogenesis." In *History and Ethnicity*, edited by Elizabeth Tonkin, 198-215. London: Routledge, 1989.

Peixoto, Antônio da Costa. *Obra nova de Lingoa g.^{al} de mina traduzida, ao nosso Igdioma por Antonio da Costa Peixoto, Naciognal do Rn.^{o} de Portugal, da Provincia de Entre Douro e Minho, do comcelho de Filgr.^{as} Que com curuzid.^{e} trabalho, e desvello, se expoz, em aprendella, p.^{a} tembem a emsignar, a q.^{m} for curiozo, e tiver von.^{de} de a saber E.^{o} Nas Minas Gerais,e Frg.^{a} de Barm.^{ou} Anno de 1741.* Lisbon: Agência Geral das Colônias, 1949.

Perdue, Charles L. Tomas Barden and Robert Phillips, ed. *Weevils in the Wheat: Interviews with Virginia Ex-Slaves.* Charlottesville: University Press of Virginia, 1992.

Pied, Révérend Père. "De Porto-Novo á Oyo- Févier-Mars 1891."*Les Missions Catholiques*, no. 1197 (1892), 231-236.

Pierson, Donald. *Negroes in Brazil, a Study of Race Contact at Bahia.* Chicago: University of Chicago Press, 1942.

Piot, Charles. *Remotely Global: Village Modernity in West Africa.* Chicago: University of Chicago Press, 1999.

Pfeiffer, Kathleen. *Race Passing and American Individualism.* Boston: University of Massachusetts Press, 2003.

Piault, Marc Henri. "Captifs du pouvoir et pouvoir des captifs." In *L'esclavage en Afrique précoloniale*, edited by Claude Meillassoux, 321-350. Paris: F. Maspero, 1975.

Platt, Virginia Bever. "The East India Company and the Madagascar Slave Trade." *William and Mary Quarterly* 26 (1969), 548-577.

Pongo, Martin Kalulambi. *Être Luba au xxe siècle.* Paris: Karthala, 1997.

Postma, Johannes M. *The Dutch in the Atlantic Slave Trade, 1600-1815.* Cambridge: Cambridge University Press, 1990.

Prado, J. F. de Almeida. *O artista Debret e o Brasil.* São Paulo: Companhia Editora Nacional, 1989.

Puri, Shalini, ed. *Marginal Migrations: The Circulation of Cultures in the Caribbean.* Oxford: Warwick University Press, 2003.

Ramírez, B. Torres. *La Compañia Gaditana de Negros.* Seville: Escuela Hispano-Americanos de Sevilla, 1973.

Ranger, Terence. *The Invention of Tribalism in Zimbabwe.* Gwelo: Mambo Press, 1985.

Ranger, Terence. "European Attitudes and African Realities: the Rise and Fall of the Matola Chiefs of South-East Tanzania." *Journal of African History* 20, no. 1 (1979), 63-82.

Raposo, Luciano. *Marcas de Escravos. Listas de Escravos Emancipados vindos a bordo de Navios Estrangeiros (1839-1841).* Rio de Janeiro: Arquivo Nacional, 1990.

Reis, João José. *Death is a Festival. Funeral Rites and Rebellion in 19th century Brazil.* Chapel Hill: University of North Carolina Press, 2003.

Reis, João José. *Slave Rebellion in Brazil: The Muslim Uprising of 1835 in Bahia.* Baltimore: Johns Hopkins University Press, 1993.

Reis, João José and Eduardo Silva, *Negociação e conflito: a resistência negra no Brasil escravista.* São Paulo: Companhia das Letras, 1989.

Ricoeur, Paul. *La mémoire, l'histoire, l'oubli.* Paris: Éditions du Seuil, 2000.

Reginaldo, Lucilene. "Os Rosários dos Angolas: Irmandades Negras, Experiências Escravas e Identidades Africanas na Bahia Setecentista." PhD Diss. Universidade Estadual de Campinas, 2005.

Robertson, Claire C., and Martin A. Klein, ed. *Women and Slavery in Africa.* Madison: University of Wisconsin Press, 1983.

Robin, Joseph Nil. *Notes historiques sur la Grande Kabylie de 1830 à 1838.*Alger: Saint Denis, Bouchène, 1999.

Robinson, Charles H. *Hausaland, or Fifteen Hundred Miles through the Central Sudan.* London: Marston, 1896.

Ross, David. "The First Chacha of Whydah: Francisco Félix de Souza." *Odu* 2 (1969), 19-28.

Rout, Leslie.*The African Experience in Spanish America: 1502 to the Present Day.* Cambridge: Cambridge University Press, 1976.

Rudnyanszky, Leslie Imre. "The Caribbean Slave Trade." PhD diss., University of Notre Dame, 1973.

Rugendas, Johann Moritz. *Malerische Reise in Brasilien*. Paris: Mülhausen Engelmann et Cie, 1835.

Rugendas, Johann Moritz. *O Brasil de Rugendas*. Belo Horizonte: Editora Itatiaia, 1998.

Rugendas, Maurice. *Voyage Pittoresque dans le Brésil*. Paris: Engelmann et Cie, 1835.

Sa°dī (al-). *Tārīkh Es-Soudan*. Translated by O. Houdas. Paris: E. Leroux, 1900.

Salau, Mohammed Bashir. "The Growth of the Plantation Economy in the Sokoto Caliphate: Fanisau 1819-1903." PhD diss., York University, 2005.

Santos, Juana Elbein dos. *Os Nàgo e a Morte: Pàde, Asèsè, e o Culto Egun na Bahia*. Petrópolis: Vozes, 1976.

Scelles, Georges. *La traite négrière aux Indes de Castile, contrats et traités d'assiento*. Paris: L. Larose and L. Tenin, 1905.

Schwartz, Stuart B. "The Economy of the Portuguese Empire." In *Portuguese Oceanic Expansion, 1400-1800*, edited by Francisco Bethencourt and Diogo Ramada Curto, 19-48. New York: Cambridge University Press, 2007.

Segurola, Basilio and Jean Rassinoux. *Dictionnaire Fon-Français*. Madrid: Société des Missions Africaines, 2000.

Semley, Lorelle. *Mother Is Gold, Father Is Glass: Gender and Colonialism in a Yoruba Town*. Bloomington, IN: Indiana University Press, 2010.

Shaw, Rosalind. *Memories of the Slave Trade: Ritual and the Historical Imagination in Sierra Leone*. Chicago: University of Chicago Press, 2002.

Sheridan, Richard B. "The Slave Trade to Jamaica, 1702-1808." In *Essays Presented to Douglas Hall: Trade Government and Society in Caribbean History, 1700-1920*, edited by Barry W. Higman, 1-16. Kingston: Heinemann Educational Books (Caribbean) Ltd., 1983.

Shyllon, Folarin. *Black People in Britain 1555-1833*. London: Oxford University Press, 1977.

Silva, Daniel Domingues. "The Coastal Origins of Slaves Leaving Angola, from the 18th to the 19th Centuries." Paper Presented at the 124th Annual Meeting of the American Historical Association, San Diego, CA. January 2010.

Silva Correa, Elias Alexandre da. *Historia de Angola*. Lisbon: Ática, 1937 [1799].

Singleton, Theresa. "The Slave Trade Remembered on the Former Gold and Slave Coasts." *Slavery and Abolition* 20, no. 1 (1999): 150-169.

Sinou, Alain. "La Valorisation du patrimoine architectural et urbain: l'exemple de la ville de Ouidah au Bénin." *Cahiers des Sciences Humaines* 29, no. 1 (1993), 33-51.

Slenes, Robert W. "African Abrahams, Lucretias and Men of Sorrows: Allegory and Allusion in the Brazilian Anti-slavery Lithographs (1827-1835) of Johann Moritz Rugendas. *Slavery and Abolition* 23, no. 2 (2002), 147-168.

Slenes, Robert W. *Na Senzala uma Flor. Esperanças e recordações na formação da familia escrava.* Rio de Janeiro: Nova Fronteira, 1999.

Slenes, Robert W. "Malungu, Ngoma Vem! África Coberta e Descoberta no Brasil." *Revista USP* 12 (1991-1992), 48-67.

Smith, Linda. *Decolonizing Methodologies: Research and Indigenous Peoples.* Dunedin: University of Otago Press, 1999.

Soares, Carlos Eugênio Líbano. *A Capoeira Escrava e Outras Tradições Rebeldes no Rio de Janeiro(1808-1850).* Campinas: Editora da Unicamp, 2001.

Soares, Mariza. "Can Women Guide and Govern Men? Gendering Politics among African Catholics in Colonial Brazil." In *Women and Slavery*. Vol. 2, edited by Gwyn Campbell, Suzanne Miers and Joseph Miller, 79-99. Athens: Ohio University Press, 2007.

Soares, Mariza de Carvalho. "A Biografia de Ignácio Montes: o Escravo que virou Rei." In *Retratos do Império: Trajetórias Individuais no Mundo Português nos séculos XVI a XIX*, edited by Ronaldo Vainfas, R. Santos and G. Neves, 47-68. Niterói: Editora da Universidade Federal Fluminense, 2006.

Soares, Mariza de Carvalho. *Rotas Atlânticas da Diáspora Africana: da Baía do Benim ao Rio de Janeiro.* Niterói: Editora da Univeresidade Federal Fluminense, 2007.

Soares, Mariza de Carvalho. "A 'nação' que se tem e a 'terra' de onde se vem." *Estudos Afro-Asiáticos* (2004), 303-330.

Soares, Mariza de Carvalho. "Descobrindo a Guiné no Brasil Colonial." *Revista do Institito Histórico Geográfico Brasileiro* 161, no. 407 (2000), 71-94.

Soares, Mariza de Carvalho. *Devotos da Cor: Identidade Étnica, Religiosidade e Escravidão no Rio de Janeiro, Século XVIII.* Rio de Janeiro: Civilização Brasileira, 2000.

Sodré, Muniz, and Luís Filipe de Lima. *Um Vento sagrado: Historia de Vida de um adivinho da Tradição Nagô-Kêtu Brasileira.* Rio de Janeiro: Mauad, 1996.

Solórzano, Juan Carlos. "El comercio de Costa Rica durante el declive del comercio Española y el desarrollo del contrabando Ingles: periodo 1690-1750." *Anuario de Estudios Centroamericanos* [Costa Rica] 20, no. 2 (1996), 71-119.

Soumonni, Élisée. *Daomé e o mundo atlântico.* SEPHIS, South-South Exchange Programme for Research on the History of Development, Centro de Estudos Afro-Asiáticos 2, 2001.

Sousa, Laura de Mello e. *Desclassificados do Ouro. A Pobreza Mineira no Século XVIII.* Rio de Janeiro: Graal, 1985.

Souza, Marina de Mello e. *Reis Negros no Brasil Escravista. História da Festa da Coroação de Rei Congo.* Belo Horizonte: UFMG, 2002.

Souza, Simone de. *La Famille de Souza du Bénin-Togo.* Cotonou: Les éditions du Bénin, 1992.

Sperling, John G. *The South Sea Company: An Historical Essay and Bibliographical Finding List.* Cambridge, MA: Harvard University Press, 1962.

Stilwell, Sean, Ibrahim Hamza and Paul E. Lovejoy. "The Oral History of Royal Slavery in Sokoto Caliphate: An Overview with Sallama Dako." *History in Africa* 28 (2001), 273-291.

Sweet, James H. "Mistaken Identities? Olaudah Equiano, Domingos Álvares, and the Methodological Challenges of Studying the African Diaspora." *American Historical Review* 114, no. 2 (2009), 279-306.

Sweet, James H. *Recreating Africa. Culture, Kinship, and Religion in the African-Portuguese World.* Chapel Hill: University of North Carolina Press, 2003.

Symanski, Luís Cláudio Pereira. "Slaves and Planters in Western Brazil: Material Culture, Identity and Power." PhD Diss. University of Florida, 2006.

Ṭaḥāwī, Abū Jaᶜfar Aḥmad b. Muḥammad. *Al-shurūṭ al-ṣaghīr mudhyy-alan bimā ᶜuthira ᶜalayhi mina 'l-shurūṭ al-kabīr*. Vol. 2. Bagdad : Maṭbaᶜat al-ᶜAnī, 1974.

Tall, Emmanuelle Kadya. "De la démocratie et des cultes voduns au Bénin." *Cahiers d'études africaines* 137 (1995), 195-208.

Tams, George. *Visita as possessões Portuguesas na Costa Occidental d'Africa*. Porto: Tipografia do Calvário, 1850.

Tavares, Ana Paula and Catarina Madeira Santos. *Africae Monumenta. A Apropriação da Escrita pelos Africanos*. Lisbon: IICT, 2002.

Taylor, Charles. *Modern Social Imaginaries*. Durham, NC: Duke University Press, 2004.

Teelock, Vijaya. "Questioning the Link between Slavery and Exclusion: The Experience of Plantation Slavery." In *L'esclavage et ses séquelles: mémoire et vécu d'hier et d'aujourd'hui, Actes du colloque international organisé par l'UOM (1998)*, 279-288. Port-Louis: M. des Arts et de la Culture, 2002.

Teelock, Vijaya. *Bitter Sugar. Sugar and Slavery in 19th Century Mauritius*. Réduit: Mahatma Gandhi Institute, 1998.

Temimi, Abdeljelil. *Sommaire des registres arabes et turcs d'Alger*. Tunis : [s.n.], 1979s.

Tereau, Lt-Col. Medicin, and Dr. Huttel. "Monographie du Hollidge." *Etudes Dahoméennes* 2 (1949), 59-72 ; 3 (1950), 7-37.

Thompson, Robert Ferris and Joseph Cornet. *The Four Moments of the Sun: Kongo Art in Two Worlds*. Washington, D.C.: National Gallery of Art, 1981.

Thornton, John. *Africa and Africans in the Making of the Atlantic World*. New York: Cambridge University Press, 1992.

Toorn, Karel van der. *Scribal Culture and the Making of the Hebrew Bible*. Cambridge, MA: Harvard University Press, 2007.

Trouillot, Michel-Rolph. *Silencing the Past: Power and the Production of History*. Boston: Beacon Press, 1995.

Turner, Jerry Michael. "'Les Bresiliens': The Impact of Former Brazilian Slaves upon Dahomey." PhD diss., Boston University, 1975.

Tyan, Émile. *Histoire de l'organisation judiciaire en pays d'islam*. Leiden: Brill, 1960.

Tyan, Émile. *Le notariat et le régime de la preuve par écrit dans la pratique du droit musulman*. Harissa: Imp. Saint-Paul, 1945.

Vail, Leroy, ed. *The Creation of Tribalism in Southern Africa.* Berkeley: University of California Press, 1989.

Vansina, Jan. *How Societies were Born: Governance in West Central Africa before 1600.* Charlottesville: University of Virginia Press, 2005.

Vansina, Jan. "Ambaca Society and the Slave Trade, c. 1760-1845." *Journal of African History* 46, no. 1 (2005), 1-27.

Vansina, Jan. *Kingdoms of the Savanna.* Madison: University of Wisconsin Press, 1966.

Vansina, Jan. *Oral Tradition as History.* Madison: University of Wisconsin Press, 1985.

Vansina, Jan. *Oral Tradition: A Study in Historical Methodology.* Harmondsworth, Middlesex: Penguin Books, 1973.

Verger, Pierre. *Os Libertos: Sete caminhos na liberdade de escravos da Bahia no século XIX.* Salvador: Corrupio, 1992.

Verger, Pierre. *Orisha: Les dieux Yoruba en Afrique et au Nouveau Monde.* Paris: A.M. Métailié, 1982.

Verger, Pierre. *Flux et reflux de la traite des nègres entre le Golfe de Bénin et Bahia de Todos os Santos, du XVIIe au XIXe siècle.* Paris: Mouton, 1969.

Verger, Pierre. "Le culte des vodoun d'Abomey aurait-il été apporté à Saint Louis de Maranhão par la mère du roi Ghèzo?" *Études Dahoméennes* VIII, Porto Novo (1952), 19-24.

Wald, Gayle. *Crossing the Line: Racial Passing in Twentieth Century U.S. Literature and Culture.* Durham, NC: Duke University Press, 2000.

Walker, Sheila S. "Are you Hip to the Jive? (Re)Writing/Righting the Pan-American Discourse." In *African Roots/American Cultures: Africa in the Creation of the Americas,* edited by Sheila S. Walker, 1- 45. New York: Rowman and Littlefield, 2001.

Walsh, Lorena. *From Calabar to Carter's Grove: The History of a Virginia Slave Community.* Charlottesville: University Press of Virginia, 1997.

Warner-Lewis, Maureen. *Central Africa in the Caribbean. Transcending Time, Transforming Culture.* Kingston: University of West Indies Press, 2003.

Wilks, Ivor. "Abu Bakr Al-Siddiq of Timbuktu." In *Africa Remembered: Narratives by West Africans from the Era of the Slave Trade*, edited by Philip D. Curtin, 152-169. Madison: University of Wisconsin Press, 1967.

Woese, Carl and Nigel Goldenfeld. "Biology's Next Revolution." *Nature* 445 (2007), arXiv:q-bio/0702015v1

Work Projects Administration of Virginia Writers' Project, *The Negro in Virginia*. Winston-Salem, North Carolina: John Blair, 1994.

Wright, Louis B., ed. *The Letters of Robert Carter: The Commercial Interests of a Virginia Gentleman.* San Marino: The Huntington Library, 1940.

Wu, Yu. "Jamaican Trade: 1688-1769, A Quantitative Study." PhD diss., Johns Hopkins University, 1995.

Yai, Olabiyi. "Texts of Enslavement: Fon and Yoruba Vocabularies from Eighteenth and Nineteenth-Century Brazil." In *Identity in the Shadow of Slavery*, edited by Paul E. Lovejoy, 102-112. London: Continuum, 2000.

Yallas, Shihāb al-Dīn (compiler). *Al-wathā'iq al-waṭaniyya: al-fahras al-taḥlīlī li-'l-wathā'iq al-tārīkhiyya 'l-jazā'iriyya li-'l-raṣīd al-ᶜuthmānī. Archives nationales: archives historiques algériennes. Inventaire analytique du fonds ottoman.* Algiers: Ministère de la culture et du tourisme, Centre national d'études historiques, 1987, 7 vols.

Notes on Contributors

ANA LUCIA ARAUJO is Assistant Professor in the Department of History at Howard University. Her research deals with the history and the memory of slavery in Brazil and the Bight of Benin. She has published *Romantisme tropical: l'aventure illustrée d'un peintre français au Brésil* (Quebec: Presses de l'Université Laval, 2008), and *Public Memory of Slavery: Victims and Perpetrators in the South Atlantic* (Cambria Press, Amherst, NY, 2010). She has also edited the volumes *Living History: Encountering the Memory of the Heirs of Slavery* (Newcastle upon Tyne: Cambridge Scholars Publishing, 2009) and *Paths of the Atlantic Slave Trade: Interactions, Identities, and Images* (Amherst: Cambria Press, 2011).

MARIANA P. CANDIDO is Assistant Professor in the Department of History, Princeton University. Her research interests encompass the history of Angola, slavery and the slave trade, and the African diaspora. She is the author of articles published in *African Economic History*, *Slavery and Abolition* and several edited volumes. Her book, *Fronteras de Esclavización: Esclavitud, Comercio e Identidad en Benguela, 1780-1850*, is published by El Colegio de México Press. Dr. Candido has been a fellow at the Gilder Lehrman Center for the Study of Slavery Resistance and Emancipation at Yale University, the John Carter Brown Library at Brown University, and Fundação Luso-Americana, in Portugal. She is also a network professor of the Harriet Tubman Institute for Research on the Global Migrations of African Peoples at York University and a collaborator in the project *Naus do Purgatório: Escravidão e Tráfico Atlântico*, hosted by the Universidade Federal Fluminense, Brazil.

SANDRA CARMIGNANI is a Social and Cultural Anthropologist. She is Research Assistant at the Institut d'anthropologie et de sociologie, Université de Lausanne, in Switzerland. Mauritius, slavery and the concepts of heritage and memory are the main topics of her PhD dissertation, which was completed in 2011.

YACINE DADDI ADDOUN received his PhD from York University in 2010 for his thesis, "Abolition de l'esclavage en Algérie, 1816-1871," and was awarded a postdoctoral fellowship at the Harriet Tubman Institute for 2010-11. He has published articles on Muhammad Kaba Saghanughu of Jamaica and is editing a volume with Bruce Hall on the intellectual and political discourse of slavery and emancipation in Islam.

NADINE HUNT is a PhD candidate in the Department of History at York University. Hunt is the recipient of several graduate scholarships and fellowships, including a Social Sciences and Humanities Research of Canada Doctoral fellowship (2006-2008). Hunt's doctoral dissertation entitled "The Caribbean trade of Jamaica: the consolidation of Atlantic networks, 1756-1807" explores how African, European, and Amerindian social, economic, and political worlds intersected in the circum-Caribbean. Her study will advance our knowledge of economic activity in eighteenth- and early nineteenth-century Caribbean and Atlantic discourse.

BOGUMIL JEWSIEWICKI is Professor Emeritus, Université Laval, and a member of the MCRI-SSHRC Project "Slavery, Memory, Citizenship." On the topic presented in this edited volume, he recently published "Mémoires et débats présents" in *Dictionnaire des esclavages*, edited by Olivier Pétré-Grenouilleau (Paris, Larousse, 2010), 18-27. He also edited the special double issue, "Réparations, restitutions, réconciliations entre Afriques, Europe et Amériques," of *Cahiers d'études africaines* 173-174 (2004).

PAUL E. LOVEJOY FRSC, Distinguished Research Professor, Department of History, York University, holds the Canada

Research Chair in African Diaspora History and is Director, Harriet Tubman Institute for Research on the Global Migrations of African Peoples. His recent publications include *Slavery, Commerce and Production in West Africa: Slave Society in the Sokoto Caliphate* (2005); *Ecology and Ethnography of Muslim Trade inWest Africa* (2005); and *The Biography of Mahommah Gardo Baquaqua: His Passage from Slavery to Freedom in Africa and America* (2nd ed., 2006). He has also edited or co-edited various volumes on the African diaspora, including *Trans-Atlantic Dimensions of Ethnicity in the African Diaspora* (2004); *Enslaving Connections: Western Africa and Brazil during the Era of Slavery* (2004); and *Slavery on the Frontiers of Islam* (2004).

MOHAMMED BASHIR SALAU, Assistant Professor of History at the University of Mississippi, received his PhD in African diaspora history at York University in 2005. He has been involved in a project to digitize archival materials, supported by the British Library Endangered Archives Programme, in Northern Nigeria. His book, *The West African Slave Plantation: A Case Study*, examines the plantation complex at Fanisau in Kano Emirate. He is currently working on a biography of Dorugu Kwage Adam, who was enslaved in the 1840s in the Central Sudan and who subsequently dictated his autobiography in Hausa, after being emancipated and traveling to Europe.

LORELLE SEMLEY is Assistant Professor of History at Wesleyan University. Her research interests in African history include gender, French imperialism, and the African diaspora. Her book, *Mother Is Gold, Father Is Glass: Gender and Colonialism in a Yoruba Town* (2010), analyzes the broader historical and political meanings of public motherhood in West Africa and traces the complex relationships between actual and symbolic mothers and fathers during three transformative processes: the Atlantic slave trade, French colonialism, and trans-Atlantic travel between West Africa and Brazil. Her current research project examines black citizenship within French colonial empire in the Americas, West Africa, and France itself.

MARIZA DE CARVALHO SOARES is Professor Associado of History, Universidade Federal Fluminense, where she teaches the history of Africa and the Atlantic world. Her research interests encompass slavery and the African diaspora. Her publications include *Devotos da Cor. Identidade étnica, Religiosidade e Escravidão no Rio de Janeiro, século XVIII* (2000) and *Rotas Atlânticas da Diáspora Africana: entre a Baía do Benim e o Rio de Janeiro* (2007). Soares has been a visiting fellow at Vanderbilt University, Yale University, Stanford University, and École des Hautes Études en Sciences Sociales. She has directed Acervo Digital Angola Brasil (2006-2009) and presently is the director of *Naus do Purgatório: Escravidão e Comércio Atlântico de Escravos* at the Universidade Federal Fluminense. She is also associated with Conselho Nacional de Desenvolvimento Científico e Tecnológico in Brazil and is a network professor of the Harriet Tubman Institute for Research on the Global Migrations of African Peoples at York University.

WENDY WILSON-FALL is an Associate Professor in Pan African Studies and Adjunct in Anthropology at Kent State University. Wilson-Fall received her PhD from Howard University's African Studies Center (1984), where she did a concentration in Social Anthropology. She received her Masters from Amadu Bello University in Zaria, Nigeria. Her current research focuses on ethnohistories in the North American African diaspora. Dr. Wilson-Fall has been a Smithsonian Fellow, a Fellow of the Rockefeller Library at the Williamsburg Foundation (Virginia), and a selected scholar/lecturer for the Virginia Foundation for the Humanities (Hanover, 2004).

Index